Mark Twain and Philosophy

Great Authors and Philosophy
General Editor: Jacob Held,
editor of *Dr. Seuss and Philosophy*

The Great Authors and Philosophy series is for anyone who ever wondered about the deeper ideas in their favorite authors' books. Comprising entertaining, concise, and accessible takes on the philosophical ideas that classic and contemporary authors and their work convey, the books in this series bring together philosophical perspectives enhanced and illuminated by beloved stories from our culture.

Current Titles in the Series
Mark Twain and Philosophy, edited by Alan Goldman
Jane Austen and Philosophy, edited by Mimi Marinucci
Stephen King and Philosophy, edited by Jacob Held

Mark Twain and Philosophy

Edited by
Alan H. Goldman

ROWMAN & LITTLEFIELD
Lanham • Boulder • New York • London

Chapter 4: "The Conscience of Huckleberry Finn" by Jonathan Bennett. *Philosophy 49* (April 1974): 123–34. Copyright © 1974 The Royal Institute of Philosophy. Reprinted with the permission of Cambridge University Press.

Published by Rowman & Littlefield
A wholly owned subsidiary of The Rowman & Littlefield Publishing Group, Inc.
4501 Forbes Boulevard, Suite 200, Lanham, Maryland 20706
www.rowman.com

Unit A, Whitacre Mews, 26-34 Stannary Street, London SE11 4AB

Distributed by NATIONAL BOOK NETWORK

British Library Cataloguing in Publication Information Available

Library of Congress Cataloging-in-Publication Data Is Available

ISBN 978-1-4422-6171-6 (paperback : alk. paper)
ISBN 978-1-4422-6172-3 (electronic)

♾™ The paper used in this publication meets the minimum requirements of American National Standard for Information Sciences—Permanence of Paper for Printed Library Materials, ANSI/NISO Z39.48-1992.

Printed in the United States of America

For all those who like to laugh
while doing serious philosophy

~

Contents

~

Introduction

ALAN H. GOLDMAN

Mark Twain is universally acknowledged to be one of America's greatest wits, the author of "the great American novel," a master of humor, irony, and dialect, a searing social critic and critic of established religion. He was also a philosopher, at least if that title is bestowed on the basis of published philosophical insight, explicit and implicit. Unlike some other psychologically and philosophically astute authors such as Jane Austen, whose philosophical insights are well hidden behind her humor and irony, Twain's philosophical seriousness is worn on its sleeve, despite equally funny humor and clever irony. This is not to say that it does not require interpretive unraveling, leaving room in its rich interpretive possibilities for acceptable critical disagreement.

This volume makes some of Twain's implicit philosophical content explicit. It is divided into five parts. Part I interprets the moral lessons to be derived from Twain's masterpiece, *Huckleberry Finn*, regarding Huck's character and moral development, the place of principle versus sentiment in determining right courses of action, and the source of moral motivation. In the first chapter, "The Conscience of Huckleberry Finn," Jonathan Bennett sees Huck as irrational in nevertheless doing the right thing. His refusal to turn Jim in to runaway slave hunters exhibits weakness of will according to Bennett. His misguided moral principles tell him only to return property to its legal owner. His sympathy for Jim simply opposes his moral principles. It is not itself a source of moral principle or insight, having no cognitive aspect.

My chapter on moral motivation presents a different picture of the place of emotions in moral decision making. Emotions such as sympathy include implicit judgments and recognition of reasons. Huck is not guilty of weakness of will as I define it, as he acts on the strongest moral reasons of which he is implicitly aware through his emotion of sympathy. What he shows us is that moral motivation is not rationally required, as he is not motivated by his explicit moral judgments, and emotions such as sympathy are not rationally required even though they might respond to reasons. In the third chapter on sympathy, conscience, and principles, Robert Fudge introduces Adam Smith into this debate. Smith holds that morality itself is based on sentiment. Actions are moral when motivated by sentiments that an impartial observer would approve of. Conscience itself does not consist of accepted principles, but in proper sentiments. In trusting to his feeling, Huck Finn morally develops.

In opposition to the first three chapters, Michael Lyons argues that moral principles should always have priority, although they must always be open to reflection and revision. Emotions such as sympathy do not override principles but may indicate a need for revision. Lyons wants to maintain the priority of principle because moral heroes stick to their considered principles, and because we need above all to discover the right ones. Finally, in "Twain's Last Laugh," Kristina Gehrman holds that seeing Huck Finn as a moral hero, as all the previous interpretations do, is a mistake. Twain's ultimate irony is his setting us up to seeing Huck that way and so revealing our own stunted moral growth in relation to race. In identifying with Huck, we do not achieve the morally mature attitude toward race relations that we think we do. Everyone recognizes the irony in Huck's renouncing of morality, but this highly original interpretation sees Twain as more deeply ironic in his portrayal of his central character and his relation to us (white liberal) readers.

In his late writings, Twain became a fierce critic of religion, drawing comparisons to Nietzsche (whom he never read). These writings remained unpublished until many years after Twain's death, and remain unknown to those who see him only as America's archetypal humorist. Part II contains essays explicating and interpreting these works. In "The Gospel According to Mark (Twain)," Craig Vasey comments on Twain's *Letters from the Earth*, Satan's comments on humanity and on inconsistencies in the Bible. Heaven, which is supposed to be supremely wonderful, has no sex but plenty of harp playing; humans suffer eternal punishment for the transgressions of Adam and Eve, who had no idea of right and wrong and death, but were created curious; God is preoccupied with individual humans (which struck Twain as ludicrous long before the size of the universe was known) and wants only to be worshipped. In the next chapter, James McLachlan explains Twain's reaction to the problem of evil and suffering, his critique of the aesthetic defense that sees suffering as contributing to the beauty and goodness of the whole of creation. After carefully laying out the defense from prominent theologians, he catalogues Twain's disdainful critique in several of his writings. Twain's Calvinist God creates humans knowing they will sin and then endlessly punishes them for being as He created them.

Part III explores nonreligious moral issues in some lesser known of Twain's writings. The range of moral issues that Twain addresses in these writings, once more often ironic and funny, exceeds that of most contemporary philosophers. Two such issues are addressed here. In "The Noble Art of Lying," James Edwin Mahon first notes Twain's claim that everyone lies, even if only by omitting to speak the truth, whether well-known or not, and even if nondeceptively and for the sake of tact and politeness. Twain's complaint is that most people lie badly. Although, as is common, it is somewhat difficult to tell when Twain is being ironic, and when he is being literal, he appears to endorse a utilitarian principle to govern the ethics of lying: all that matters is whether we are helping or harming people by lies or truth.

Emily E. VanDette explores Twain's opposition to animal experimentation in writings that are polemical, satirical, and sentimental, some from the animals' perspective as narrators. As a strong animal rights advocate, Twain predates later philosophers who take up the same cause, turning Darwinian theory on its head, seeing humans as at least morally inferior, and refuting earlier philosophers' mechanistic view of animals. His championing of animals parallels his passionate opposition to imperialism and social and economic oppression.

Twain was a master humorist and ironist. Humor, satire, and irony were his primary tools with which to express his social, moral, and religious critiques. Part IV explicates these literary devices as he used them to such weighty purpose. In a chapter on Twain's serious humor, Chris Kramer explains how trenchant philosophical critique can go hand in hand with laugh-out-loud humor, both of which are evidenced in the same passages in Twain's writings. Twain opposed the solemn seriousness that equates with arrogance and certainty, vices of the religious indoctrinators and political oppressors. His humor is equally but differently serious in attacking these vices that account for so much suffering in the world.

In what I assume was the last essay Dale Jacquette wrote before his untimely death, he clearly and carefully explains the nature of irony generally and then argues that Twain's is of the Socratic variety. Fortunately this essay required little or no editing, as Dale passed away before the editorial process began. His chapter focuses on a lesser known work about Joan of Arc and on *The Innocents Abroad* to illustrate Twain's use of Socratic irony in his critique of Christianity.

Part V contains essays comparing Twain to earlier and later philosophers. In "The American Diogenes," Brian Earl Johnson compares Twain to the ancient Cynic who famously sought an honest man. Both humorously satirize religion, bogus morality, superstition, and hypocrisy. Both engage in what Johnson describes as sacred profanity: profaning the pseudo-sacred and making honest profanity itself sacred. Continuing the comparison to ancient philosophers, Jennifer Baker likens Twain to the Epicureans, early virtue ethicists. Twain shares their attitude toward death and their disdain of material wealth (at least as expressed by characters such as Huck Finn). But the Epicureans opposed false and scary stories. Twain opposes them too in the Bible, but he is guilty, as are his characters, of making up a few of his own.

In one of Twain's wilder and funnier stories, the narrator kills his conscience, who has tormented him in an almost random fashion. The story is clearly philosophical, although its philosophy is not so clear. Frank Boardman offers both Nietzschean and Humean interpretations, both of which have some plausibility in tying aspects of the story together, as well as some problems in capturing Twain's intent.

Finally, Jeffrey Dueck compares Twain to a more contemporary philosopher, Edward Bullough, who proposed a theory of "psychical distance" as necessary for aesthetic appreciation. As opposed to ethics and religion, which were major concerns of Twain in many of his writings, one might be surprised that he expressed views in line with contemporary aesthetics. But in certain passages of *Life on the Mississippi*, he strongly anticipates Bullough's fuller exposition of the nature of aesthetic appreciation and its prerequisites in the right amount of emotional attachment and distance from its object. Dueck notes both this connection and Twain's genius as a writer to create the conditions for aesthetic appreciation in his audience.

This volume, of course, does not exhaust the philosophical insight of Mark Twain. I myself would have liked to have seen more reference to *Pudd'nhead Wilson*, for example. But the variety of chapters here, many of which address Twain's later and lesser known stories, do bring to light the breadth of his vision on social, religious, moral, and aesthetic issues, much of which was far ahead of his time. Twain's biting humor was an apt tool for his philosophical insight and social criticism. As the range of interpretations of *Huckleberry Finn* in the first section illustrates, his work offers the same rich possibilities of interpretation that typifies other of the greatest works of literature. In Twain's case, such interpretive criticism inevitably addresses profound philosophical issues.

PART I

MORALITY IN
HUCKLEBERRY FINN

CHAPTER ONE

~

The Conscience of Huckleberry Finn[1]

Jonathan Bennett

In this chapter, I shall present the conscience not just of Huckleberry Finn but of two others as well. One of them is the conscience of Heinrich Himmler. He became a Nazi in 1923; he served drably and quietly, but well, and was rewarded with increasing responsibility and power. At the peak of his career, he held many offices and commands, of which the most powerful was that of leader of the SS—the principal police force of the Nazi regime. In this capacity, Himmler commanded the whole concentration camp system and was responsible for the execution of the so-called final solution of the Jewish problem. It is important for my purposes that this piece of social engineering should be thought of not abstractly but in concrete terms of Jewish families being marched to what they think are bathhouses, to the accompaniment of loud-speaker renditions of extracts from *The Merry Widow* and *Tales of Hoffman*, there to be choked to death by poisonous gases. Altogether, Himmler succeeded in murdering about four and a half million of them, as well as several million gentiles, mainly Poles and Russians.

The other conscience to be discussed is that of the Calvinist theologian and philosopher Jonathan Edwards. He lived in the first half of the eighteenth century and has a good claim to be considered America's first serious and considerable philosophical thinker. He was for many years a widely renowned preacher and Congregationalist minister in New England. In 1748, a dispute with his congregation led him to resign (he couldn't accept

3

their view that unbelievers should be admitted to the Lord's Supper in the hope that it would convert them). For some years after that he worked as a missionary, preaching to Indians through an interpreter. Then, in 1758, he accepted the presidency of what is now Princeton University, and within two months died from a smallpox inoculation. Along the way he wrote some first-rate philosophy: his book attacking the notion of free will is still sometimes read. Why I should be interested in Edwards's *conscience* will be explained in due course.

I shall use Heinrich Himmler, Jonathan Edwards, and Huckleberry Finn to illustrate different aspects of a single theme, namely the relationship between *sympathy* on the one hand and *bad morality* on the other.

All that I can mean by a "bad morality" is a morality whose principles I deeply disapprove of. When I call a morality bad, I cannot prove that mine is better; but when I here call any morality bad, I think you will agree with me that it is bad; and that is all I need.

There could be dispute as to whether the springs of someone's actions constitute a *morality*. I think, though, that we must admit that someone who acts in ways that conflict grossly with our morality may nevertheless have a morality of his own—a set of principles of action that he sincerely assents to, so that for him the problem of acting well or rightly or in obedience to conscience is the problem of conforming to *those* principles. The problem of conscientiousness can arise as acutely for a bad morality as for any other: rotten principles may be as difficult to keep as decent ones.

As for "sympathy": I use this term to cover every sort of fellow-feeling, as when one feels pity over someone's loneliness, or horrified compassion over his pain, or when one feels a shrinking reluctance to act in a way that will bring misfortune to someone else. These *feelings* must not be confused with *moral judgments*. My sympathy for someone in distress may lead me to help him, or even to think that I ought to help him; but in itself, it is not a judgment about what I ought to do but just a *feeling* for him in his plight. We shall get some light on the difference between feelings and moral judgments when we consider Huckleberry Finn.

Obviously, feelings can impel one to action, and so can moral judgments; and in a particular case sympathy and morality may pull in opposite directions. This can happen not just with bad moralities but also with good ones like yours and mine. For example, a small child, sick and miserable, clings tightly to his mother and screams in terror when she tries to pass him over to the doctor to be examined. If the mother gave way to her sympathy, that is to her feeling for the child's misery and fright, she would hold the child close and not let the doctor come near; but don't we agree that it might be wrong for her to act on such a feeling? Quite generally, then, anyone's moral principles may apply to a particular situation in a way that runs contrary to the particular thrusts of fellow-feeling that he has in that situation. My immediate concern is with sympathy in relation to bad morality, but not because such conflicts occur only when the morality is bad.

Now, suppose that someone who accepts a bad morality is struggling to make himself act in accordance with it in a particular situation where his sympathies pull him another way. He sees the struggle as one between doing the right, conscientious thing, and acting wrongly and weakly, like the mother who won't let the doctor come near her sick, frightened baby. Because we don't accept this person's morality, we may see the situation very differently, thoroughly disapproving of the action he regards as the right one, and endorsing the action that from his point of view constitutes weakness and backsliding.

Conflicts between sympathy and bad morality won't always be like this, for we won't disagree with every single dictate of a bad morality. Still, it can happen in the way I have described, with the agent's right action being our wrong one, and vice versa. That is just what happens in a certain episode in chapter 16 of *The Adventures of Huckleberry Finn*, an episode that brilliantly illustrates how fiction can be instructive about real life.

Huck Finn has been helping his slave friend Jim to run away from Miss Watson, who is Jim's owner. In their raft journey down the Mississippi River, they are near to the place at which Jim will become legally free. Now let Huck take over the story:

Jim said it made him all over trembly and feverish to be so close to freedom. Well, I can tell you it made me all over trembly and feverish, too, to hear him, because I begun to get it through my head that he *was* most free—and who was to blame for it? Why, *me*. I couldn't get that out of my conscience, no how nor no way. . . . It hadn't ever come home to me, before, what this thing was that I was doing. But now it did; and it stayed with me, and scorched me more and more. I tried to make out to myself that *I* warn't to blame, because *I* didn't run Jim off from his rightful owner; but it warn't no use, conscience up and say, every time: "But you knowed he was running for his freedom, and you could a paddled ashore and told somebody." That was so—I couldn't get around that, no way. That was where it pinched. Conscience says to me:

"What had poor Miss Watson done to you, that you could see her nigger go off right under your eyes and never say one single word? What did that poor old woman do to you, that you could treat her so mean? . . ." I got to feeling so mean and so miserable I most wished I was dead.

Jim speaks of his plan to save up to buy his wife, and then his children, out of slavery; and he adds that if the children cannot be bought he will arrange to steal them. Huck is horrified:

> Thinks I, this is what comes of my not thinking. Here was this nigger which I had as good as helped to run away, coming right out flat-footed and saying he would steal his children—children that belonged to a man I didn't even know; a man that hadn't ever done me no harm. I was sorry to hear Jim say that, it was such a lowering of him. My conscience got to stirring me up hotter than ever, until at last I says to it: "Let up on me—it ain't too late, yet—I'll paddle ashore at first light, and tell." I felt easy, and happy, and light as a feather, right off. All my troubles was gone.

This is bad morality all right. In his earliest years, Huck wasn't taught any principles, and the only ones he has encountered since then are those of rural Missouri, in which slave-owning is just one kind of ownership and is not subject to critical pressure. It hasn't occurred to Huck to question those principles. So the action, to us abhorrent, of turning Jim in to the authorities presents itself *clearly* to Huck as the right thing to do.

For us, morality and sympathy would both dictate helping Jim to escape. If we felt any conflict, it would have both these on one side and something else on the other—greed for a reward, or fear of punishment. But Huck's morality conflicts with his sympathy, that is, with his unargued, natural feeling for his friend. The conflict starts when Huck sets off in the canoe toward the shore, pretending that he is going to reconnoiter, but really planning to turn Jim in:

> As I shoved off, [Jim] says: "Pooty soon I'll be a-shout'n for joy, en I'll say, it's all on accounts o' Huck I's a free man . . . Jim won't ever forget you, Huck; you's de bes' fren' Jim's ever had; en you's de *only* fren' old Jim's got now."
> I was paddling off, all in a sweat to tell on him; but when he says this, it seemed to kind of take the tuck all out of me. I went along slow then, and I warn't right down certain whether I was glad I started or whether I warn't. When I was fifty yards off, Jim says:
> "Dah you goes, de ole true Huck; de on'y white genlman dat ever kep' his promise to ole Jim." Well, I just felt sick. But I says, I *got* to do it—I can't get *out* of it.

In the upshot, sympathy wins over morality. Huck hasn't the strength of will to do what he sincerely thinks he ought to do. Two men hunting for runaway slaves ask him whether the man on his raft is black or white:

I didn't answer up prompt. I tried to, but the words wouldn't come. I tried, for a second or two, to brace up and out with it, but I warn't man enough—hadn't the spunk of a rabbit. I see I was weakening; so I just give up trying, and up and says: "He's white."

So Huck enables Jim to escape, thus acting weakly and wickedly—he thinks. In this conflict between sympathy and morality, sympathy wins.

One critic has cited this episode in support of the statement that Huck suffers "excruciating moments of wavering between honesty and respectability." That is hopelessly wrong, and I agree with the perceptive comment on it by another critic, who says:

> The conflict waged in Huck is much more serious: he scarcely cares for respectability and never hesitates to relinquish it, but he does care for honesty and gratitude—and both honesty and gratitude require that he should give Jim up. It is not, in Huck, honesty at war with respectability but love and compassion for Jim struggling against his conscience. His decision is for Jim and hell: a right decision made in the mental chains that Huck never breaks. His concern for Jim is and remains *irrational*. Huck finds many reasons for giving Jim up and none for stealing him. To the end Huck sees his compassion for Jim as a weak, ignorant, and wicked felony.[2]

That is precisely correct—and it can have that virtue only because Mark Twain wrote the episode with such unerring precision. The crucial point concerns *reasons*, which all occur on one side of the conflict. On the side of conscience, we have principles, arguments, considerations, ways of looking at things:

> It hadn't ever come home to me before what I was doing.

> I tried to make out that I warn't to blame.

> Conscience said "But you knowed . . ."—I couldn't get around that.

> What had poor Miss Watson done to you?

> This is what comes of my not thinking.

> Children that belonged to a man I didn't even know.

On the other side, the side of feeling, we get nothing like that. When Jim rejoices in Huck, as his only friend, Huck doesn't consider the claims of friendship or have the situation "come home" to him in a different light. All that happens is: "When he says this, it seemed to kind of take the tuck all out of me. I went along slow then, and I warn't right down certain whether I was glad I started or whether I warn't." Again, Jim's words about Huck's "prom-ise" to him don't give Huck any *reason* for changing his plan: in his morality, promises to slaves probably don't count. Their effect on him is of a different kind: "Well, I just felt sick." And when the moment for final decision comes, Huck doesn't weigh up pros and cons: he simply *fails* to do what he believes to be right—he isn't strong enough, hasn't "the spunk of a rabbit." This pas-sage in the novel is notable not just for its finely wrought irony, with Huck's weakness of will leading him to do the right thing, but also for its masterly handling of the difference between general moral principles and particular unreasoned emotional pulls.

Consider now another case of bad morality in conflict with human sym-pathy: the case of the odious Himmler. Here, from a speech he made to some SS generals, is an indication of the content of his morality:

> What happens to a Russian, to a Czech, does not interest me in the slight-est. What the nations can offer in the way of good blood of our type, we will take, if necessary by kidnapping their children and raising them here with us. Whether nations live in prosperity or starve to death like cattle interests me only in so far as we need them as slaves to our *Kultur*; otherwise it is of no in-terest to me. Whether [ten thousand] Russian females fall down from exhaus-tion while digging an antitank ditch interests me only in so far as the antitank ditch for Germany is finished.[3]

But has this a moral basis at all? And if it has, was there in Himmler's own mind any conflict between morality and sympathy? Yes there was. Here is more from the same speech:

> I also want to talk to you quite frankly on a very grave matter . . . I mean . . . the extermination of the Jewish race. . . . Most of you must know what it means when [one hundred] corpses are lying side by side, or [five hundred], or [one thousand]. To have stuck it out and at the same time—apart from exceptions caused by human weakness—to have remained decent fellows, that is what has made us hard. This is a page of glory in our history which has never been written and is never to be written.[4]

Himmler saw his policies as being hard to implement while still retaining one's human sympathies—while still remaining a "decent fellow." He is saying that only the weak take the easy way out and just squelch their sympathies, and is praising the stronger and more glorious course of retaining one's sympathies while acting in violation of them. In the same spirit, he ordered that when executions were carried out in concentration camps, those responsible "are to be influenced in such a way as to suffer no ill effect in their character and mental attitude."[5] A year later, he boasted that the SS had wiped out the Jews

> without our leaders and their men suffering any damage in their minds and souls. The danger was considerable, for there was only a narrow path between the Scylla of their becoming heartless ruffians unable any longer to treasure life, and the Charybdis of their becoming soft and suffering nervous breakdowns.[6]

And there really can't be any doubt that the basis of Himmler's policies was a set of principles that constituted his morality—a sick, bad, wicked *morality*. He described himself as caught in "the old tragic conflict between will and obligation."[7] And when his physician Kersten protested at the intention to destroy the Jews, saying that the suffering involved was "not to be contemplated," Kersten reports that Himmler replied:

> He knew that it would mean much suffering for the Jews. . . . "It is the curse of greatness that it must step over dead bodies to create new life. Yet we must . . . cleanse the soil or it will never bear fruit. It will be a great burden for me to bear."[8]

This, I submit, is the language of morality.

So in this case, tragically, bad morality won out over sympathy. I am sure that many of Himmler's killers did extinguish their sympathies, becoming "heartless ruffians" rather than "decent fellows"; but not Himmler himself. Although his policies ran against the human grain to a horrible degree, he did not sandpaper down his emotional surfaces so that there was no grain there, allowing his actions to slide along smoothly and easily. He did, after all, bear his hideous burden, and even paid a price for it. He suffered a variety of nervous and physical disabilities, including nausea and stomach convulsions, and Kersten was doubtless right in saying that these were "the expression of a psychic division which extended over his whole life."[9]

This same division must have been present in some of those officials of the Church who ordered heretics to be tortured so as to change their theological opinions. Along with the brutes and the cold careerists, there must have been some who cared, and who suffered from the conflict between their sympathies and their bad morality.

In the conflict between sympathy and bad morality, then, the victory may go to sympathy as in the case of Huck Finn, or to morality as in the case of Himmler.

Another possibility is that the conflict may be avoided by giving up, or not ever having, those sympathies that might interfere with one's principles. That seems to have been the case with Jonathan Edwards. I am afraid that I shall be doing an injustice to Edwards's many virtues, and to his great intellectual energy and inventiveness; for my concern is only with the worst thing about him—namely his morality, which was worse than Himmler's.

According to Edwards, God condemns some men to an eternity of unimaginably awful pain, though he arbitrarily spares others—"arbitrarily" because none deserve to be spared:

> Natural men are held in the hand of God over the pit of hell; they have deserved the fiery pit, and are already sentenced to it; and God is dreadfully provoked, his anger is as great towards them as to those that are actually suffering the executions of the fierceness of his wrath in hell . . . ; the devil is waiting for them, hell is gaping for them, the flames gather and flash about them, and would fain lay hold on them . . . ; and . . . there are no means within reach that can be any security to them. . . . All that preserves them is the mere arbitrary will, and un covenanted unobliged forebearance of an incensed God.[10]

Notice that he says "they have deserved the fiery pit." Edwards insists that men *ought* to be condemned to eternal pain; and his position isn't that this is right because God wants it, but rather that God wants it because it is right. For him, moral standards exist independently of God, and God can be assessed in the light of them (and of course found to be perfect). For example, he says:

> They deserve to be cast into hell; so that . . . justice never stands in the way, it makes no objection against God's using his power at any moment to destroy them. Yea, on the contrary, justice calls aloud for an infinite punishment of their sins.[11]

Elsewhere, he gives elaborate arguments to show that God is acting justly in damning sinners. For example, he argues that a punishment should be exactly as bad as the crime being punished; God is infinitely excellent, so any crime against him is infinitely bad; and so eternal damnation is exactly right as a punishment—it is infinite, but, as Edwards is careful also to say, it is "no more than infinite."[12]

Of course, Edwards himself didn't torment the damned; but the question still arises of whether his sympathies didn't conflict with his *approval* of eternal torment. Didn't he find it painful to contemplate any fellow human's being tortured forever? Apparently not:

> The God that holds you over the pit of hell, much as one holds a spider or some loathsome insect over the fire, abhors you, and is dreadfully provoked; . . . he is of purer eyes than to bear to have you in his sight; you are ten thousand times so abominable in his eyes as the most hateful venomous serpent is in ours.[13]

When God is presented as being as misanthropic as that, one suspects misanthropy in the theologian. This suspicion is increased when Edwards claims that "the saints in glory will . . . understand how terrible the sufferings of the damned are; yet . . . will not be sorry for [them]."[14] He bases this partly on a view of human nature whose ugliness he seems not to notice:

> The seeing of the calamities of others tends to heighten the sense of our own enjoyments. When the saints in glory, therefore, shall see the doleful state of the damned, how will this heighten their sense of the blessedness of their own state. . . . When they shall see how miserable others of their fellow-creatures are . . . ; when they shall see the smoke of their torment, . . . and hear their dolorous shrieks and cries, and consider that they in the mean time are in the most blissful state, and shall surely be in it to all eternity; how they will rejoice![15]

I hope this is less than the whole truth! His other main point about why the saints will rejoice to see the torments of the damned is that it is *right* that they should do so:

> The heavenly inhabitants . . . will have no love nor pity to the damned. . . . [This will not show] a want of a spirit of love in them . . . ; for the heavenly inhabitants will know that it is not fit that they should love [the damned] because they will know then, that God has no love to them, nor pity for them.[16]

The implication that *of course* one can adjust one's feelings of pity so that they conform to the dictates of some authority—doesn't this suggest that ordinary human sympathies played only a small part in Edwards's life?

Huck Finn, whose sympathies are wide and deep, could never avoid the conflict in that way; but he is determined to avoid it, and so he opts for the only other alternative he can see—to give up morality altogether. After he has tricked the slave hunters, he returns to the raft and undergoes a peculiar crisis:

> I got aboard the raft, feeling bad and low, because I knowed very well I had done wrong, and I see it warn't no use for me to try to learn to do right; a body that don't get *started* right when he's little, ain't got no show—when the pinch comes there ain't nothing to back him up and keep him to his work, and so he

gets beat. Then I thought a minute, and says to myself, hold on—s'pose you'd a done right and give Jim up; would you feel better than what you do now? No, says I, I'd feel bad—I'd feel just the same way I do now. Well, then, says I, what's the use you learning to do right, when it's troublesome to do right and ain't no trouble to do wrong, and the wages is just the same? I was stuck. I couldn't answer that. So I reckoned I wouldn't bother no more about it, but after this always do whichever come handiest at the time.

Huck clearly cannot conceive of having any morality except the one he has learned—too late, he thinks—from his society. He is not entirely a prisoner of that morality, because he does after all reject it; but for him that is a decision to relinquish morality as such; he cannot envisage revising his morality, altering its content in face of the various pressures to which it is subject, including pressures from his sympathies. For example, he does not begin to approach the thought that slavery should be rejected on moral grounds, or the thought that what he is doing is not theft because a person cannot be owned and therefore cannot be stolen.

The basic trouble is that he cannot or will not engage in abstract intellectual operations of any sort. In chapter 33, he finds himself "feeling to blame, somehow" for something he knows he had no hand in; he assumes that this feeling is a deliverance of conscience; and this confirms him in his belief that conscience shouldn't be listened to:

It don't make no difference whether you do right or wrong, a person's conscience ain't got no sense, and just goes for him *anyway*. If I had a yaller dog that didn't know no more than a person's conscience does, I would pison him. It takes up more room than all the rest of a person's insides, and yet ain't no good, nohow.

That brisk, incurious dismissiveness fits well with the comprehensive rejection of morality back on the raft. But this is a digression.

On the raft, Huck decides not to live by principles, but just to do whatever "comes handiest at the time"—always acting according to the mood of the moment. Because the morality he is rejecting is narrow and cruel, and his sympathies are broad and kind, the results will be good. But moral principles are good to have, because they help to protect one from acting badly at moments when one's sympathies happen to be in abeyance. On the highest possible estimate of the role one's sympathies should have, one can still allow for principles as embodiments of one's best feelings, one's broadest and keenest sympathies. On that view, principles can help one across intervals when one's feelings are at less than their best, that is, through periods of misanthropy or meanness or self-centeredness or depression or anger.

What Huck didn't see is that one can live by principles and yet have ultimate control over their content. And one way such control can be exercised is by checking of one's principles in the light of one's sympathies. This is sometimes a pretty straightforward matter. It can happen that a certain moral principle becomes untenable—meaning literally that one cannot hold it any longer—because it conflicts intolerably with the pity or revulsion or whatever that one feels when one sees what the principle leads to. One's experience may play a large part here: experiences evoke feelings, and feelings force one to modify principles. Something like this happened to the English poet Wilfred Owen, whose experiences in the First World War transformed him from an enthusiastic soldier into a virtual pacifist. I can't document his change of conscience in detail, but I want to present something that he wrote about the way experience can put pressure on morality.

The Latin poet Horace wrote that it is sweet and fitting (or right) to die for one's country—*dulce et decorum est pro patria mori*—and Owen wrote a fine poem about how experience could lead one to relinquish that particular moral principle.[17] He describes a man who is too slow donning his gas mask during a gas attack—"As under a green sea I saw him drowning," Owen says. The poem ends like this:

In all my dreams before my helpless sight
He plunges at me, guttering, choking, drowning.
If in some smothering dreams, you too could pace
Behind the wagon that we flung him in,
And watch the white eyes writhing in his face, His hanging face, like a devil's
    sick of sin;
If you could hear, at every jolt, the blood Come gargling from the froth-
    corrupted lungs, Bitter as the cud
Of vile, incurable sores on innocent tongues,—
My friend, you would not tell with such high zest
To children ardent for some desperate glory,
The old Lie: Dulce et decorum est
Pro patria mori.

There is a difficulty about drawing from all this a moral for ourselves. I imagine that we agree in our rejection of slavery, eternal damnation, genocide, and uncritical patriotic self-abnegation; so we shall agree that Huck Finn, Jonathan Edwards, Heinrich Himmler, and the poet Horace would all have done well to bring certain of their principles under severe pressure from ordinary human sympathies. But then we can say this because we can say that all those are bad moralities, whereas we cannot look at our own moralities and declare them bad. This is not arrogance: it is obviously incoherent for someone to declare the system of moral principles that he *accepts* to be *bad*, just as one cannot coherently say of anything that one *believes* it but it is *false*.

Still, although I can't point to any of my beliefs and say "That is false," I don't doubt that some of my beliefs *are* false; and so I should try to remain open to correction. Similarly, I accept every single item in my morality—that is inevitable—but I am sure that my morality could be improved, which is to say that it could undergo changes that I should be glad of once I had made them. So I must try to keep my morality open to revision, exposing it to whatever valid pressures there are—including pressures from my sympathies.

I don't give my sympathies a blank check in advance. In a conflict between principle and sympathy, principles ought sometimes to win. For example, I think it was right to take part in the Second World War on the allied side; there were many ghastly individual incidents that might have led someone to doubt the rightness of his participation in that war; and I think it would have been right for such a person to keep his sympathies in a subordinate place on those occasions, not allowing them to modify his principles in such a way as to make a pacifist of him.

Still, one's sympathies should be kept as sharp and sensitive and aware as possible, and not only because they can sometimes affect one's principles or one's conduct or both. Owen, at any rate, says that feelings and sympathies are vital even when they can do nothing but bring pain and distress. In another poem, he speaks of the blessings of being numb in one's feelings: "Happy are the men who yet before they are killed/Can let their veins run cold," he says. These are the ones who do not suffer from any compassion which, as Owen puts it, "makes their feet/Sore on the alleys cobbled with their brothers." He contrasts these "happy" ones, who "lose all imagination," with himself and others "who with a thought besmirch/Blood over all our soul." Yet the poem's verdict goes against the "happy" ones. Owen does not say that they will act worse than the others whose souls are besmirched with blood because of their keen awareness of human suffering. He merely says that they are the losers because they have cut themselves off from the human condition:

> By choice they made themselves immune
> To pity and whatever moans in man
> Before the last sea and the hapless stars;
> Whatever mourns when many leave these shores;
> Whatever shares
> The eternal reciprocity of tears.

CHAPTER TWO

~

Huckleberry Finn
and Moral Motivation[1]

ALAN H. GOLDMAN

Many philosophers and critics have claimed that novels can provide philosophically interesting ethical theses, but few have offered plausible examples.
Huckleberry Finn is often cited as an example of such a novel, but the moral
lessons abstracted from it have not been for the most part very interesting,
and where they have been, the interpretations in my view have not been correct. Many philosophers have also claimed, following Kant, that moral motivation is rationally required, that rational agents must be motivated to act on
their moral judgments or must be concerned for the interests of others. I will
argue here that Huck Finn shows us otherwise. I will argue against several
prominent interpretations that Huck is not irrational at the crucial relevant
points in the novel. In one sense, he is not morally motivated either, showing directly that moral motivation in that sense is not rationally required. In
another sense, he is morally motivated, but the nature of his motivational
state is such that it is not rationally required either. The philosophically
interesting conclusion is that, because Huck Finn is a rational agent who is
not morally motivated in any way that is rationally required, and as there
is no other normal route to moral motivation, such motivation is itself not
required of rational agents.

In the first half of the chapter, I will argue that Huck is not irrational in
being unmotivated to follow his explicit judgments of rightness and wrongness. It follows, of course, that rational agents need not be so motivated. As

opposed to my view, philosophers have previously judged Huck to be irrational, subject to weakness of will, in being unable to act on his moral judgment. But their interpretation rests on incorrect analyses of weak will and of the emotions on which Huck does act. I will also argue that, surprisingly, my refutation of moral judgment internalism, the thesis that these judgments must be motivating for agents, including rational agents who sincerely make them, does not eliminate expressivism as a meta-ethical theory, the theory that moral judgments express emotions. We can save expressivism in large part despite denying motivational force to all moral judgments by drawing a distinction between core judgments and others.

In the second half of the chapter, I will describe the way in which Huck is morally motivated by his sympathetic feeling toward his friend, the runaway slave Jim, but will argue that such emotion-based motivation is not of the kind that could be rationally required. This will require a brief examination of the relation of emotions to reasons. I will argue that Huck's emotion of sympathy reflects awareness of moral reasons without itself being required by them. Having this emotion, he is inconsistent in several ways in his moral attitudes, but I will maintain that this inconsistency does not amount to irrationality. I will argue as well that Huck's route to moral motivation is in an important sense the usual one, as is his view of the source of moral requirements, although the relation between the two is certainly unusual in his case. The thesis that rational agents need not be morally motivated is both philosophically controversial and interesting as well as implied by the character of Huckleberry Finn.

Huck's Explicit Moral Judgments

In borrowing his moral judgments from corrupt sources, Huck Finn justifiably fails to be moved by them, although he accepts their status as reflecting genuine moral requirements. He sincerely believes in a strict moral requirement to return all stolen property to its rightful owner, and he believes that his friend Jim, a runaway slave, is rightfully owned. He therefore accepts that he has a moral obligation to return Jim to his owner. But having become Jim's friend on the raft they share, when the opportunity arises to turn him in, Huck finds himself unable to do so. He therefore decides to wash his hands entirely of moral requirements as he sees them and risk an eternity in Hell. Having renounced morality, it is not that his desire to help Jim overrides his motivation to follow his moral judgments: he has no remaining motivation to do what he believes morality requires. If Huck is rational in this attitude, then rational agents need not be motivated at all by their explicit judgments of rightness and wrongness.

Prominent earlier interpretations of the text by philosophers, however, see Huck as irrational in failing to turn in Jim, as a victim of weak will, a paradigm form of irrationality. If Huck's decision is irrational given his moral attitudes and judgments, then, of course, his case fails to show that rational agents need not be morally motivated. In his seminal article on the topic, Jonathan Bennett sees Huck as weak-willed in being unable to resist acting on his feeling of sympathy for Jim as opposed to his considered, even if bad, judgment of what is morally required of him.[2] A bare feeling propels him to act against his moral principles, however corrupt those principles may be. Feelings, for Bennett, are themselves irrational (he might have better said arational), while moral reasons derive from principles that enter into deliberation about what one ought to do. Huck does not deliberate and does not view his feeling for Jim as providing him with any moral reasons. He simply cannot resist acting on his feeling against his moral judgment. The moral reasons as he sees them all lie on one side; only an irrational feeling opposes them. He is weak-willed in acting against what he takes to be his strongest, indeed in the circumstances, his only reasons. In a much more recent article, Nomy Arpaly and Timothy Schroeder agree that Huck is weak-willed, albeit commendably so, in that he believes one action to be right and yet does another. He is incapable of doing what he judges to be overall right, and this meets the definition of irrational weakness of will.[3]

But this interpretation of Huck as irrational rests on a simplistic view of emotions in Bennett's case, and on an incomplete definition of weakness of will. Regarding the latter, weakness of will is not best characterized simply as failure to do what one explicitly or consciously believes one ought to do, but instead as failure, usually resulting from an irresistible bare urge, to act on the strongest reasons of which one is in some sense aware. When agents suffer from this malady, they feel torn by conflicting motivations and unable to muster the courage to act on their strongest reasons or to resist the urge to take the easy way out. Neither of these descriptions fits Huck Finn. He requires courage *not* to turn his friend in, and continuing to hide him is not the easy way out for Huck or the way of least resistance to an urge. In regard to his emotion of sympathy, it is not a bare feeling or urge. Even if we are not cognitivists about all emotions, we should recognize that intentional emotions, those directed at persons or objects, represent their objects as having certain properties. They contain implicit judgments[4] and therefore an implicit awareness of reasons. Sympathy is such an emotion.

These judgments implicit in emotions do not typically arise from or alter in response to reasons in the way that conscious judgments or beliefs do. In fact, the adaptive value of emotions lies precisely in their bypassing ordinary rational deliberation in prompting more automatic and immediate reactions.[5] Nevertheless, these implicit judgments may be seen to reflect an awareness of reasons when the emotions are fitting or appropriate reactions to their objects. In bypassing rational deliberation or weighing of reasons, emotions can threaten or defeat rational judgment, but they can also implicitly embody the contents of such judgments. When I fear a large snake, this fear causes me to flee immediately without deliberating about the reasons for doing so (and this may be a good thing for me). Nor does my fear necessarily disappear if I learn that the snake is not dangerous and therefore gives me no reason to flee. My belief adjusts to my altered recognition of reasons, but my emotion may not. My fear implicitly judges the snake to be dangerous, although I may at the same time consciously recognize that it is not. The implicit judgment is not the product of weighing reasons. However, when the judgment is correct, when the snake is dangerous and I have reason to flee, the judgment can be seen to reflect the reason of which I am implicitly aware.

Huck's guiding emotion is sympathy for his friend Jim. Sympathy contains the implicit judgment that a person needs help in light of his situation. In Huck's case, this emotion is entirely fitting, and its implicit judgment reflects awareness of the reasons to help Jim escape from slavery. In reflecting such reasons, this is a moral emotion, containing a judgment about the right thing to do, although Huck does not consciously recognize it as such because of his very limited view of what morality requires. Moral emotions are those that typically prompt or reflect moral behavior: guilt, anger, and disgust, but also empathy, sympathy, and pride. In Huck's case, it is clear that his trip on the river and away from the corrupt society he flees constitutes and in the novel symbolizes a moral transformation, and that this transformation is prompted by his developing emotional attachment to Jim.[6] Having developed this sympathetic relation, Huck is implicitly aware of the reasons to help Jim, although he does not conceive them as moral reasons. As a moral emotion, Huck's sympathy reflects reasons constitutive of the rightness of his action of continuing to hide Jim. The action's being right consists in its being a reaction to the injustice of slavery and to his friendship. In being implicitly aware of these reasons through his emotion, Huck is implicitly aware of the rightness of his action, although he explicitly judges it to be wrong at the same time. He is aware of the moral reasons that require him to act as he does, although this awareness is not conscious or explicit, and he does not conceive of these reasons as moral.

Rational agents are those who act on the strongest reasons of which they are aware. These reasons reflect their deepest or most important concerns at the time, although priorities among concerns can certainly shift over time. Deliberation, the conscious weighing of reasons, is not required in the normal course of rational actions. It normally occurs only in those relatively rare occasions in which agents become aware of serious conflicts among the reasons on which they could act. Normally what we do automatically reflects our concerns at the time and so reflects the reasons that indicate ways of satisfying those concerns in the circumstances. Normally we act rationally without having to think or debate with ourselves about our reasons. We remain focused on our objectives and not on our reasons, which motivate us automatically by indicating how to achieve those objectives. But if most (or all) reasons derive internally from the rational concerns we have, and if they typically motivate us automatically, we might wonder how we can ever fail to be motivated by them, how we can ever fail to be rational. The answer is that our deepest and most general concerns can fail to translate into specific desires or motivations, or those specific desires can fail to generate actions because of various interfering factors. In weakness of will, the interfering factor is usually an urge that is incoherent with one's deeper and more stable concerns but is, as the term indicates, more urgently felt.

In Huck Finn's case, the judgment implicit in his sympathy reflects a deeper concern than his concern for morality as he conceives it. Indeed, as emphasized earlier, he is not concerned with or motivated by morality as he conceives it at all. Usually, when an emotion opposes a considered, conscious judgment, it is the latter that reflects one's deeper and more stable concerns and the former that temporarily clouds one's more sober and rational judgment. One must then try to control or suppress one's emotion. But that is not always the case: sometimes one should instead trust to one's feeling as indicative of the rational course of action. This is the case with Huck. His reasons for helping Jim are stronger than his reason for turning him in and returning him to slavery. Although Huck does not engage in moral deliberation, does not consciously weigh the moral reasons on both sides, he does act on his strongest reasons deriving from his friendship and his implicit sense of justice as reflected in his sympathetic feeling. Agents can have reasons of which they are not consciously aware and be motivated by or act on such reasons without conceiving of them as such. Again, this is the case with Huck Finn. Because he acts on his strongest reasons and is implicitly aware of them, he is not weak-willed, although he may think that he is. His own description of his situation might mislead interpreters, but the description is ironic.

Indeed, as pointed out earlier, it takes strong will to risk his own freedom by continuing to hide Jim. Just as the genuine moral reasons all lie on that side, so does the danger to his own welfare, and so his action is courageous as opposed to weak-willed. He does not see himself as courageous even though he takes himself to be risking eternal damnation, but like his misguided in-terpreters, he simply misinterprets his own action. This misinterpretation is a large part of the irony in this part of the novel, irony that is partly missed by those who see him as weak-willed. Despite his own denial, Huck is clearly morally motivated, as we infer from his behavior. He is only not conscious of being morally motivated because he does not act on his explicit judgment that his action is wrong. In the same way that he is moved by moral consid-erations, one who appreciates an artwork might be moved immediately by its beauty without conceiving of the aesthetic reasons to be moved as such. One would then be sensitive to and responding to these reasons emotionally without being explicitly conscious of them. Huck responds to Jim's moral status and to his morally abhorrent condition in the same way. He is aware of and responding to the moral reasons he has (while not conceiving of them as such), and so he is not weak-willed. If he is not weak-willed, then he is not irrational, as this is the only form of irrationality of which the interpreters accuse him. Mark Twain himself is neither approving of irrationality here nor condemning Huck for being irrational; instead, he is being ironic in having Huck describe the incident as he does.

One must conclude, then, because Huck's motives do not track his judg-ment that his action is wrong, even though he is rational and virtuous, that rational agents need not be motivated by their explicit judgments of right-ness and wrongness. It might be objected that it is crucial to this example that Huck is mistaken in what he takes the moral requirement to be. If my account of Huck's mental condition is accepted, it might be claimed that he fails to be motivated by his moral judgment of wrongness because he implicitly recognizes that it is in error. But in fact he does not doubt his judgment, instead fully buying into the corrupt attitude toward slaves of his society as reflecting what morality requires. That this is his view of morality is supported rather than being refuted by his wholesale dismissal of moral obligations as guides to his conduct. It is true, as I have been emphasizing, that he implicitly recognizes opposing moral reasons to help Jim escape, and that this recognition in large part explains his dismissal of what he takes to be his moral obligations. But, as I have also been emphasizing, it is important here that he does not recognize these reasons as moral reasons. That is why he does not recognize the inconsistency in his judgments or attitudes, does not see it as an inconsistency in moral judgments. Instead, he fully trusts his judgment that hiding Jim is wrong as representative of morality in general, which is why he is willing to dismiss the whole business. So he does not implicitly sense an error in moral judgment, and he is not irrational for generalizing from his judgment to the conclusion that morality itself is not worthy of allegiance. A proper inference from a false belief is not thereby irrational.

Error might be claimed to be crucial to the example in a different way that still disqualifies it from refuting a rational requirement to be motivated by one's judgments of rightness and wrongness. If an agent only falsely believes that she has a reason R to do something, then R is not a reason to do it. And if R is not a reason, then it can be claimed that there is no rational requirement to be moved by it. A daughter might believe that she has a moral obligation to do whatever her father orders her to do, but she might be rationally unmotivated to adhere to some outlandish parental demand. This would not show that she need not be motivated by genuine moral requirements. Similarly, it can be claimed that Huck is not rationally required to be moved by his false moral judgment that hiding Jim is wrong, but this does not show that agents can rationally fail to be moved by judgments that reflect genuine moral reasons.

In reply, we can point out first that Huck is relevantly different from the recalcitrant daughter. He not only fails to be moved by his judgment of what he ought to do with Jim; generalizing from this attitude, he fails to be moved by any explicit judgments of rightness and wrongness, many of which will be correct. And once more, although this attitude is based on a generalizing inference from a particular false judgment about what morality requires, it is not thereby rendered irrational. Perhaps more relevant is that we all believe that our moral judgments are correct from the moral point of view when we sincerely make them. Some of these judgments may well be incorrect or, unbeknown to us, inconsistent with others that we make. But we cannot be rationally required to be motivated only by our actually correct judgments, when we do not know that our incorrect judgments are incorrect. Rationality depends on our reactions to our reasons as we are aware of them, assuming that we have arrived at our judgments of reasons in ways that are not themselves irrational. Either we must be motivated by all our sincere moral judgments that are not irrationally formed, or there is no such rational requirement at all. A requirement of rationality must be able to be followed: it must be used to guide rational agents. We cannot be guided by a requirement to obey only our correct moral judgments. As for Huck Finn, he may be mistaken in his belief that the demands of his society are genuine moral demands, but he is not irrational to accept them as such. Conventionalism may be a false meta-ethical theory, but those who hold it explicitly or implicitly are again not thereby irrational.

Thus it does not seem to matter to the connection between rationality and moral motivation that Huck is mistaken in his moral judgment. His case still shows that rational agents need not be motivated by their explicit judgments of moral rightness and wrongness. But we are not free yet from objections on grounds of meta-ethical considerations. Moral judgment internalists can still offer their standard reply to lack of motivation: that agents who are not moved by their moral judgments do not make genuine moral assertions but judge only in an inverted commas sense. Huckleberry Finn's judgments simply mimic those of his corrupt society, they will point out. In simply mouthing his society's moral principles, he is quoting their morality without sincerely adapting it as his own. Hence, he is not making genuine moral assertions and that is why he is not, and need not be, motivated by them.

But this appeal to pseudo-moral judgments is an ad hoc invention of the defenders of moral judgment internalism, as the case of Huck Finn again makes clear. The only evidence possible for the claim that his judgment of wrongness is not genuine is his failure to be motivated by it. Citing this as evidence is, of course, circular or question begging. Huck's explicit moral assertions are borrowed from his society and his religious education, but then so are the moral judgments of most people. That the judgments derive from these sources does not begin to show that they are not ordinary or sincere. These are the only moral beliefs that Huck knows as such, and he is entirely sincere in taking them to be expressions of what morality requires. As noted in the previous paragraphs, that they are wrong or corrupt is irrelevant to the question of whether, in sincerely believing them, Huck ought to be motivated by them.

Moral judgment internalists are most often expressivists: they take moral judgments to be intrinsically motivating because they take them to express positive or negative attitudes or emotions, and these attitudes or emotions are themselves motivational, including within them dispositions to certain behaviors (as well as implicit judgments, as emphasized earlier). If expressivism is the correct meta-ethical theory, then all agents are motivated by their sincere moral judgments, and the question whether rational agents need be so motivated is moot. Does the Huck Finn example then refute expressivism? Not entirely. I have said that Huck's sympathy implicitly involves the judgment that Jim ought to be helped. Huck is implicitly aware of the rightness of helping Jim; he implicitly judges it right to do so, although he does not consciously accept this as a moral judgment. Despite not conceiving it as moral, he also implicitly recognizes this to be a stronger reason than any reason he might have to turn Jim in, as it reflects a deeper concern and he is motivated to act on it. Despite not tracking his explicit moral judgments,

Huck's motives do track his concrete judgment about what is owed to his friend. We can therefore characterize these emotional judgments as core moral judgments for Huck, as opposed to those moral beliefs borrowed from his society that fail to motivate him. His core moral judgments express the emotion of sympathy. Thus, they suggest expressivism as a meta-ethical theory instead of refuting it.

But these core moral beliefs are not Huck's only moral judgments. He has other moral beliefs that fail to motivate him and which are inconsistent with his regard for Jim. And in addition to these two sets of moral beliefs, there are others that Huck ought to hold on grounds of consistency with his core beliefs that he fails to hold, for example that all slaves deserve the same moral regard and ought to be helped. If the core judgments of more typically morally minded people also express such emotions as sympathy, guilt, pride, anger, and disgust, for them too these are not the only sources of moral judgments. They are also rationally required to accept a constraint of consistency or coherence on their moral beliefs: they must not judge cases differently without being able to specify a morally relevant difference between them.[7] And the judgments outside the core to which they are committed by this constraint may not express the same emotional commitments as those in the core, even if they accept these judgments as Huck does not. Whether this lack of commitment amounts to irrationality will be addressed below. The point here, and the final one of this section, is that a distinction can be drawn between core moral judgments that express deeply felt attitudes and other judgments that agents take to be moral, or to which they are committed on grounds of consistency, that need not express such attitudes. Thus, my interpretation of the Huck Finn case and his failure to be motivated by his explicit moral judgments do not imply a rejection of expressivism or acceptance of either conventionalism or realism on the meta-ethical level.

Expressivism may well provide the best account of our core moral judgments. But this core varies from individual to individual and may be vanishingly small for some. Thus the analysis so far also leaves open the question whether a rational person must be motivated by moral demands at all. Huck Finn is morally motivated and rational but is his sort of motivation rationally required?

Huck's Moral Motivation

In the first section I argued that Huck Finn's core moral judgments are implicitly contained in his emotion of sympathy for Jim. I pointed out that emotions in general, at least intentional ones, contain such implicit judgments or beliefs as well as dispositions to react to their objects. We may add to these aspects bodily changes or symptoms and sensations, sometimes analyzed as perceptions of these bodily changes. When I fear a snake, I implicitly judge it to be dangerous, am disposed to flee, might tremble and feel increased heart beat, or feel a chill run through me. Our focus, however, is on the judgments implicit in emotions, and especially on the moral judgments implicit in moral emotions such as sympathy. These emotions, I argued, may reflect genuine moral reasons, but they do not typically arise through the deliberate weighing of the reasons that would justify the judgments.

When I am sympathetic to the plight of another person, my sympathy may be fitting in relation to her plight, may involve implicit awareness of the moral reasons to help her. But I might also feel sympathy for Jim, whom I, unlike Huck, know to be only a fictional character. Such emotions arise immediately from cues often subconsciously processed, and they prompt immediate reactions, or at least dispositions to react. These dispositions can be suppressed when it is known that action is out of place or impossible, but the other aspects of the emotions do not necessarily alter in response to the recognition that the reasons that may be reflected in their judgments do not exist in particular cases. I might continue to fear a snake after being informed by a reliable source that it is not dangerous, and I might continue to feel sympathy for Jim when I know he is not real. Such feelings can be condemned as irrational, but they may be better seen as indicating again the largely arational nature of emotions.

Might certain emotions and the judgments implicit in them nevertheless be rationally required by the reasons that make them appropriate when they are? In general, this seems again not to be the case. When fear is appropriate in the face of danger, we nevertheless do not typically blame or hold the person to be irrational who faces the danger fearlessly. We are more likely to praise her unusual courage (although we also sometimes condemn fearless actions as rash or unnecessarily risky). Likewise, when anger at a slight would be fitting, we do not condemn as irrational the person who remains calm or forgiving; and when pride would be warranted, it is not irrational to remain modest or even self-effacing. Thus, in general, emotions seem not to be rationally required even when they would be fitting or appropriate, even when there appear to be reasons to feel fear, anger, or pride.

Huck Finn's sympathy is entirely appropriate and reflects the genuine reasons to help Jim escape his plight. Might there be something about moral emotions, and specifically about the concern for others expressed in this emotion of sympathy, that makes them rationally required when other emotions are not? Put another way, is it irrational to lack this emotion, when it might be not only rationally permitted, but praiseworthy, to lack others? Answering this question requires brief further analysis of rationality, irrationality, and the rational constraint on moral judgments mentioned earlier. Once more we may narrow the task by focusing on Huck Finn's case.

I have argued that Huck is not irrational in the way that previous interpreters have held him to be. Practical irrationality consists in self-defeat, just as does irrationality in belief. The aim of belief is truth. Thus, an irrational belief is one that flies in the face of known or available evidence, as evidence indicates truth. An irrational belief is defeating of its own aim in the way that it is acquired or persists. The aim of action is the fulfillment of the prioritized motivations that prompt the actions. We act in order to fulfill our concerns or motives in acting. Irrational people defeat their own strongest concerns or deepest aims by failing to specify them when they are general or by failing to act on them when they are specific, usually by acting on a more superficial urge instead. They fail to act on those reasons that indicate ways to satisfy these deepest concerns. Rational people avoid such self-defeat. They are coherent in their motivations and actions, acting on the strongest reasons that exist in light of these motivations. Priorities among desires change with contexts and opportunities for satisfying them, but rational agents do not sacrifice satisfaction of deeper concerns, those that connect with many others, to more superficial urges.

Huck Finn does not appear to be irrational in the ways just described. He acts on his emotion of sympathy instead of on his explicit moral judgment, but I claimed that this emotion reflects a stronger moral reason for him, in that his concern for Jim and their friendship is deeper than his concern (or lack of it) for doing what his society deems right, for following the only moral requirements as he conceives them. In acting on his stronger reasons, he is perfectly rational, coherent in his motivations and actions, and not self-defeating. But I also pointed earlier to a rational constraint on moral judgments that Huck does violate. We must ask whether in violating this constraint he is practically irrational in a way that shows moral concern to be rationally required.

The constraint in question requires not judging cases differently without being able to find a morally relevant difference between them. To judge one case right and another wrong when they are similar in every morally relevant respect is to promote and defeat the same moral value at stake in the same way, again a form of incoherence. Huck violates this constraint first by failing to grant the same moral regard to other slaves that he grants to Jim. His sympathy for Jim is personalized—it grows directly from his personal relationship with his friend—and it does not generalize to other slaves, who of course deserve equal moral status simply in virtue of being human. When asked whether anyone was hurt in a boat accident that Huck made up, he responds, "No'm. Killed a nigger." He certainly is guilty of moral inconsistency here. And second, he is guilty of an even more obvious though less easily detectable form of inconsistency in implicitly sensing the strong moral reasons to hide Jim while explicitly judging that he ought to turn him in. (Again, there is irony in this inconsistency, as the far more common form is to be explicitly fair or nonracist but implicitly or subconsciously racist.) He judges the same case in incompatible ways without reconciling these conflicting attitudes. He is morally incoherent in these two ways, the first being the more common form, but is he thereby practically irrational?

If he is, then first, his case may once more fail to show that rational agents need not be motivated by their moral judgments, and second, his case may instead show that some moral concerns are rationally required, given other concerns. It is indeed very tempting to assimilate moral incoherence of the sort suffered by Huck Finn to practical irrationality as characterized above. Both are forms of incoherence, which is why we can describe the constraint on moral reasoning as a rational constraint. And moral judgments, after all, are typically intended to guide actions, and are therefore practical. But there is a crucial difference in that, while moral incoherence amounts to promoting and failing to promote the same moral value in relevantly similar contexts, it does not amount to self-defeat for the agent himself, as does genuine practical irrationality. To see this, we may first consider a more typical case and then return to the case of Huck Finn.

Moral incoherence occurs when an agent fails to extend a concern to others who fall under the same relevant description as those who enjoy such status, as Huck Finn fails to extend moral concern to all slaves. A common form of such incoherence occurs these days in our attitudes toward animals. A meat eater who considers it seriously wrong to eat dogs might well be incapable of finding a morally relevant difference in this regard between dogs and pigs, although he enjoys his BLTs completely guilt free. While his omnivorous action lacks justification by his own lights, it does not defeat any aim or purpose that he accepts as his own. In fact, it satisfies his desire for gustatory pleasure, although it balances that desire in an arbitrary way against the reasons for not killing, accepting an arbitrary subclass of these reasons as his own. If practical irrationality consists in self-defeat, then a failure to respond to such moral reasons does not appear to be practically irrational, unless it is itself a case of weakness of will, which many such cases are not. The meat eater in question is not giving in to an irresistible urge at the expense of a deeper concern when he orders his bacon. He has no concern for the pigs. He may even recognize that what he does is wrong in this instance by his own lights, but that recognition will not move him to abstention. He is morally inconsistent, as he may acknowledge, but his inconsistency amounts simply to a narrowing of the scope of his accepted moral values in an arbitrary way, in a way that cannot be defended by appeal to any moral reasons.

Moral values may have limited motivational force for agents who must balance them against nonmoral concerns. These limits may be expressed in ways that are morally arbitrary but that enable agents to better achieve their personal aims. If the latter is true, then the agents who limit their moral concerns in these ways are not defeating their strongest aims and are not practically irrational. Even if they cannot justify limiting their concerns to those relatively few people they care about, they do not defeat their own aims in doing so. They fail to extend the motivational force behind their core moral beliefs to other judgments implied or supported by those core judgments, but this does not defeat any motivations they have and may even serve to better fulfill them.

Huck Finn is not motivated by self-interest in failing to extend his moral regard to slaves other than Jim. He may in fact be serving his self-interest by his attitude in better fitting in to his corrupt society and limiting the risks he takes, but this is not his motive. But neither is he defeating his own aims and motivations by his inconsistency. If the meat eater is not practically irrational, then neither is Huck. He suffers from an extreme form of a moral malady, a lesser form of which infects most of us nonsaints: a failure to extend moral concern or sympathy and resultant altruistic action to all those who are not relevantly different from those whose distresses we do seek to alleviate. When I convince my ethics class students that they morally ought to contribute substantially to the alleviation of hunger in distant areas of the world, the vast majority even of those who acknowledge this obligation remain unmoved to fulfill it. To hold us all practically irrational for such moral failings is to extend the notion of irrationality far beyond its standard use and meaning.

Thus, failure to extend moral concerns in a fully coherent way does not amount to practical irrationality any more than would failure to extend aesthetic taste in a transparently coherent way. Appreciating Haydn but not Mozart, or Haydn's Symphony 101 but not 104, would be highly unusual, aesthetically arbitrary, and even incomprehensible and indefensible, if the aesthetic reasons to appreciate the 101st apply also to the 104th. But once more, unless the listener had the unusual aim of appreciating all Haydn symphonies or all composers in the classic tradition, her arbitrarily limited taste would not be practically irrational. If asked why she passed up a chance to hear the 104th in concert, an acceptable response would be "I do not care for that symphony." Her lack of appreciation cannot be defended by appeal to aesthetic reasons, but it does not defeat her own aims and may serve them better if she has other things to do. Neither then is Huck's arbitrarily limited moral concern practically irrational.

If extending such concern coherently is not required by practical rationality, then lack of a rational requirement seems even clearer for those who lack moral concerns altogether. They are not guilty of moral inconsistency, of narrowing the scope of moral values they accept in an arbitrary way. Such persons, complete amoralists, are classified as psychopaths, however. Arguments against the claim that moral concern is rationally required often appeal to such characters. But they are widely recognized to be abnormal and psychologically impaired. Debate then ensues whether their impairment is affective or cognitive, or both, and again, whether they use moral terms in the same way we do.[8] Given the inconclusiveness of this debate, the argument is better made by appeal to more psychologically normal individuals, such as Huckleberry Finn and us.

While Huck is not unusual in seeing all moral demands as imposed by society and God, he is atypical in having his core moral judgments expressed only implicitly in his sympathetic feeling for Jim and so failing to translate into explicit judgments of right and wrong. Most people's core judgments largely overlap with their society's ethical code, and most people's judgments of right and wrong derive from more concrete reactions to right- and wrong-making properties. These judgments might seem to derive at least in part from social programming or education, although the origin of their motivational force might lie elsewhere. It might be claimed in light of efforts at moral education that, independent of emotional development, there is another more purely cognitive route to moral maturity that rational people must take. But one of the central moral lessons of Twain's novel lies in his showing us precisely how moral concern develops through emotional attachment in personal relationships. Our concerns for others, like Huck's, also develop outward as our relationships expand, until, unlike him, we come to an appreciation of common humanity. Developing affect is the key to such moral development, as it is in Huck's case, not coming to appreciate newly learned arguments.

If there is a route to required moral motivation through an argument that all rational people can grasp, no one has given the argument. When my students fail to extend concern to distant people or future generations, demonstrating the most common form of partial amorality, their fault is not a failure to understand the argument that such people are not relevantly different from others. The students' fault is not a fault of reason, but of lack of real sympathy, predictable from lack of personal contact. If moral concern were a requirement of reason that all rational people could grasp, then, as my students are rational people, all I would need to do to get them to feed the starving in Africa would be to present them with the simple argument just indicated. Despite the desires or pretensions of classes in ethics, such is not the case.

For Huck Finn, by contrast, all the arguments he knows fall on the wrong side, but as Mark Twain himself noted in a journal, his heart is fortunately in the right place, at least when it comes to Jim on the river. Huck is not unlike Everyman: a bit more corrupted by his corrupt society than is Everyman these days (does Trump's popularity say otherwise?), but a bit better in his ability to escape its rules and trust to his natural moral feelings when out on the river. Most important, his route to real moral motivation is that of Everyman. It is by way of developing moral emotions toward other people and their actions, emotions that embody implicit awareness of moral reasons without being rationally required.

CHAPTER THREE

Sympathy, Principles, and Conscience

Getting to the Heart of Huck Finn's Moral Praiseworthiness

ROBERT FUDGE

"Persons attempting to find a motive in this narrative will be prosecuted; persons attempting to find a moral in it will be banished; persons attempting to find a plot in it will be shot."[1] So wrote Mark Twain in the Notice preceding chapter 1 of *Adventures of Huckleberry Finn*. I must then admit up front that this paper subjects me to banishment, for I, like many philosophers past and present, seek to draw a moral from the novel. I am not so presumptuous, however, as to try to divine some grand message that Twain sought to impart to us through his work. Rather, I will focus on the much more restricted, but equally interesting, question of what we are to make of Huck Finn's conscience and what his ostensibly acting against his conscience portends for how we think of Huck morally.

Huck's Dilemma

The relevant passages concerning this topic appear in chapter 16, as Huck and Jim are floating down the Mississippi toward Cairo. The prospect of reaching a free town has distinctively different effects on them:

> Jim said it made him all over trembly and feverish to be so close to freedom. Well, I can tell you it made me all over trembly and feverish, too, to hear him, because I begun to get it through my head that he *was* most free—and who was to blame for it? Why, me. I couldn't get that out of my conscience, no

30

how nor no way. It got to troubling me so I couldn't rest; I couldn't stay still in one place. It hadn't ever come home to me before, what this thing was that I was doing. But now it did; and it stayed with me, and scorched me more and more. I tried to make out to myself that *I* waren't to blame, because *I* didn't run Jim off from his rightful owner; but it warn't no use, conscience up and says, every time, "But you knowed he was running for his freedom, and you could 'a' paddled ashore and told somebody." That was so—I couldn't get around that no way. That was where it pinched. Conscience says to me, "What had poor Miss Watson done to you that you could see her nigger go off right under your eyes and never say one single word? What did that poor old woman do to you that you could treat her so mean? Why, she tried to learn you your book, she tried to learn you your manners, she tried to be good to you every way she knowed how. *That's* what she done.[2]

Quite unequivocally, Huck reports that he considers what he is doing wrong and as a result he is having pangs of conscience. This response is entirely consistent with the moral principles that he has learned and that he has observed in those around him. He only comes to feel worse as Jim tells of how, once free, he will work to earn enough money to buy his wife and then together they will either buy or steal back their children:

I was sorry to hear Jim say that, it was such a lowering of him. My conscience got to stirring me up hotter than ever, until at last I says to it, "Let up on me— it ain't too late yet—I'll paddle ashore at the first light and tell." I felt easy and happy and light as a feather right off.[3]

His resolve to do what he considers right clearly eases his conscience. And yet, Huck's determination wavers as he sets off from the raft to turn in Jim, who calls out:

Pooty soon I'll be a-shout'n' for joy, en I'll say, it's all on accounts o' Huck; I's a free man, en I couldn't ever ben free ef it hadn't ben for Huck; Huck done it. Jim won't ever forgit you, Huck; you's de bes' fren' Jim's ever had; en you's de *only* fren' old Jim's got now.[4]

As Huck reports, this "seemed to kind of take the tuck" right out of him; nevertheless, he remained resolved to do what's right: "I *got* to do it—I can't get *out* of it." Despite the sympathies that have been aroused within him, Huck is determined to act in accordance with his moral principles. But then, something extraordinary happens. When Huck has the opportunity to give Jim up, his resolve fails him and Jim is spared.

Even at this stage, Huck does not feel good about what he has done; he has, after all, violated his moral principles. At the same time, he recognizes that were he to have acted differently, he would feel equally bad. As a result, he chooses the only course he thinks open to him—he resolves to reject morality altogether:

> They went off and I got aboard the raft, feeling bad and low, because I knowed very well I had done wrong, and I see it warn't no use for me to try to learn to do right; a body that don't get *started* right when he's little ain't got no show—when the pinch comes there ain't nothing to back him up and keep him to his work, and so he gets beat. . . . Well then, says I, what's the use you learning to do right when it's troublesome to do right and ain't no trouble to do wrong, and the wages is just the same? I was stuck. I couldn't answer that. So I reckoned I wouldn't bother no more about it, but after this always do whichever come handiest at the time.[5]

What, then, do philosophers have to say about all this?

Huck's (Alleged) Weakness of Will

In one influential treatment of these passages, Jonathan Bennett argues that what Huck experiences is a classic case of weakness of will, or what the ancient Greeks called *akrasia* (literally, "lack of mastery").[6] As explained by Aristotle, we act akratically when we act against reason because of some pathos (that is, emotion or feeling). In some cases of akrasia, the agent acts impetuously, meaning that she does not deliberate before the fact but simply acts from emotion. In other cases, the person does deliberate but nevertheless acts from weakness; his passions overwhelm his reason. Given the reasoning he engages in before setting off to betray Jim, it is this second form of akrasia to which Huck seemingly succumbs.

Of course, as Bennett notes, there are times when reason or principle should trump our sympathies. A parent who feels great distress for her child who is about to undergo a painful yet necessary medical procedure must overcome her feelings and do what reason tells her is right. To succumb to akrasia in such a case would subject the parent to moral blame. What distinguishes the case of Huck Finn from the sympathetic parent is that we approve of Huck's actions despite his weakness of will, because his sympathies for Jim lead him to act contrary to a bad morality, specifically, a morality that treats slaves as the rightful property of others and as not worthy of moral consideration. We praise Huck's action, because in saving Jim we know Huck has acted rightly, despite his going against his conscience.

Central to Bennett's analysis is an explicit account of what it means to act according to conscience; namely, it means nothing more than acting according to one's principles.

On the side of conscience we have principles, arguments, considerations, ways of looking at things:

"It hadn't ever come home to me before what I was doing"

"I tried to make out that I warn't to blame"

"Conscience said 'But you knowed . . .'—I couldn't get around that"

"What had poor Miss Watson done to you?"

"This is what comes of my not thinking"

"Children that belonged to a man I didn't even know"[7]

When Huck goes against these principles, he does not formulate and weigh contrary reasons but simply notes that Jim's words "seemed to kind of take the tuck out of him." His sympathies, in other words, override his principles. His will to do what he considers right simply fails him, and this is what subsequently leads him to feel bad about what he has done.

The upshot of all this, according to Bennett (although he doesn't put it in precisely these terms), is that acting according to conscience is not a reliable guide to moral conduct, and so it does not always make us morally praiseworthy. To be sure, morality at times requires us to act on principle against our sympathies: "moral principles are good to have, because they help to protect one from acting badly at moments when one's sympathies happen to be in abeyance."[8] At other times, however, morality requires that our sympathies override our principles: "experiences evoke feelings, and feelings force one to modify principles."[9] Huck's feelings for Jim lead him to reject his prejudicial morality—at least in this one instance—just as nowadays we frequently hear how a personal relationship with a gay person (whether a friend, coworker, fellow student, or family member) often leads people to reject principles unfriendly to gays.

Bennett deserves credit for raising a host of important issues that pertain to these passages. Nevertheless, something about his analysis doesn't seem quite right. Weakness of will, after all, is generally understood to be a kind of character flaw, even when it leads to a praiseworthy action. As Bennett tells us, Huck's failure to act according to his bad morality is due simply to a lack of conviction with respect to what he believes is right. We are relieved when Huck fails to turn Jim over to the slave hunters (Huck has certainly done the right thing), but this does not make Huck's weakness, or Huck himself, praiseworthy. Yet the fact that Huck does seem deserving of praise suggests that there's something more going on here than just akrasia.

Nomy Arpaly and Timothy Schroeder provide an alternative interpretation of these passages that they believe better accounts for Huck's praiseworthiness.[10] While their analysis is in many ways sympathetic to Bennett's, particularly as they see Huck's actions as akratic and thus as being irrational, they argue that Huck's action is best understood as an instance of what they term "inverse akrasia" and that understanding it this way can help explain why it is not merely Huck's action but also his character that is praiseworthy.

As already suggested, standard cases of akrasia involve an agent who rightly believes an action is right, but whose sentiments nevertheless lead him not to perform the action. In such cases, failure to perform the action opens the agent to blame. The conditions of standard akrasia can then be laid out as follows:

1. Person P rightly believes x is a right action.
2. P wants to do what she believes is right.
3. P's sentiments override her will to do what she believes to be right (P fails to do x).
4. P's failure to do x is blameworthy.

Someone who rightly believes that she owes a friend an apology but whose cowardice causes her to fail in her duty exhibits blameworthy akrasia.

An inverse akratic's actions, however, are not blameworthy because they fall under a significantly different description:

1. Person P wrongly believes x is a right action.

Importantly, then, the inverse akratic adheres to a bad morality. The next two conditions are the same as for the standard akratic:

2. P wants to do what she believes is right.
3. P's sentiments override her will to do what she believes to be right (P fails to do x).

But now, the difference in condition 1 leads to a difference in condition 4:

4. P's failure to do x is praiseworthy.

At this point, we might wonder what, exactly, is deserving of praise. One possibility is that only the action warrants praise. The agent, after all, does not consider it right, and it is only through a failure of will that she did it. On this interpretation, Huck performed a right action, but he personally does not deserve praise.

As already noted, something does not quite feel right about this. It's because Huck goes against his principles—even though he judges doing so to be wrong—that we praise *him*. As Arpaly and Schroeder put it, we regard "Huckleberry's action as saying something important about Huckleberry's self. The reader of Twain's novel tends to see Huckleberry's action not as an accidental good deed done by a bad boy, but as indicative of the fact that Huckleberry is, in an important sense, a good boy, a boy with his heart in the right place."[11] In other words, we intuit that there is something commendable about Huck's character, and so we are right to praise Huck and not just his behavior.

The question now is how to make full sense of this, given that we consider the standard akratic's character blameworthy. One place to begin is with an account of what actions properly reflect an agent's self. The model Arpaly and Schroeder adopt is called a whole-self theory, according to which "other things being equal, an agent is more praiseworthy for a good action, or more blameworthy for a bad action, the more the morally relevant psychological factors underlying it are integrated within her overall personality."[12] A psychological factor is well integrated when it is deep (that is, resists easy revision) and doesn't conflict with other deep psychological factors. These psychological factors might include intentions, schemas, scripts, emotions, moods, and one's stream of consciousness, but to keep things simple I will focus on just beliefs and desires.

Consider the example of a kleptomaniac who strongly desires to overcome his condition. The desires that lead him to steal, we may imagine, are quite deep, but so are the psychological factors underlying his desire to change. He has, in other words, a divided self, and this is what helps mitigate our negative judgment of him when he akratically steals. If he lacked the desire to change, his desire to steal would be a much more integrated part of his self, and so his character would be much more blameworthy. (Of course, his stealing would also no longer be akratic.)

In the case of Huck Finn, the fact that Huck's feelings of loyalty and friendship toward Jim conflict with his stated moral ideals, along with the fact that these feelings cause him to disavow morality altogether—which, of course, is ironic, because he most certainly doesn't do this—suggest that these feelings are deep. Further, the fact that Huck would so easily give up his moral convictions suggests that they are not a very well integrated part of him. As Arpaly and Schroeder put it, "his convictions regarding slavery are not nearly as well-integrated—they strike one as no more than the accidental result of unexamined early education; while Huckleberry is not introspective enough to openly question the 'truths' believed by every authority figure he knows, or examine their consistency with his other beliefs, it is clear that racism does not 'go deep' into his heart and rarely, if ever, motivates him to action."[13] We find Huck praiseworthy, then, because we sense that his true self is determined more by the qualities of loyalty, friendship, and sympathy than by the racist beliefs he professes to hold. So, while Huck remains an inverse akratic—while his desire to act from principle is not strong enough to resist his sentiments—both he and his actions are nevertheless praiseworthy.

While Arpaly and Schroeder can account for Huck's moral merit in a way that Bennett cannot, they nevertheless accept Bennett's twin claims that Huck acted irrationally and, thus, akratically. Both of these claims can be challenged, but to do so, we need an alternative account of conscience and moral action. For that, I suggest we look to the writings of the eighteenth-century moral philosopher Adam Smith.

The Man within the Breast

Like many philosophers of the Scottish Enlightenment, Smith thought that the rightness/wrongness (or propriety/impropriety) of actions is determined not by whether the actions conform to some abstract moral principle but rather by whether they are motivated by sentiments with which properly situated observers can sympathize. The term "sympathize" here can be misleading, for while we generally use it (as Smith himself notes) to refer to "feeling for" another, Smith uses it instead to refer to "feeling with" another. Sympathy, then, need not refer simply to our sharing in the suffering of others, but "may . . . without much impropriety, be made use of to denote our fellow-feeling with any passion whatever."[14] We judge others' sentiments (and the actions that follow from them) proper, then, when we recognize that we would feel (and act) similarly, were we in the other's situation. Conversely, we judge others' sentiments and actions improper when we find ourselves unable to sympathize with them.

Of course, given our biases, not everyone's judgments concerning a particular situation should count equally. We are just as likely to rationalize the sentiments and behavior of those we like, as we are to fail to give the benefit of the doubt to those we hold in contempt. To get around this problem, Smith embraced the notion of the impartial spectator, which, roughly speaking, represents someone who has no stake in the situation at hand (or who has a stake but is nevertheless able to set these considerations aside by effectively projecting herself imaginatively into the position of one who is impartial). The standard of morality then consists of the concurring judgment of every impartial spectator: "But these, as well as all the other passions of human nature, seem proper and are approved of, when the heart of every impartial spectator entirely sympathizes with them, when every indifferent by-stander entirely enters into, and goes along with them."[15] Actions, in turn, are deemed proper when motivated by sentiments approved of by impartial spectators.

The sympathetic impartial spectator is similarly central to Smith's notion of conscience. This differs fundamentally from Bennett, who treats conscience as consisting of one's accepted principles and accompanying reasons. Similarly, while Arpaly and Schroeder rightly argue that the principles Huck espouses don't seem a central part of his whole self, they do seem to accept Bennett's claim that Huck goes against his conscience when he acts against his principles. Smith, by contrast, presents an account of conscience that is decidedly less cognitive:

> But though man has, in this manner, been rendered the immediate judge of mankind, he has been rendered so only in the first instance; and an appeal lies from his sentence to a much higher tribunal, to the tribunal of their own consciences, to that of the supposed impartial and well-informed spectator, to that of the man within the breast, the great judge and arbiter of their conduct.[16]

For Smith, then, one's conscience seems more like an internal guide that produces emotive responses in the face of (proposed) actions. Though moral principles can and often should play a role in guiding one's conscience, they need not; conscience, like moral judgment itself, can be understood on the basis of sentiment.

None of this is to say that moral principles play no role in Smith's moral theory. They do. However, Smith understood these as nothing more than generalizations formed from our sympathetic responses to others: "Our continual observations upon the conduct of others, insensibly lead us to form to ourselves certain general rules concerning what is fit and proper either to be done or to be avoided."[17] Of course, this is not the only source of our moral principles. Especially while we're young, we readily adopt principles taught to us by our parents, friends, culture, and so on. In Huck we see a fascinating example of a young person whose moral sentiments conflict with the bad moral principles taught him by his racist society. He has not risen to the level of replacing his bad principles with better ones, choosing instead (ironically) to reject morality altogether, but he has revealed the morality that lies at his core.

Huck's Morally Praiseworthy Conscience

The conflict that Huck experiences, and the consequent pangs of conscience that he feels, are real. Huck recognizes that he has certain duties to Miss Watson and others (in this sense he is going against his conscience), but he also recognizes (or perhaps senses) that his duties to his friend are equally important, if not more so. But as Anders Schinkel notes, this conflict seems due to Huck's inability to articulate his sentiment-based moral convictions: "Huck's inner conflict . . . is the result of a split conscience, where only one half has the whole of Huck's moral vocabulary at its disposal."[18] Huck does not have the linguistic resources to articulate why sparing Jim is morally praiseworthy, and so when he acts against the explicit principles that he can and does articulate and recognizes that he would have felt equally bad had he turned Jim in, he sees no option except to throw off morality. But of course what he has in fact done is embrace the moral sentiments and corresponding principles that lie at the core of his self.

One might object here that Huck is nevertheless acting akratically, as his emotions overrule what reason tells him is right. Alan Goldman challenges this on the grounds that it is an inadequate understanding of akrasia: "weakness of will is not best characterized simply as failure to do what one explicitly or consciously believes one ought to do, but instead as failure, usually resulting from an irresistible bare urge, to act on the strongest reasons of which one is in some sense aware."[19] On this account, the kleptomaniac discussed earlier still acts akratically, because he is driven by a strong urge to steal, against all of the good reasons he has not to. But Huck's situation is altogether different, as his action is motivated not by a bare desire or urge, but by sympathy.

Bennett treats sympathetic feelings as mere feelings and so as fundamentally different from reasons. He describes the feeling of sympathetic distress for a friend as "just a feeling for him in his plight."[20] But Goldman, following Jenny Teichman's lead, argues that this is a gross oversimplification. For both of these writers, certain emotions contain implicit judgments. Specifically, "intentional emotions, those directed at persons or objects, represent their objects as having certain properties. They contain implicit judgments, and therefore an implicit awareness of reasons. Sympathy is such an emotion."[21] This helps us understand how Huck comes to feel *for* Jim precisely because he feels *with* him. And this occurs, not because Huck engages in an intentional action of imaginatively projecting himself into Jim's position, but because of simple emotional contagion. Huck feels what Jim is going through, he has a pre-linguistic understanding of Jim's plight, he feels the duties of friendship pressing upon him, and this takes the tuck right out of him.

Even if Huck's sympathetic response is cognitively very basic, Goldman's point about its involving an implicit awareness of reasons still applies. If Huck were not at some level aware of Jim's humanity (or dignity, if you will), of his caring for Huck as well as for his family, in short of his being a person worthy of moral concern, then Huck would arguably not so readily have overridden and subsequently given up his principles to save Jim. Indeed, it's not even a stretch to say that Huck was aware of these reasons when he reflects on the fact that, had he given up Jim, "I'd feel bad—I'd feel just the same way I do now."[22] Were he not aware of these reasons at some level, then it would be much harder to understand this claim.

The upshot of all of this is that Huck is not, in fact, acting akratically or purely irrationally, and he is not acting against his conscience. The sympathetic feelings that motivate Huck to save Jim are reason-based and so, contrary to how it first appears, he is not acting akratically, inversely or otherwise. And, given that these sentiments are at the heart of Huck's moral sensibility, he cannot be said to be going against his conscience. Instead, what we witness in this powerful scene is a significant growth in Huck's moral character. Though he thinks that his actions contradict his conscience and that he in fact is making his life easier by jettisoning his moral principles, he is wrong about this and is instead molding his conscience to better reflect the values, feelings, and beliefs that constitute his whole self. All that is left is for him to develop principles that reflect his conscience. And for this, he deserves our praise.

~

CHAPTER FOUR

Huckleberry Finn's Struggle between Sympathy and Moral Principle Reconsidered

Michael Lyons

As relatable and likeable as Huckleberry Finn might be as a character, it is quite clear why he might be regarded as more of an anti-hero than a traditional hero. Struggling with the norms of the society into which he finds himself trying to integrate, Huckleberry in the end decides to give up on his journey towards becoming "civilized," and makes plans to head out West.

In his paper, "The Conscience of Huckleberry Finn,"[1] Jonathan Bennett uses chapter 16 of *The Adventures of Huckleberry Finn*[2] to analyze the interaction between acting from moral principle and "sympathy" (specifically by looking at Huckleberry's struggle with this interaction in himself). Although we tend to assume that acting from moral principle is a higher form of moral behavior, and that acting from extraneous sentiments indicates a lack of moral strength, Bennett argues that in Huckleberry's case (that of failing to respect Miss Watson's "property rights" over the slave Jim, in favor of humane sympathy toward him), the opposite appears to be the case.

Moreover, Bennett uses the real-life case of the Nazi Heinrich Himmler to highlight a reverse case to that of Huckleberry's, in order to indicate how moral atrocities can be defended out of so-called moral principle. Bennett here seems to be trying to undermine the pedestal that we put our moral principles on, and consequently to urge us to use our sense of human sympathy to keep our moral principles in check when necessary.

While I would agree that our moral principles should always be subject to scrutiny, I will be arguing here that the concerns Bennett raises can be answered with the pedestal intact. In fact, while I grant that it is not necessary for moral heroes (or indeed, moral agents in general) to stick rigorously to any set of moral principles, it is nevertheless a possible feature of heroes that deserves the highest moral admiration.

First of all, I argue that Huckleberry's sympathy is sufficient for his own heroism, although his moral status would be much higher if it derived from moral principle. I then explain how the case of Himmler need not undermine the importance of moral principles, and, finally, use other cases of heroism to show the feature that moral principles produce to elevate agents to the highest heroic status, that being, incorruptibility.

"The wages is just the same": The Adventures of Huckleberry Finn, Chapter 16

Up to this point, Huckleberry has been helping the slave Jim run away from his owner, Miss Watson, who is presented from Huckleberry's perspective in a reasonably positive light (she tried to school him during the "civilizing" process, as it's referred to in the book). Jim and Huckleberry are on a raft heading down the Mississippi, getting close to the state border, beyond which lies Jim's legal freedom.

For Huckleberry, this is where the gravity of the situation seems to become apparent. He starts to become "all over trembly and feverish"[3] about the matter, and explains the attack of conscience he is experiencing about distancing a slave from his "rightful owner."[4] He starts having a go at himself: "Conscience says to me, 'What had poor Miss Watson done to you. . . . What did that poor old woman do to you, that you could treat her so mean?'"[5] He feels so "mean and so miserable"[6] that he almost wishes he were dead. His guilt only grows when Jim discusses his plan to buy his wife and children's freedom as well. Despite all the guilt, and the subsequent brief change of mind he has to turn Jim in after all, he fails to go through with this course of action. He decides to leave Jim on the pretense of reconnaissance, but actually sets out to turn him in. He ends up running into two men looking for runaway slaves, giving him the opportunity to betray Jim. They ask him whether the man he left on the raft was black or white, and out of what he feels to be weakness in his own will, he says "he's white."[7] This chapter in the book is the really significant one for this discussion.

"Poor devil, there's something in that": Bennett on Acting from Moral Principle and Sympathy

Jonathan Bennett's paper uses this scene from *Huckleberry Finn* to draw conclusions on how we ought to think about morality—more specifically, on the interaction between our moral principles and our sense of sympathy. When we say "*our* moral principles," neither Bennett nor I are committing ourselves to any particular view on what exactly the nature of morality is, or more specifically on whether the validity or truth of moral principles are in any way dependent on the agents who assent to them. These are relevant and interesting questions to ask, but they are not under discussion here.

When Bennett speaks of "moral principles" he means: "A set of principles of action which he [the agent] sincerely assents to, so that for him the problem of acting well or rightly or in obedience to conscience is the problem of conforming to *those* principles."[8] In Huckleberry's case, his moral principles appear in the form of his conscience's voice, telling him that he is wronging Miss Watson by facilitating Jim's escape. He uses the term "sympathy," on the other hand, "to cover every sort of fellow-feeling, as when one feels pity over someone's loneliness, or horrified compassion over his pain, or when one feels a shrinking reluctance to act in a way that will bring misfortune to someone else."[9] In chapter 16 of *Huckleberry Finn*, it's Huckleberry's sympathy for Jim that is in conflict with his moral principles.

Now Bennett is very clear that moral principles and sympathy are quite distinct. That isn't to say that there is never any kind of overlap or agreement between them. Bennett almost certainly doesn't mean to rule out any possibility that moral principles can guide you in the same direction as sympathy. He does however want to show some interesting things that happen when they do disagree.

Finn's case is one of three cases that Bennett raises of "bad morality" battling with "sympathy." Although in Finn's case, his sympathy luckily won over his bad morality, this is not what happens in the cases of Heinrich Himmler (leader of the SS, the main Nazi police force) and Jonathan Edwards (1703–1758), the Calvinist theologian and philosopher. Himmler effectively managed and supervised the killing of millions of Jewish people (possibly as many as six million),[10] "as well as several million gentiles, mainly Poles and Russians."[11] Himmler, according to Bennett, suppressed his sympathy toward those whom he was responsible for killing in order to follow his moral principles, so bad morality won in a conflict with sympathy.

Jonathan Edwards, on the other hand, according to Bennett, did not put much value in human sympathy in the first place, and so his bad morality had nothing to really compete against. He apparently claimed: "God condemns some men to an eternity of unimaginably awful pain, though he arbitrarily spares others—'arbitrarily' because none deserve to be spared."[12] Moreover, "Edwards insists that men *ought* to be condemned to eternal pain; and his position isn't that this is right because God wants it, but rather that God wants it because it is right."[13] So although this isn't a question of what wrong he did, it's that his principles claim that we all deserve this eternity of unimaginably awful pain.

Although I won't be discussing the Edwards case in any greater detail here, I do think it's worth looking at why Bennett uses this third case in the first place. One might think the case to be irrelevant, as it's not a question of Edwards trying to decide what to do in the face of a conflict between moral principle and sympathy, and simply following bad morality irrespective of sympathy. It's just that his principles are so bad, and he is so absent of sympathy, that according to Bennett his morality is worse than Himmler's, because he lacks conscience.[14] The reason I think Bennett raises this case is because he wants to show that it's not just that there can be cases of "bad morality" when your moral principles are in conflict with your sympathy, but also that you can have bad morality without that conflict being generated. In other words, the danger isn't specifically coming from the conflict; rather, it is coming from simply treating our moral principles as the unconditional authority for our actions. In order therefore to come to the defense of moral principles in the face of the danger that Bennett is pointing to here, his view that Edwards's morality is worse than Himmler's needs to be contested.

It is worth noting here that I fully accept Bennett's evaluation of Edwards's lack of sympathy as presented, and I see why it is worse from the perspective of conscience to lack sympathy when it's necessary to correct erroneous moral principles, but I think Bennett mistakenly fails to evaluate a person's morality based on their actions, as well as simply on how they manage their interaction between moral principle and sympathy (or lack thereof).[15]

I do not think it unreasonable to disagree with Bennett here; to claim that the morality of a man responsible for the death of millions is better than the morality of a man who had no direct responsibility for anyone's death seems at the very least to be potentially mistaken, irrespective of whether the second man had any sympathy for anyone else on the planet. Simply having deeply irrational beliefs that might widely appear to be abhorrent does not seem comparable to actually causing the kind of harm that Himmler did. That is not to say that Edwards and his ideas were harmless, but it is at least theoretically possible that he could have been both entirely apathetic to all humanity in virtue of these beliefs, *and* completely harmless.

At any rate, Bennett subsequently judges Huckleberry to be the most morally worthy of the three cases, followed by Himmler, and with Edwards being the least morally worthy. While I have indicated some reasons for disagreeing with Bennett that Edwards is the least morally worthy, I do agree that Huckleberry is without doubt the most worthy. My aim will be to defend this view without using Bennett's reasoning, so I can avoid his conclusions. As for what conclusions Bennett actually tries to draw from these cases, I will try first of all to show that the matter is a little unclear. While a lot of the argument that Bennett makes is very clearly put, as well as the general conclusion, it's not quite as clear just how far he takes his argument to go, and therefore how far his conclusion actually reaches. In order to explain this potential room for interpretation, I will start by looking at Bennett's argument in greater detail.

"Always do whichever come handiest at the time": Bennett's Argument

It's worth starting with a summary of Bennett's argument in his own words:

> [Finn, Himmler, and Edwards] would all have done well to bring certain of their principles under severe pressure from ordinary human sympathies. But then we can say this because we can say that all those are bad moralities, whereas we cannot look at our own moralities and declare them bad. This is not arrogance: it is obviously incoherent for someone to declare the system of moral principles that he accepts to be *bad*, just as one cannot coherently say of anything that one *believes* it but it is *false*.
>
> Still, although I can't point to any of my beliefs and say "That is false," I don't doubt that some of my beliefs *are* false; and so I should try to remain open to correction. Similarly, I accept every single item in my morality—that is inevitable—but I am sure that my morality could be improved, which is to say that it could undergo changes which I should be glad of once I had made them. So I must try to keep my morality open to revision, exposing it to whatever valid pressures there are—including pressures from my sympathies.
>
> I don't give my sympathies a blank cheque in advance. In a conflict between principle and sympathy, principles ought sometimes to win. . . . Still, one's sympathies should be kept as sharp and sensitive and aware as possible . . . because they can sometimes affect one's principles or one's conduct or both.[16]

Here are the four key claims to take out from this extract:

1. Finn, Himmler, and Edwards "would all have done well to bring certain of their [moral] principles under severe pressure from ordinary human sympathies."

2. "We can say this because we can say that all those are bad moralities, whereas we cannot look at our own moralities and declare them bad."
3. "I am sure that my morality could be improved, which is to say that it could undergo changes which I should be glad of once I had made them. So I must try to keep my morality open to revision, exposing it to whatever valid pressures there are—including pressures from my sympathies."
4. "I don't give my sympathies a blank cheque in advance. In a conflict between principle and sympathy, principles ought sometimes to win. . . . Still, one's sympathies should be kept as sharp and sensitive and aware as possible . . . because they can sometimes affect one's principles or one's conduct or both."

The lesson that Bennett would have Huckleberry learn here, for instance, is that, by rejecting the voice of his conscience and refraining from turning Jim in, he is right to act from sympathy over acting from moral principle. However, Huckleberry should allow his sympathy to *inform* and hence improve the voice of his conscience, rather than give up on his conscience altogether.

It is worth noting at this point that (3) and (4) potentially represent two different conclusions to draw about the conflict between moral principle and sympathy. The stronger one undermines the pedestal on which moral principles sit. I'm definitely not objecting to the weaker reading of Bennett here, according to which all (3) is saying is that we should use other factors such as our sympathies in certain situations to test and evaluate our moral principles, and if something is wrong with them, correct them. That doesn't in any way entail the possibility that there are cases where our sympathies should be listened to over our moral principles, leaving the principles themselves intact, albeit less authoritative. That might instead be said to be implied from (4). Looking carefully at the final sentence, Bennett suggests that sympathies "can sometimes affect one's principles *or one's conduct*, or both." So according to this suggestion, it's not just that one's principles might be affected by sympathy, and at the same time our conduct might be affected, but potentially our sympathies can (and Bennett potentially implies should) affect our conduct *without* affecting our principles that conflict with them. It's this possibility that lessens the authority of moral principles, advocating a rejection of them as an unconditional authority over how we should act. It is this conclusion that I wish to not only avoid but reject.

"All right then, I'll go to hell":
Principle and Sympathy Reconsidered

So what I want to do here in response to Bennett's argument is show that we don't have to accept the possibility of sympathy needing to affect our conduct without also affecting our moral principles. We can keep moral principles on the pedestal, and I will suggest some reasons why they should be on this pedestal. In order to do this, I will now try to put together what I think are the claims behind Bennett's argument to construct what I consider to be the "stronger" version of his argument that tries to defend the stronger conclusion I wish to reject (i.e., the removal of moral principles from their pedestal). I do not take this argument to be one that Bennett would definitely advocate, let alone what he actually intended to advocate in his paper. However, considering this argument will allow me to clarify why I think the stronger conclusion can be rejected without rejecting what Bennett has to say altogether. In any case, the "stronger" argument is as follows.

The Stronger Argument
    (1) In order to behave morally, one should always act in accordance with one's moral principles.
    (2) If (1) is true, then one's moral principles are the best primary guide on how to behave morally in every situation.
    (3) There are cases of "bad morality," where one's "sympathy" is a better primary guide on how to behave morally than one's moral principles.

Conclusion (1) Therefore, one's moral principles are not the best primary guide on how to behave morally in every situation.

Conclusion (2) Therefore, premise (1) is false.

Premise (1) is one way of formulating what I have been calling the "pedestal" on which we put our moral principles, insofar as premise (1) is stating that moral principles are meant to be the predominant method of determining how we ought to conduct our actions. Premise (2), I think, is a reasonable entailment from premise (1). If our moral principles are the primary authority over our actions, then they need to always point us in the right direction.

By "best primary guide" here, what I mean is *the guide that suggests the course of action that fits most closely with what we genuinely ought morally to do.* If you were behaving in a morally ideal way, for instance, you would do everything that was morally required of you, without doing anything that was morally wrong. In effect, you would have to rule out anything that would be morally impermissible, and fulfill all moral obligations by how you chose to act. Then any other aspects of your behavior could be determined by other factors, such as sympathy. So the best primary guide here would be whatever would suggest you act in a way that would either achieve this, or provide the best approximation. To use Huckleberry's case as an example, it seems reasonable to claim that the best primary guide for Huckleberry is his sympathy (for Jim), because it stops him from turning Jim in. Although his conscience tells him that he ought to turn Jim in, Huckleberry is actually morally required to do the opposite, because the right thing for him to do, contrary to what he might believe, is to refrain from preventing Jim's escape. At any rate, according to premises (1) and (2), following your moral principles is the best way to do what is morally required of you.

Premise (3) is really where Bennett's point comes in, and what his argument fundamentally hinges on. It seems as if Bennett claims that our sympathies should in some situations be the predominant factor of our decision making. Moral principles should in other words just be knocked off their pedestal (as Conclusion 2 effectively states). This I think is very dangerous, because it makes the project of the moral agent that much harder. Not only does one have to conduct generally difficult deliberations to determine what moral principles one should adhere to, and how it is best to understand and apply them, but one can't even be sure even at that stage that you should be following those principles *at all*. In other words, behaving morally doesn't just involve performing a moral calculus and acting in accordance with whatever the output might be; one has to consider all of the factors in play (well, certainly at least one's sympathies) before determining how to act.

Because I agree with premises (1), (2), and (3) and do not deny that the first conclusion follows from them, I can only reject this stronger argument by denying that the second conclusion follows from it. What I really think is the problem is how premise (2) and subsequently premise (3) are stated. The reason why I think they are problematic is because they don't seem to acknowledge the need for any kind of defeasibility when it comes to our moral principles. That is exactly the lesson that needs to be learned from Bennett's paper—that we can't just take our moral principles as true and unconditionally reliable. So with that in mind, I believe the following "adjusted" version of the argument might be how the argument can be restated to fit in line with the weaker reading of Bennett.

The Adjusted Argument

(1) In order to behave morally, one should always act in accordance with one's moral principles.

(2) If (1) is true, then one's moral principles *should be* the best primary guide on how to behave morally in every situation. *If they do not turn out to be in any particular cases, then they need to be corrected to agree with the better primary guide(s).*

(3) There are cases of "bad morality," where one's "sympathy" is a better primary guide on how to behave morally than one's moral principles *as they currently stand.*

Conclusion *Therefore, there are cases of "bad morality" when one's moral principles are not the best primary guide on how to behave morally in their current form, so they need to be corrected to agree with the better primary guide(s).*

This argument I think manages to encapsulate the weaker reading of Bennett's argument, but it also leaves the pedestal we put moral principles on intact. Although they can be undermined and corrected, moral principles are still the first place to start when considering how one should act.

"No more about reforming": The Pedestal of Moral Principles

There are two potential objections to my adjusted argument, both of which I think are worth responding to. The first is that my adjusted argument as a suggested interpretation of Bennett's argument relies in a way that Bennett's argument does not on the view that there are objectively correct moral principles that we need to do our best to both identify and act from. This is a view called moral realism. Moral realism is not easy to define, but here is a reasonable attempt from Russ Shafer-Landau:

Some moral views are better than others, despite the sincerity of the individuals, cultures, and societies that endorse them. Some moral views are true, others false, and my thinking them so doesn't make them so. My society's endorsement of them doesn't prove their truth. Individuals, and whole societies, can be seriously mistaken when it comes to morality. The best explanation of this is that there are moral standards not of our own making.[17]

To use Huckleberry's case as an example, one might think that in chapter 16 Huckleberry incorrectly believes he ought to turn Jim in, and by failing to turn him, he has actually done the morally right thing. Moreover, the fact that it is the right thing for him to do isn't dependent on our individual attitudes, or the collective attitudes of our society, any more than it is dependent the collective attitude of Huckleberry's society. The view that it is the right thing for Huckleberry to do is *objectively* true.

Any reliance on this view could be problematic because it could potentially undermine the very lesson that we are supposed to be learning from Bennett's paper, which is that we should not be simply following our moral principles. If we claim there are objectively correct moral principles to be discovered, there is a temptation to simply reject any other guides for action like sympathy once we take ourselves to have discovered the relevant correct moral principles. This is exactly what the cases of Himmler and Edwards were meant to challenge.

Moreover, one might take issue with the view that there are objectively correct moral principles in the first place. This need not even require a rejection of objective moral truths about what we ought to do, but only the existence of any kind of objective moral principles. Rejecting the latter without the former could for instance involve accepting a *particularist* approach to morality, which is most famously defended by Jonathan Dancy. Here are his reasons for doing so: "Moral life, it can be said, is just too messy, and the situations we encounter differ from each other in subtle ways that no panoply of principles could ever manage to capture. Principles deal in samenesses, and there just aren't enough samenesses to go round."[18]

In response to this objection, I think first of all that actually my adjusted argument is completely compatible with rejecting the existence of independent moral standards, either due to rejecting the existence of objective moral truths or defending their existence without defending moral principles. This is because correcting one's own moral principles might not be a matter of making them comply with independent moral standards. It might instead be only a matter of making them comply with the standards of a certain culture or society, for instance.

The second and potentially more significant objection is that even the stronger argument I drew out from Bennett's paper did not actually draw a sufficiently strong conclusion—an even stronger potential conclusion that would undermine my attempt to keep moral principles on a pedestal. This conclusion would be that not only should sympathy be guiding our actions rather than moral principles, but in fact what determines whether we are doing the right thing isn't moral principle at all. It might instead be the *consequences* of our actions (this view is known as *consequentialism*). The most well-known example of this view is classical utilitarianism, defended most famously by Jeremy Bentham (1748–1852) and J. S. Mill (1806–1873), where morally good actions are those that cause happiness, and morally bad actions cause suffering.

Once again though, I would argue that even a consequentialist account of morality would be consistent with my adjusted argument. Moral principles are completely compatible with utilitarian accounts of morality, the fundamental principle being the utilitarian principle itself. Therefore there is no substantial reason why the conflict between moral principle and sympathy should be at all significantly changed by this kind of account of morality.

"De on'y white genlman dat ever kep' his promise to ole Jim": Huck's Struggle Revisited

So how do we reconcile Huckleberry's deliberations and his subsequent decisions? I don't think there's any problem diagnosing Himmler's wrong-doings; he completely failed to correct horrific moral principles in light of his far more sensible sympathies. But under the weaker reading, it seems like Huckleberry was still doing something wrong in failing to stick to his own moral principles (as they should still sit on a pedestal, even if he fails to correct them).

I think that Bennett himself actually provides some of the answer to this question, for he accepts that "Huck clearly cannot conceive of having any morality except the one he has learned—too late, he thinks—from his society."[19] And so he chooses to give up on it:[20]

> Then I thought a minute, and says to myself, hold on,—s'pose you'd a done right and give Jim; would you felt better than what you do now? No, says I, I'd feel bad—I'd feel just the same way I do now. Well then, says I, what's the use you learning to do right, when it's troublesome to do right an ain't no trouble to do wrong, and the wages is just the same? I was stuck. I couldn't answer that. So I reckoned I wouldn't bother no more about it, but after this always do whichever come handiest at the time.[21]

This still seems as if Bennett is wrongly trying to knock moral principles from their pedestal, but I think he is not appreciating the story Mark Twain is telling about morality. While there are always discussions about how Twain is depicting the struggle between nature and nurture in the book,[22] I think that actually he was to an extent applying that struggle to how morality ought to be understood (whether there are inherent moral principles we just inherently know, or whether we simply learn them from society). I think Twain would say that it's a bit of both. There are clearly good behaviors that Huckleberry never learns from society (although it might be a controversial point to make, Huckleberry sees people lying all around him, and never really seems to have any problem with it, and thus clearly fails to learn the value of honesty). However, his sympathy for Jim reflects an inherent requirement to respect other people as individuals that is undermined by society's acceptance of slavery. Furthermore, although Huckleberry could never conceive of it himself, it reflects a kind of raw, natural morality, not a societal construction, but a morality grounded in a sense of *humanity*.

So I think one of the biggest lessons that we can learn from *Huckleberry Finn* is that while there is a clear need to learn certain moral principles as we develop as moral agents, there is a certain inherent or "natural" morality that is reflected in our human sympathies. While Huckleberry does abandon the societal "nurtured" morality, he doesn't abandon the natural morality. So by moving West and giving up on civilization, he hopefully can still keep his natural morality, expressed in a set of correct principles, while divorcing himself from the moral principles about slavery, the "deformed conscience that the good citizens had attempted to instill into him."[23] In Bennett's own words, "What Huck didn't see is that one can live by principles and yet have ultimate control over their content. And one way such control can be exercised is by checking one's principles in the light of one's sympathies."[24]

You could, I think, ask at the end of all of this why I went through all of this trouble to defend the pedestal on which we put our moral principles. One of the biggest reasons why I think the pedestal ought to be kept is because I think finding the right moral principles, and sticking to them no matter what, is perhaps a feature of the most admirable kind of heroes, the kind that those like Huckleberry can aspire to become.

Now I take a hero to be someone who performs an action that is far greater in moral value/worthiness than those made by others in a similar context. So we tend to think of a soldier jumping on a grenade to protect others as a hero. Even if we don't accept that action as being entirely beyond the call of duty, we still accept that it's not to be expected—most would not make that same sacrifice.

But in my mind, the heroes I admire most tend to never compromise on what they think they ought to do, irrespective of the circumstances. There are lots of examples from history. This isn't to say that they have to be perfect in all respects, but one cannot deny the heroism of exercising nonviolent means of protest even in the most atrocious of circumstances, where violence might be understandable. Heroes of this kind are, in a word, incorruptible, and that incorruptibility is what allows them to set an example to us all, in showing the intrinsic value of finding and defending the right moral principles.

Ultimately though, the lesson that *Huckleberry Finn* gives us is not a warning against putting moral principles first as the guide for your actions; instead it "celebrates, not the loss of a child's vision through the experience of a sordid and brutal world, but Huck's wary rejection of the Southern beliefs he knows he ought to hold, and the triumph of his innocence."[25]

CHAPTER FIVE

~

Twain's Last Laugh

KRISTINA GEHRMAN

Novels naturally invite their readers to identify with their protagonists, and this invitation is especially compelling when the novel is narrated in the first-person. Nabokov's *Lolita* or Dostoevsky's *Notes from Underground*, for example, are so challenging and controversial because they draw the reader to identify with someone whom the reader simultaneously finds to be loathsome and morally reprehensible. Mark Twain's *The Adventures of Huckleberry Finn*, in contrast, has no doubt earned the honorific title of The Great American Novel in part because a certain kind of American reader identifies so readily and so warmly with the novel's youthful protagonist and narrator, Huck.

What is it to "identify" with someone? It is to see oneself in the other person *and to see the other person in oneself* in a way that is a condition for the possibility of empathy. This idea of identification is adapted from the philosopher Arne Naess, who argued that "with sufficient comprehensive maturity, we cannot help but identify ourselves with all living things, beautiful or ugly, big or small, sentient or not."[1] To support this radical claim, Naess tells a story about coming to identify with a creature very far removed indeed from the human form of life:

> I was looking through an old-fashioned microscope at the dramatic meeting of two drops of different chemicals. At that moment, a flea jumped from a lemming that was strolling along the table. The insect landed in the middle of the acid chemicals. To save it was impossible. It took minutes for the flea to die.

The tiny being's movements were dreadfully expressive. Naturally, I felt a painful sense of compassion and empathy. But the empathy was *not* basic. Rather, it was a process of identification: I saw myself in the flea.[2]

We need not agree with Naess that true identification is possible even across the exo-endoskeletal divide in order to believe that great works of literature *do* provide us with precisely the sort of experiences that make identification possible.[3] To the extent that a reader identifies with a novel's protagonist, the hero's successes become the reader's successes, his pains are her pains; his redemption (or lack thereof) becomes her own. But even though identification makes empathy possible, it does not always involve *sympathy*, or positive regard. We can identify with *Lolita*'s Humbert Humbert even while we find him horrifying. That is why in reading *Lolita* we are so discomfited by the ugly and disturbing qualities of the novel's protagonist. We are upset to see ourselves in this human flea, but in the process of identifying with him we are forced to a different, more complicated, hopefully more honest view both of our own humanity, and that of a hopeless pedophile. Identification, then, amounts to this: one sees oneself (even) in the flea.

I am going to assume for the purposes of this essay that Mark Twain wrote *Huckleberry Finn* with a White, American, literate audience in mind. It is readers like this—readers like myself—to whom the novel issues its compelling invitation to identify with Huck. And its remarkable success with this audience makes the novel what it is, and gives it its place in American culture and history. And here, unlike with Humbert Humbert, the identification is welcome. Although of course there are individual exceptions, by and large Huck strikes the novel's target audience as appealingly innocent and naïve and utterly unpretentious; and though he is far from perfect, he is generally kind and well-intentioned. He is remarkably persistent in the face of real trouble, and he triumphs over adversity when, at the novel's close, he is freed from Pap and, with his help, his beloved friend Jim is freed from slavery.

Above all, to the novel's target audience Huck personifies a critical moral struggle—and the eventual moral redemption—of the America both of his time, and of ours: namely, the struggle to overcome anti-Black racism and the poisonous legacy of American slavery. Thanks to his friendship with Jim, Huck seems gradually (if inarticulately) to overcome his socially inculcated racism, eventually coming to love Jim and learning to prioritize Jim's well-being. In the novel's climactic moment, Huck declares his willingness to "*go to hell*" rather than send Jim back into slavery, finally defying unequivocally the corrupt moral code of his society.[4]

To the target audience, this uplifting reading of Huck's moral progress represents and makes plausible a correspondingly hopeful and comforting narrative about American society at large. Like Huck's racism, American anti-Black racism is largely based in ignorance and is therefore largely inadvertent or innocent. And like Huck's racism, which cannot withstand Huck's relationship with Jim, American racism cannot withstand being confronted with the simple fact of the humanity of Black people. It will therefore inevitably be transcended in the course of American history, in a series of dramatic steps toward greater integrity (the Civil War, *Brown v. Board of Education*, the Civil Rights Movement, potentially the Black Lives Matter movement, etc.). In the process of identifying with Huck, the target reader thus finds reason to believe that "we"—Americans, America—are not to blame for missteps in our past; nor are we a lost cause when it comes to our future. The reader is glad to identify with this young hero; he elicits both sympathy and empathy.

Reading Huck Developmentally

Although it is still the dominant reading of the novel, this pat inspirational reading of *Huckleberry Finn*, and of Huck's character in particular, can be challenged in a number of ways. For instance, the triumphalist, optimistic parallel between Huck and American society presupposes that *America is White*, or that (archetypal) Americans are White. This supposition is quite hard to reconcile with the rosy vision of a colorblind America that has no further stake in White supremacy. It is also difficult to maintain the same cheerful view of Huck's moral progress if one attends realistically to the novel's depiction of its only major Black character, Jim. For as DonnaRae McCann and Fredrick Woodard have argued, in many ways (though not always), Jim instantiates a familiar, nineteenth-century racist caricature of an implausibly cheerful and willingly servile Black person.[5] And even if the reader sees through this mask to some extent, Huck himself certainly does not. For this reason it can hardly be said that in Jim, Huck is confronted with a faithful, realistic, and entirely inoffensive portrait of Black humanity that teaches him to see Black people for the full equal persons that they really are. Finally, although Huck does come to love Jim, a more sophisticated conception of what racism is like shows that his affection for Jim is fully compatible with continued, and even strengthened, racism on Huck's part. As Peaches Henry puts it, "There is no denying the rightness of Huck's decision to risk his soul for Jim. But there is no tangible reason to assume that the regard Huck acquires for Jim . . . is generalized to encompass all blacks. . . . His emancipatory attitudes extend no further than his love for Jim. [W]ere he given the option of freeing other slaves, Huck would not necessarily choose manumission."[6]

These challenges to the inspirational, "Great American Novel" reading of Huck Finn are serious, and they deserve serious consideration. But in this chapter, I wish to explore a different sort of challenge, a challenge that the novel poses, especially for readers inclined to identify warmly with Huck. The challenge is a *moral* challenge, a test of integrity. And it stems from the fact that the surface-level reading of Huck, according to which he personifies a successful American struggle with racism, is *ironic*. It is made available by the author precisely to lure the novel's target audience into acting out a defining American self-deceit that the novel then mocks mercilessly.

To recognize the irony in the surface reading of *Huckleberry Finn*, we need to adopt what I have elsewhere called a *developmentally attuned* perspective on Huck's character and his moral capacities.[7] We can adopt such a perspective by first taking a cue from Aristotle, who emphasized the importance of upbringing to moral character. Then, with Aristotle's views in mind, we can employ what the philosopher and novelist Iris Murdoch calls "just and loving" *attention* to arrive at a more faithful reading of Huck's character, in both the literary and the moral sense of the word.[8]

Aristotle observed that we learn to be good people by first doing what is good under another's guidance: "For the things we have to learn *before* we can do them, we learn *by* doing them, e.g., men become builders by building and lyre-players by playing the lyre; so too we become just by doing just acts, temperate by doing temperate acts, brave by doing brave acts."[9] Unfortunately, however, "it is from playing the lyre that both good *and* bad lyre-players are produced,"[10] and the same is true of moral character. If a person practices injustice and cowardice from youth, for instance, they will grow up knowing how to be unjust and cowardly, and they will have no idea how to be just and brave even if they want to be. For this reason, "it makes no small difference whether we form habits of one kind or of another from our very youth; it makes a very great difference, or rather *all* the difference."[11]

Now if we, as readers, wish to arrive at a fair and accurate estimation of Huck's moral character and abilities as they are presented in the novel, then we need to know more than just that upbringing is *generally* important to character. We need in particular to become intimately familiar with Huckleberry Finn himself, the individual (fictional) person. And with both fictional and living persons, this is often not an easy thing to do. Nothing less than the demanding, morally challenging practice of paying just and loving attention to another, described by Iris Murdoch, is required in order to bring the reader into a more intimate, more just, and more compassionate relationship with Huck.

Murdoch introduces the idea of just and loving attention with the example of a mother-in-law who does not like or respect her daughter-in-law, but who suspects that her judgment may be clouded, and who says to herself, "Let me look again." This mother-in-law is "an intelligent and well-intentioned person, capable of self-criticism, capable of giving careful and just *attention*" to something or someone that matters.[12] As this mother attends carefully to her daughter-in-law, she is "engaged in an internal struggle," attempting "not just to see [her daughter-in-law] accurately but to see her justly and lovingly." Exercising attention in this way can be a "struggle" in part because it is such a morally weighty act for the one who attends. It provides opportunities for humbleness or arrogance, self-deceit or self-reckoning, emotional openness or rigidity, and a range of related morally significant choices and actions. It is an intrinsically open-ended and fallible activity; it is "essentially something progressive, something infinitely perfectible. . . . [One] is engaged in an endless task."[13]

Now, what happens if the reader seeks to pay Huck the sort of just and loving attention that Murdoch here describes? When we attend to Huck in this way, we are forced to realize that his story is not the inspiring and comforting story of a young White man who triumphs over his own socially inculcated anti-Black racism. Instead, Huck's story is the tale of a traumatized child whose upbringing has left him deeply damaged: he is largely bewildered about the difference between right and wrong, he is incapable of acting in ways that are consistent with his own choices and values, and he is just as racist as the other White members of his community.

The first thing to note is that Huck is still so young that he is—most appropriately—very morally immature and not yet really able to have the kind of transformative, autonomous crisis of conscience that is so often attributed to him in connection with his decision to go to hell rather than betray Jim. We know he is prepubescent because he can convincingly pass for a girl, but his general lack of moral sophistication and deference to moral authority are also what we would expect from a child of his age. Huck tends not to distinguish easily between more and less serious infractions of moral laws, and he takes on the moral norms and restrictions of his elders and of society at large without any deep understanding of the reasons behind those rules. It does not occur to Huck, for example, that a moment when Jim truly feared that Huck was dead is no time for practical jokes. Huck needs to have this pointed out to him, just as children often need their parents to teach them when something is really serious and no laughing matter.[14] And, although he chafes at the Widow's and Aunt Sally's attempts to "civilize" him, he does not question their view that the behaviors they seek to instill in him are, in fact, civil.[15]

And yet Huck's difficulty making sense of his society's moral code goes beyond what we would expect from a normal child of his age. There is no doubt that Huck's upbringing was terribly abusive and neglectful—it is only when Pap actually tries to kill Huck in an episode of alcohol-induced psychosis that Huck finally runs away. But it often goes unnoticed that Huck consistently and realistically manifests the traumatic effects of such an upbringing. Huck is simultaneously passive and manipulative, constantly seeking to "lay low" and constantly telling lies. In these respects he is not like a normal, healthy preadolescent; he displays what contemporary psychologists would recognize as the posttraumatic behaviors associated with abuse and neglect. Abused children behave with an odd combination of passivity and manipulativeness, both because they have not learned normal, positive, mutually trusting modes of social interaction, and because such behavior is best suited to keeping them safe under high-risk and totally unpredictable circumstances (such as one would encounter living with an abusive or neglectful parent). True to form, when Huck works himself up to telling Mary Jane the truth about the King and the Duke, he marvels at how "strange and irregular" it is that the truth in this instance is "better and actually *safer* than a lie."[16] On the other hand, there's no question about how to deal with the King and the Duke themselves: "I never said nothing, never let on; kept to myself; it's the best way; then you don't have no quarrels, and don't get into no trouble. . . . If I never learnt nothing else out of pap, I learnt that the best way to get along with his kind of people is to let them have their own way."[17]

The finishing touch to Huck's comprehensive moral miseducation lies in the fact that he is tragically well-socialized in one crucial respect: namely, he is an unquestioning racist whose background racism is not significantly altered by his relationship with Jim. It is true that Huck comes to love, trust, and even respect Jim, who is the only adult in the world of the novel who empathizes with Huck and treats him with real kindness. And Huck himself is very kind and very responsive to kindness. But, as we have already noted, this does not automatically mean that Huck has renounced his standing, more general racist beliefs and attitudes.[18] Sure enough, again and again Huck makes bizarre (but not unusual) *exceptions* for Jim. For example, though he hears—and emotionally comprehends—Jim grieving for his wife and children, left behind in slavery, Huck's discovery of Jim's humanity is the discovery of Jim's surprising similarity to White people: "I do believe he cared just as much for his people as white folks does for their'n. It don't seem natural, but I reckon it's so."[19] At the last, when Jim risks lynching to save the feverish Tom, Huck concludes in a flush of pride, "I knowed he was White inside."[20] This sort of exception-granting is a familiar and banal strategy for explaining away evidence that would otherwise systematically undermine one's racism.

Twain's Last Laugh

A developmentally attuned reading of *Huckleberry Finn* reveals a starkly different young person than the Huck of the dominant, inspiring reading: a child whose trauma, vulnerability, and racism are fundamental to what he does and what he believes. This child faces far more serious obstacles to both his own personal security and his own prospects for developing good character than the dominant reading of him recognizes. The difference is so stark, in fact, that it is natural to feel a sense of loss at the prospect of accepting this new reading of Huck. What happened to the intrepid, innocent boy contentedly hanging a line and one bare foot off the edge of a raft? But accepting the developmentally attuned reading of Huck does not require us to deny the innocent, kind, and adventuresome aspects of Huck's character. Nor should it lead us to write him off as a lost cause, without any prospect of further growth or change. Though it is painfully at odds with the cheerful, adventuresome surface narrative of the text, the developmentally attuned reading honors Huck's innocence by allowing the reader to see through his uncomplaining, un-self-aware rendition of things to the true circumstances under which he maintains such equanimity. This insight allows the reader to adopt a more just and more loving attitude toward a vulnerable, sadly unloved, morally lost and stunted child. The developmentally attuned reading is also compatible with continuing to see Huck as admirable for his doggedness, his childlike innocence, and his remarkable capacity for real kindness given its near-total absence in his world.

But if the developmentally attuned reading helps us to see Huck with a greater measure of justice and love, it is also the key to what is surely the novel's greatest irony. For if this understanding of Huck Finn, the basically kind but morally and emotionally damaged child, is the most just and loving reading of his character, then where does this leave the reader who has identified so warmly and optimistically with Huck?

Let us imagine a reader who had succumbed to the novel's invitation, and identified him- or herself with Huckleberry Finn. When this reader attends carefully to Huck and comes to see him with a greater measure of justice and love, what sorts of changes to her self-conception will ensue? If the reader continues to see herself in Huck, she is revealed as the child of a deeply immoral, self-deceiving, callous, and neglectful society, for one. She also now seems to be a person who remains significantly in the grip of racist ideology while congratulating herself on its opposite, who lacks moral maturity or a reliable, autonomous moral compass, and who is ultimately unable to stand up for what she believes in even when she finally makes up her mind about what that is. Above all, the reader who naively identifies with Huck is revealed as someone who lacks self-knowledge where it matters most: namely, in her estimation of her own moral character.

The identification is no more favorable if Huck holds up a mirror to American society at large. Are Americans deluded about the continued extent and depth of our society's own anti-Black racism? Is the national moral character developmentally damaged by our cruelty-steeped past—perhaps irreversibly? Are we as a society less able to do the right thing in certain respects than we might have been had our nation not been founded in slavery and dedicated for so long to the proposition that some persons are more equal than others? Perhaps most frighteningly of all, are we, like the lost and vulnerable Huck, at great risk of failing altogether to develop into a mature, morally just society—precisely in the areas where we have been most harmed by our disturbed and disturbing past? There is no doubt in my mind that Mark Twain, at any rate, would answer these questions in the affirmative. His target audience is right to see themselves in Huck. The mistake is to be untroubled by that identification.

This is Twain's last laugh: a brilliant, *living* act of irony that is reiterated each time the novel is read, taught, or lauded in keeping with the surface narrative of Huck's triumphant moral overcoming. What is particularly stunning is that the irony in question is not contained entirely within the pages of the novel; it characterizes the *relationship* between the novel and a reader who commits a certain interpretive act. This is why I say that it is a "living" act of irony. By exploiting and encouraging the natural tendency of a reader to identify with a novel's protagonist, Twain skewers his presumptively White American readership, leading them to endorse their own blinkered perspective on reality and to misapprehend and mischaracterize it as a moral triumph. And because the reader may never be aware of this particular ironic aspect of the novel's structure, Twain's is a joke that may well be only ever on, and never for, the reader.

But things only get worse from here. For now suppose the reader, realizing the joke, recoils from his initial identification with Huck. Where, then, in the world of the novel, is the reader meant to place himself? Must he identify with Aunt Sally, the Widow? With *Pap*? (I assume that a novel which afforded *no* opportunities for identification would reveal next to nothing about the human condition, and would thus be far from "great" in its genre.) Here, it matters that, with the sole exception of Jim, the neglect and miseducation that Huck experiences at the hands of adults is utter and complete. It includes not just the horrible physical and emotional abuse heaped on him by his father, but also Miss Watson's terrifying warnings about the fiery Hell toward which Huck is bound, and the Widow's and Aunt Sally's kindly meant but deeply unempathetic, emotionally and physically stifling attempts to "civilize" Huck. That is: it's not just the obvious villains—Pap and the King and the Duke—who perpetrate Huck's neglect, abuse, and moral miseducation. If anything, their treatment of Huck is *less* morally significant for our purposes, because Huck does not accept them as moral authorities; he tries only to limit their impact on his well-being. No, Huck's not being properly brought up also includes the broader social miseducation that he receives from all of the White adults in the novel: adults who are, in various ways, wholly indifferent to the suffering of Black persons and of all children. Even at the novel's close, Huck's plan to "light out for the Territory" lest Aunt Sally adopt and "civilize" him ensures that he will continue to wander in a moral wilderness in the company of indifferent adults straight through into his own adulthood.[21] Thus the reader trying to see Huck with justice and love cannot escape the humbling implications for himself by seeking refuge in identification with the novel's unfeeling White adults.

What about Jim? Jim now emerges clearly as the only just, kind, and morally mature person in the world of the novel, in virtue of the simple fact that he is the only person who knows how to treat children properly.[22] He is unfailingly gentle, kind, and patient with Huck. He protects him from experiences that children should not have to have—such as the sight of his murdered father's body—and he firmly but kindly insists upon terms of mutual respect in their father-son relationship on the raft. He alone is tenderly, physically affectionate toward Huck. He is of course also the only person in the novel who dares to think that a Black man and his family should be free and treated as full autonomous persons. Surely, then, Jim is the person with whom the reader should most wish to identify.

But Twain's portrayal of Jim, together with the actual social and psychological identity of the reader whose predicament we are discussing, combine to make this desirable identification, if not impossible, then all but impossible, and certainly inappropriate. To begin with, precisely in falling for the surface reading of Huck, the reader has shown herself to be *unlike* Jim in the most relevant respect: she has shown herself to be largely oblivious to Huck's youthful vulnerability, his trauma, his moral confusion, and the other important things about Huck that Jim attends to with such care. What's more, the reader is obliged to ask herself an uncomfortable question: if Jim is really so much wiser and more admirable, so much more worthy of emulation than all of the other characters in the novel, then why didn't I instinctively identify with Jim all along?

Here, the reader may find to his dismay that latent racism figures to some extent in his failure to see both Huck and Jim with justice and love. It would seem to be latent racism, for example, that leads to Jim being so often characterized as Huck's *equal*, not as his surrogate parent—Jim is usually described as Huck's friend, Huck's companion, Huck's comrade, Huck's "partner in crime," and so on.[23] By giving Jim the social and moral status of a child, such characterizations obscure Jim's actual role in Huck's life—namely, that of surrogate parent and guardian. The effect is to obscure Jim's singular moral wisdom and disguise it as innocence, while simultaneously helping Huck's all-too-real youth and moral immaturity to escape the reader's notice.

But it is not only possible racism on the part of the reader that blocks identification with Jim; the racially fraught way in which Jim is presented bears some responsibility as well. Identifying with a character in a novel is a way of learning about oneself by seeing oneself in that character—seeing, that is, one's shared humanity. And Jim, as we know, is not presented in a particularly humanizing way. He is demeaningly painted as gullible, superstitious, childlike, and subservient. Thus, even while he is the only mature, morally wise person in the novel, he is simultaneously depicted precisely as lacking the adult moral maturity and autonomy that the reader wants to identify with and emulate. And this poses a serious obstacle, not just to the target audience, but to *any* reader's attempt to identify with Jim. Just as we couldn't get away with seeing only what we want to see in Huck, we can't pick and choose which aspects of Jim's character we attend to.

It is a subject of debate whether Mark Twain meant the reader to see through the caricatured aspects of Jim's character, to recognize them as Huck's perception, and not as the author's perception, of black male adulthood. But even if Twain's portrayal of Jim is ironic, that in itself does not clear the way for his target audience to identify with Jim's underlying positive qualities. We know that Jim's reality must have been a life of terrible, suffocating oppression, of constant vulnerability to physical and emotional violence, and of the terrible pain of being unable to protect his loved ones from the same. That pain and suffering, however, is almost entirely invisible in the novel's portrayal of Jim (unsurprisingly, as it was all but invisible to Huck). The fact that these aspects of Jim's human reality are hidden means that it would be *too easy* for the reader to identify with him as he is presented;

the positive self-association would be too cheap. The reader doesn't have to bear the cost that Jim has had to bear, of preserving his integrity and his capacity to love and to empathize under his actual life circumstances. Part of coming to see Jim with justice and love, therefore, is coming to see that his story simply hasn't been told in *The Adventures of Huckleberry Finn*. That means that his humanity hasn't been fully expressed in this novel; it has been suppressed, even though he has been presented as a morally admirable figure. To attempt to identify with Jim, therefore, would be in some sense to accept a partial, less-than-fully humanized character as an acceptable mirror for one's own humanity.

If racism and race are factors in the reader's having misconstrued both Huck and Jim, then that is bound to be a bitter pill for her to swallow, considering that she identified with Huck in the first place because he (supposedly) so bravely and sincerely overcame his own racism in response to Jim's humanity. But having once begun the fraught and humbling process of paying just and loving attention to Huck, the reader cannot now simply decide to ignore its less pleasant implications for her own character. In the end, the reader who said to herself, "let me look again," is forced to face up to the appropriateness of her original identification with Huck—who is, of course, now greatly altered. And here, I think, we have found the barb on the end of the hook with which Twain has snagged his reader. The reader *should* want to be like Jim with respect to his admirable moral qualities. The fact that this identification is so vexed by American racial realities as to be effectively blocked for Twain's target audience completes the novel's ironic gesture.

Ethical Implications and the Status of the Novel

The reader who has used just and loving attention to arrive at this new understanding of *Huckleberry Finn* now finds himself in a challenging—but potentially rewarding—position. A reader who understands himself to be the butt of Twain's joke has shown himself to be, like Murdoch's mother-in-law, "a well-intentioned person, capable of self-criticism, capable of giving careful and just *attention*" to Huck and Jim, even at his own expense. He has successfully identified with Huckleberry Finn, even when that identification turned out to reveal things about both himself and Huck that are less than sympathetic. In this respect, warranted identification with Huck is a mark of the moral and personal "maturity" that Arne Naess described. But at the same time, this reader has also shown himself to be selectively blind: capable of buying into a self-serving and therefore less-than-compassionate reading of one of his culture's defining works of literature. For this reason, while he is capable of becoming *less* blind to his own flaws (and thereby less flawed), it doesn't follow that he will ever become excellent in those places where he has the most work to do, just as Huck may never entirely overcome the miseducation of his youth. More probably, the habits he has acquired and practiced from youth will dog him, and he will have to be endlessly on guard against them.

What about *Huckleberry Finn*'s status as one of the great American novels? Certainly Huck's tale does not teach us to believe in and celebrate America's certain triumph over its own unjust past. If the novel can still be considered one of the great works of American literature, then its greatness is not triumphant or celebratory, but rather *Socratic*.

In Plato's *Apology*, Socrates tells the Athenian jurors, "I was attached to this city . . . as upon a great and noble horse which was somewhat sluggish because of its size and needed to be stirred up by a kind of gadfly."[24] The Athenians were meant to be "stirred" by Socrates's relentless and often humiliating questioning for the good of their souls, to teach them to love virtue and to prioritize good character and good deeds above all else. But Socrates's sting was not entirely therapeutic: he provoked and humiliated his fellow Athenians not only for the good of their souls but also to amuse himself at their expense. Perhaps Socrates's fellow ironist, the American Mark Twain, has done much the same thing for his own society with this, his most scathing work.

But to say the novel is great and to say that it captures something definitively American is not to say that it is perfect, nor is it *complete* as a treatment of racial injustice in America. Socrates spoke his immortal words to an Athenian assembly of native-born, upper-class, politically enfranchised men, and most decidedly *not* to slaves, immigrants, or even his own wife and children (who were shuffled unceremoniously out of his presence in the final hours of his life). And as we have seen, Mark Twain wrote *Huckleberry Finn* not just about but also most decidedly *for* the target readership whose struggles we have been discussing here. The novel shows us how slavery, racism, and general callousness toward those who are vulnerable all harm the person who enslaves, who is racist, and who is callous toward the vulnerable.[25] But this obviously does not amount to a complete reckoning with the relevant moral issues. The stories of those who are enslaved and those who are otherwise *oppressed* by racism, not corrupted by it—those stories have yet to be told, as far as this novel is concerned. For this reason, the novel does not speak to all Americans in the same way, and this fact must be weighed in discussions of the novel's status and stature.

We began by observing that novels characteristically invite their readers to identify with their protagonists, to dwell upon and become vulnerable to their shared humanity. There's nothing particularly subtle about the way in which a novel like *Lolita* or *Notes from Underground* exploits this tendency, however brilliant these works may be. The reader knows that they are being invited to find common human ground with a despicable, contemptible protagonist. One isn't really engaging seriously with literature like this—one doesn't become vulnerable to learning from it—unless one does a bit of soul-searching along the way. But the invitation is *explicit*.

In *Huck Finn,* on the other hand, the invitation to "look again" is buried so deep in irony that the reader may easily miss it entirely. But if it is once perceived, that irony allows the novel to make an extremely powerful moral and political argument. The irony is the mechanism by which the novel proves to certain readers that some soul-searching is called for, first luring them in with a surface reading and then showing them the character flaws in themselves and their society—the flaws that made that surface reading first seem reasonable. These readers are left engaged in the "endless task" of trying to see themselves, their country, and the character of Huckleberry Finn with a greater measure of justice and love.[26]

PART II

TWAIN ON RELIGION

~

CHAPTER SIX

The Gospel According to Mark (Twain)

CRAIG VASEY

While banished from Heaven for speaking sarcastically of some of God's creations, Satan made a visit to Earth to see how the experiment called "man" was coming along. His eleven letters from the Earth to the archangels Michael and Gabriel report on what he finds there at the end of the nineteenth century.

Mark Twain wrote *Letters from the Earth* (and "Letter to the Earth") in 1909 and seems not to have intended it for publication, as it stops with the end of the eleventh letter and there is no overview or summarizing perspective to give it a sense of completeness. Regardless, it provides us with a pretty clear picture of what he thought of religion and God.

On September 4, 1907, he dictated a statement for his autobiography concerning a letter received from Professor Henderson in England about his privately and anonymously published book, *What Is Man?* The letter compared Twain's ideas to those of George Bernard Shaw, Henrick Isben, and Friedrich Nietzsche. Twain commented:

> I have not read Nietzsche or Ibsen, nor any other philosopher, and have not needed to do it; I have gone to the fountainhead for information—that is to say, to the human race. Every man is in his own person the whole human race, with not a detail lacking. I am the whole human race without a detail lacking; I have studied the human race with diligence and strong interest all these years in my own person.[1]

Whether or not we find this claim convincing—that everyone embodies "every quality and every defect" that is discoverable among humans—he goes on to claim that *everyone is a coward*, afraid to differ from the dominant opinions of his or her society. If he means this seriously, it would seem to detract somewhat from what the reader experiences as the otherwise inspiring call for intellectual integrity that Twain's later writings, like *Letters*, implicitly express.

Letters from the Earth addresses a variety of things, but chiefly it addresses the inconsistencies of the God story as the Bible tells it, and it addresses the general gullibility of human beings and their virtual will to be deceived. Though written in 1909, *Letters from the Earth* was not published until 1962, a fate it shared with several other writings from Twain's later years.[2] This chapter will relate the main ideas of *Letters from the Earth* and present the case for seeing these suppressed writings not as the misanthropic rants of a frustrated old man but as a great writer's stand on the importance of critical thinking.

Satan's Letters, Twain's Critique

The premise of the text is a bit shocking to the first-time reader: The *Letters* are written in Satan's voice, and Satan is presented as a reasonable, if skeptical, personality, with whom the reader is intended to identify. In setting the stage for the letters, Mark Twain tells of the archangels Satan, Michael, and Gabriel witnessing the creation of the contents of the universe and their reactions to it. Specifically, the great miracle they see in the creation is the invention of what they call "automatic law," to be known as God's Law and the Law of Nature: "exact and unvarying law—requiring no watching, no correcting, no readjusting, while the eternities endure."[3] They marvel at this, at the basic fact of there being *stuff*, and that the stuff is self-regulating, embodying obedience to the law. Gabriel mentions that God intends later on to create animals, and they are all puzzled by this, because they have never heard of animals before.

Hundreds of years later, God begins creating animals, and explains to the archangels that animals are an experiment in "Morals and Conduct": each is a being created with a certain nature that it is unable to not obey: the lack of courage in the rabbit, for example, and the ferocity of the tiger, cause them to behave as they do, and they are completely blameless for their actions.

> After a long time and many questions, Satan said, "the spider kills the fly and eats it; the bird kills the spider and eats it; the wildcat kills the goose; the—

well, they all kill each other. It is murder all along the line. Here are countless multitudes of creatures, and they all kill, kill, kill, they are all murderers. And they are not to blame, Divine One?"

"They are not to blame. It is the law of their nature."[4]

Then God creates man, and he explains that man is a different experiment. Instead of having just one distinguishing quality, like courage or ferocity, man will have all the qualities, and this fact of having them all will constitute the nature of the individual. Some will be dominated by evil qualities, some by good and noble ones. God explains that these two experiments are something that time will show the value of; maybe they will be worthwhile, maybe just a waste of time.

In Twain's story, Satan is soon ordered into banishment—and not for the first time, though this is the first time since the creation of worlds—so he has options on places to go to spend his time, and he decides to find Earth and see how the experiment is going.

In the first two letters, he reports on the utter insanity that characterizes humanity: the absurd self-understanding that humans have made up for themselves, and the place of God and Heaven in that self-understanding. Satan knows, as do the other archangels, that God created these animals and humans as an experiment, and pays no particular attention to them. Now he finds that on Earth, humans think God is paying *constant* attention to them:

> He thinks he is the Creator's pet. He believes the Creator is proud of him; he even believes the Creator loves him; has a passion for him; sits up nights to admire him; yes, and watch over him and keep him out of trouble. He prays to Him, and thinks He listens. Isn't it a quaint idea? Fills his prayers with crude and bald and florid flatteries of Him, and thinks He sits and purrs over these extravagancies and enjoys them. . . . I must put one more strain upon you: he thinks he is going to heaven! He has salaried teachers who tell him that.[5]

Satan's comments on the relationship that humans have dreamed up between themselves and God contains two major elements: the belief that God is preoccupied with humans, and the belief that God needs to be constantly told that He is loved and adored by them. Satan finds both of these to be incredible. The absurdity of the notion that each human being is more interesting to God than he or she was even to his or her own parents, somehow is believable to most humans. Equally absurd is the belief that someone who is as far superior to us as God would care in the slightest what we thought about Him and whether we even *were* thinking about Him (something akin, perhaps, to how likely it would be that our feelings could be hurt if we found out that paramecia don't like us!). To hold such beliefs and to live by them seems insane to Satan, and presumably to Mark Twain as well.

Twain lampoons this conceit delightfully in "Letter to the Earth" (a different, much shorter text) written to Abner Scofield, Coal Dealer, Buffalo NY, by the Recording Angel, Dept. of Petitions in Heaven. The angel recounts the prayers Abner has submitted—which ones are granted, and which put on hold. For instance:

1. for weather to advance hard coal [fifteen] cents a ton. Granted.
2. for influx of laborers to reduce wages 10 [percent]. Granted.

But later in the text, the angel explains:

Prayer for weather mercifully tempered to the needs of the poor and the naked. Denied. This was a Prayer-meeting prayer. It conflicts with Item 1 of this report, which was a Secret Supplication of the heart. By a rigid rule of this office, certain sorts of Public Prayers of Professional Christians are forbidden to take precedence of Secret Supplications of the Heart.[6]

And he concludes with an account of how impressed everyone in Heaven was when Scofield wrote his impoverished widowed cousin a check for fifteen dollars after balancing his books and confirming a forty-five thousand dollar profit for the month from his three mines:

There was not a dry eye in the realms of bliss; and amidst the handshakings, and embracings, and praisings, the decree was thundered forth from the shining mount, that this deed should out-honor all the historic self-sacrifices of men and angels, and be recorded by itself upon a page of its own for that the strain of it upon you had been heavier and bitterer than the strain it costs ten thousand martyrs to yield up their lives at the fiery stake; and all said "What is the giving up of life, to a noble soul, or to [ten thousand] noble souls, compared with the giving up of [fifteen dollars] out of the greedy grip of the meanest white man that ever lived on the face of the Earth?"

This letter ends:

And Peter weeping, said "He shall be received with a torchlight procession when he comes"; and then all heaven boomed, and was glad you were going there. And so was hell. Signed, the Recording Angel.[7]

The other element in the self-understanding of humanity is the place of Heaven. First, Satan thinks it is absurd that humans think they will be going there; but Satan is talking about the real Heaven, the one he is temporarily banished from, the home of God and the angels and archangels. But more to the point, Satan cannot believe how they have conceptualized this Heaven for themselves. For they have conceptualized a Heaven for themselves—it is supposed to be their greatest reward and happiness—in which the one thing they prize most highly is missing, and in which most of the things they are unhappy about on Earth are in abundance. The former, he matter of factly says, is sex.

> The very thought of it excites him; opportunity sets him wild; in this state he will risk life, reputation, everything—even his queer heaven itself—to make good that opportunity and ride it to the overwhelming climax. From youth to middle age all men and all women prize copulation above all other pleasures combined, yet it is actually as I have said: it is not in their heaven; prayer takes its place.[8]

"The very thought of it excites him." We know that all too well. So Satan finds it very strange that, instead of imagining that in Heaven sex is more abundant, longer lasting, more varied, more interesting, more enjoyable, humans instead imagine that in Heaven there is *no sex at all*. But, as if to make up for this in some bizarre way, most of the things they are unhappy about on Earth are in full supply! What Satan has in mind here are being in church, singing hymns, playing a musical instrument (harp), being with the kind of people you really hate ("All nations hate each other, and every one of them hates the Jew"[9])—and having absolutely nothing to occupy your mind, nothing to do. The most dreadful tedium and boredom.

Mark Twain has a point. This is a very odd self-understanding. What is going on when a species understands itself in terms of a goal that amounts to achieving the opposite of the things it values and enjoys? What is going on when a species understands itself so narcissistically that it thinks the creator of the universe will have His feelings hurt if you don't tell Him how wonderful He is? A virtual will to be deceived, perhaps. Or a serious inferiority complex and overdeveloped sense of shame.

Satan goes on to recount the Judeo-Christian account of the creation of humanity, that God created a young man and a young woman, who had no idea what anything was. After all, as they arrived uneducated, they certainly had no idea what death was (because they had never seen an example of death), nor any idea what good and evil were. They are told by God not to eat the fruit of a certain tree or they will die. Mark Twain recounts this at length in another text, *Interpolated Excerpts from Eve's Diary*, which are part of the *Papers of the Adam Family*.

Adam said it was the tree of knowledge of good and evil.

"Good and evil?"

"Yes."

"What is that?"

"What is what?"

"Why, those things. What is good?"

"I do not know. How should I know?"

"Well, then, what is evil?"

"I suppose it is the name of something, but I do not know what."

"But Adam, you must have some idea of what it is."

"Why should I have some idea? I have never seen the thing, how am I to form any conception of it? What is your own notion of it?"

Of course I had none, and it was unreasonable of me to require him to have one. There was no way for either of us to guess what it might be. It was a new word, like the other; we had not heard them before, and they meant nothing to us. My mind kept running on the matter, and presently I said, "Adam, there are those other new words—die and death. What do they mean?"

"I have no idea."

"Well then, what do you think they mean?"

"My child, cannot you see that it is impossible for me to make even a plausible guess concerning a matter about which I am absolutely ignorant? A person can't think when he has no material to think with. Isn't that true?"

"Yes—I know it; but how vexatious it is. Just because I can't know, I want all the more to know."

We sat silent a while turning the puzzle over in our minds: then all at once I saw how to find out, and was surprised that we had not thought of it in the beginning, it was so simple. I sprang up and said, "How stupid we are! Let us eat of it; we shall die, and then we shall know what it is, and not have any more bother about it."[10]

Twain's point here—and it is one he makes in several of his writings—is how absurd it is to think that God creates humans of such a nature that they are curious and then orders them not to follow their nature. In *Eve's Diary*, one of the most entertaining elements is her account of how they go about learning various things, such as that fish prefer not to be on dry land[11] and that water always runs down hills but never up.[12]

Now, being ignorant they do not know what death is, with which they are threatened as punishment. So they follow their nature, which they cannot help but do, and are punished for doing so. In *Letters*, Satan points out that not only are they punished, they are not even given the slightest break:

> He requires his children to deal justly—and gently—with offenders, and for-give them seventy and seven times; whereas he deals neither justly nor gently with anyone, and he did not forgive the ignorant and thoughtless first pair of juveniles even their first small offense, and say "you may go free this time, I will give you another chance." On the contrary! He elected to punish their children, all through the ages to the end of time, for a trifling offense commit-ted by others before they were born.[13]

That God would make things a certain way and then be angry at them for being the way He made them is the absurdity with which Satan charges the Christian account of God. In Letter VIII, he specifically addresses the absurdity that God would forbid sexual experience and condemn adultery. He somewhat provocatively points out that the difference between the physical sexual nature of man and of woman is such that in some cases it might take ten men to satisfy a woman sexually, and that she can be sexually active her entire life, but—in those pre-Viagra days—"his candle is increas-ingly softened and weakened by the weather of age as the years go by, until at last it can no longer stand, and is mournfully laid to rest in the hope of a blessed resurrection which is never to come."[14] So he denounces the rule set out in the Bible that restricts a woman to a single man, saying it is no more appropriate than to blame the goat for being a goat or to praise the tortoise for its lack of passion.

In Letter X, Satan goes after the Biblical story of God's treatment of the Midianites; he speculates that God had all the Midianites slaughtered be-cause of one of three possible offenses. Either one of them committed the sin of Onan and spilled his seed upon the ground, or maybe one of them pissed against a wall, or maybe one of them left his paddle home—and so would be unable to follow the injunction to dig and cover up "that which cometh from thee" when "thou wilt ease thyself abroad."[15]

Satan's attention to flies is noteworthy. The Gospel, according to Mark Twain, makes it clear that everything that is, is as it is because God has made it so: "nothing can happen without his knowing beforehand that it is going to happen; nothing happens without his permission; nothing can happen that he chooses to prevent."[16] Twain makes this observation right after a paragraph describing God's invention of disease:

> The fear that if Adam and Eve ate of the fruit of the Tree of Knowledge, they would "be as gods" so fired his jealousy that his reason was affected. . . . To this day his reason has never recovered from that shock; a wild nightmare of vengefulness has possessed him ever since, and he has almost bankrupted his native ingenuities in inventing pains and miseries and humiliations and heart-breaks wherewith to embitter the brief lives of Adam's descendants. Think of the diseases he has contrived for them. . . . The human being is a machine. . . . It is composed of thousands of complex and delicate mechanisms, which perform their functions harmoniously and perfectly. . . . For each one of these thousands of mechanisms the Creator has planned an enemy, whose office is to harass it, pester it, persecute it, damage it, afflict it with pains and miseries, and ultimate destruction. Not one has been overlooked. From cradle to grave, these enemies are always at work; they know no rest, night or day. They are an army: an organized army; a besieging army; an assaulting army; an army that is alert, watchful, eager, merciless; an army that never relents, never grants a truce.[17]

Like the catalogue of miseries that David Hume recites in Part X of his *Dialogues Concerning Natural Religion*, the point of the passage is to bring home something we all already know: the senselessness and relentlessness of human suffering in face of the assertion that our creator is our benevolent Father.

Satan puts it to his archangel friends:

> It is as I tell you. He equips the Creator with every trait that goes to the making of a fiend, and then arrives at the conclusion that a fiend and a father are the same thing![18]

Satan tells about the presence of flies on Noah's ark, and how, despite the fact that all other animals each wound up in one particular climate or continent,

> the fly is of no nationality: all the climates are his home, all the globe is his province, all creatures that breathe are his prey, and unto them all he is a scourge and a hell.
>
> To man he is a divine ambassador . . . the Creator's special representative. He infests him in his cradle; clings in bunches to his gummy eyelids; buzzes and bites and harries him, robbing him of his sleep and his weary mother of her strength in those long vigils which she devotes to protecting her child from this pest's persecutions. The fly harries the sick man in his home, in the hospital, even on his deathbed at his last gasp. Pesters him at his meals; previously

hunts up patients suffering from loathsome and deadly diseases; wades in their sores, gaums its legs with a million death-dealing germs; then comes to that healthy man's table and wipes these things off on the butter, and discharges a bowel-load of typhoid germs and excrements on his batter-cakes. The housefly wrecks more human constitutions and destroys more human lives than all God's multitude of misery-messengers and death-agents put together.[19]

Twice in the first four Letters, Satan talks about human gullibility: with respect to the Heaven that humans have conceptualized, he says,

They dream of it, they talk about it, they think they think they are going to enjoy it—with all their simple hearts they think they think they are going to be happy in it!
It is because they do not think at all; they only think they think. Whereas they can't think; not two human beings in ten thousand have anything to think with.[20]

And commenting on the absurdity of the punishment of Adam and Eve, he writes

In your country and mine, we should have the privilege of making fun of this kind of morality, but it would be unkind to do it here. Many of these people have the reasoning faculty, but no one uses it in religious matters.[21]

The second remark is almost understanding, indulgent: we shouldn't make fun of the stupidity of these people because it is so severe, that would just be cruel. Many of them actually *can* reason, they just don't. This strikes me as similar to the injunction to not take candy from a baby. Your equals are those whom you might engage in challenging and taunting for their mistakes, especially your intellectual equals. But you don't do that sort of thing to imbeciles, any more than you take candy from a baby: it's just unseemly.

The first remark is more entertaining, because of the double meaning of "think" that is going on: they *don't* think, they only *think* they think; they don't have anything to think with, so they can only think that they are thinking.

Obviously, thinking that you are thinking *is* thinking already. But there's thinking and then there's thinking! Most humans are perfectly happy without really thinking, without anything close to critical reflection; as long as their minds are occupied with something, that's enough. That keeps boredom away, that keeps depression away, that keeps you distracted from the possibility—which would be potentially very upsetting to your routine and your life—that you don't really know why it is that you are doing what you are doing, believing what you are believing, or living as you are living. As long as you feel somewhat important, and you have something to do, things are good.

The Suppression of *Letters from the Earth*

Twain wrote this text in 1909; he died in 1910, and they were finally published in 1962. What was so inappropriate about publishing them? His daughter Clara reportedly had them held back when an editor was preparing to bring them out in 1939, supposedly for the reason that she thought they misrepresented her father's views.[22] Today, with the publication of the complete *Autobiography of Mark Twain*, I think we can safely dispute that reason, for in volume III there are numerous places where he indicates that the views he expresses here (and in *What Is Man?*) have been his private views for decades.

> I have talked my gospel rather freely in conversation for twenty-five or thirty years and have never much minded whether my listeners liked it or not, but I couldn't get beyond that—the idea of actually publishing always brought me a shudder: by anticipation I could not bear the reproaches which would assail me from a public which had been trained from the cradle along opposite lines of thought.[23]

It appears that Clara objected to the publication of *Letters* for a reason quite similar to one Mark Twain frequently gave: not because they distorted his views but precisely because they expressed them! Still, one wonders: is this only because they are blasphemous, sarcastic, and mocking? Is this only because in them Twain denounces Christianity as insane? That may well be a good part of it, but I'd propose that there's more to it. It seems that Mark Twain had no illusions about his fellows: that there's something about mainstream American culture that makes it difficult, awkward, and maybe even unwise to be the kind of intellectual and critical person that he was and wanted people to be. It seems he feared the anti-intellectualist streak in the public.

"Not two humans in ten thousand have anything to think with."[24] He's denouncing human stupidity. Human stupidity is obvious and enthusiastically embraced. The aim of this critique of Christianity is to undermine its believability to anyone who will challenge himself to think about it critically. But it is not limited to Christianity.

In 2016, it's a little easier than in Twain's time to believe we don't need to believe in God in order to be moral. A little easier, a little less difficult. In general, people today are still raised to respect and fear violence, and the threat of violence is still the most often-invoked rationale to be moral: "Thou shalt not . . . or thou shalt go to Hell." Otherwise intelligent adults are still frightening their children with those threats, because they themselves are still unwilling and unprepared to grow up and take responsibility for themselves: they need to invoke a higher authority in order to be able to believe in their own authority. The Gospel, according to Mark Twain, is an expression of something even more disturbing than the jealous rage and violence of the *Old Testament*. God the father may have been petty, jealous, vengeful, indiscriminant in His violence, and irrational in His hygienic requirements, but once you died (or He killed you) it was all over.[25] Satan points out that according to the Bible, when God came to Earth as Jesus, and presented himself in the name of love, He brought with him a new phenomenon: life after death. With life after death, the persecution of an offender need never end; God could now have the satisfaction of killing him but not give up the satisfaction of persecuting him—He can have him tortured. It is hard to think otherwise than Nietzsche on this: The strongest motivation for creating this story would be the wish to identify with the one who takes revenge, the wish to be the one who gets back at those others. All in the name of love, all under the rubric of "saving man."[26]

What Twain's narrative of Satan's reflections tells us about God is really what it tells us about the human "need" for God. I put "need" in quotation marks to indicate that it is doubtful that it is a genuine and irreducible human need. We don't need electricity in order to live the same way that we need food. And we don't need God in order to be moral the same way that we need competent and caring caretakers. We do need competent and caring caretakers: none of us would have survived the first or second twenty-four hours of life without minimally competent caretakers; and from them we all learned, ideally, love, respect, obedience, obligation, and gratitude.

But just as my son's preschool teacher would say grace before they could have their snack, thanking God for the food that the parents had baked or bought and brought in—so too, people are prone to overlook the human role in giving humans a motivation to be good. *They think they think* about what it is to be good, but they don't really, and *when they think they're thinking* about it, they think that the reason to be good is to please God—not to maintain and strengthen the bonds and institutions that make human coexistence possible and that give life its joys and satisfactions.

Time to Grow Up?

Questions about God and the meaning of life have always mattered to human beings and have been explored by literary authors, playwrights, artists, and songwriters—not only by "official" or academic philosophers. But the audience is often not expecting to see the writer shift from his usual subjects to these questions, quite likely a consideration in the nonpublication of Twain's *Letters from the Earth*. Perhaps something similar took place when, soon after The Beatles broke up in 1970, John Lennon released a solo album containing a song titled *God*, not a subject previously addressed in the group's musical repertoire. Because of the enormous popularity of The Beatles, the group's break up was very big news, and Lennon's activities were newsworthy. Besides the controversial *God*, in 1970 he was emerging as an important voice in the anti-war or Peace Movement. The central lyric of the song was "God is a concept by which we measure our pain." Whether this idea was original with him or not, it brought an interesting and provocative claim into popular culture and was an invitation to take up serious subjects. Some may take it to mean that our hopes for salvation by God are the result of our mortal pain and limits. I go in another direction. Our pain is varied, and we measure it in various ways. Our pain is daily and hourly; it can be our envy, our resentment, or our desire; our weakness, our disappointment, or our uncertainty; our anger, our cowardice, our mortality, or our mediocrity. Our conception of God offers us a way to measure, to take stock of, our pain. But it's a special kind of taking-stock, because it is a taking-stock that does not take responsibility. To put it briefly, and perhaps too briefly, when we measure our pain through God, we either blame ourselves for it—in the Christian approach, we deserve to suffer because we are guilty of sin—or—at least according to Nietzsche's reading—we blame the gods themselves (the Greek approach).[27] But I don't think that finding someone to blame is taking responsibility; scapegoating, even scapegoating oneself, is not facing up to one's agency. Facing up is living differently, making a new beginning.

I propose this as the meaning of Lennon's line: that when we are unsure if we are right about things, the pain of that uncertainty can be measured by (i.e., you can gauge the degree to which we are troubled by it by) the grandiosity of the projection we concoct. The pain—the anxiety and uncertainty—of not knowing exactly how to live one's life, what to believe, whom to love and whom to fear, is measured by the harshness of the rules we willingly impose on ourselves and others in the name of a vengeful, jealous celestial fantasy. I would say that what Twain's text tells us about God, or rather, what it tells us about the human "need" for God, is very much the same message that Socrates offered when he told his fellow citizens in Athens that "the unexamined life is not worth living for man." It is undignified, and it is unworthy of our potential as beings who by their nature are able to take responsibility for themselves, that we resort to blame and to stories about the will of higher powers to make sense of existence. We are beings whose greatest task and responsibility is to grow up! And what a remarkable possibility it is!

This is what I think Mark Twain means by his frequent attack on humanity's lack of thinking and willful childishness. The Gospel, according to Mark Twain, is a catalog of *excuses* for human suffering, and the scandal of humanity is that it embraces such catalogs, and all the irrationality and inconsistency of that story, when there is an alternative—thinking!

At the beginning of this chapter, I alluded to the inspiring character of Mark Twain's critical stance and his call for intellectual integrity, and I have just invoked the spirit of Socrates in coming to my conclusion. We can find evidence in the *Autobiography*, however, to give us pause at the prospect of grouping Twain with Socrates. He might be calling upon us all to live up to an ideal of intellectual integrity in our private thinking, but it is not clear that he would take this to the next step. In January 1908, recalling a conversation he had with a young woman asking for his public support on a controversy (which he declined to give), he observed:

> The fact is, she was brought up just like the rest of the world, with the ingrained and stupid superstition that there is such a thing as *duty for duty's sake*. . . . She believed that when a man held a private unpleasant opinion of an educational sort, which would get him hanged if he published it, he ought to publish it anyway, and was a coward if he didn't.[28]

He apparently did not disagree with her assessment: "The human race is a race of cowards; and I am not only marching in that procession but carrying a banner."[29]

CHAPTER SEVEN

~

Mark Twain and the Problem of Evil

The Mysterious Stranger, Letters from the Earth, and The Diaries of Adam and Eve

JAMES M. MCLACHLAN

Strange! that you should not have suspected years ago—centuries, ages, eons, ago!—for you have existed, companionless, through all the eternities. Strange, indeed, that you should not have suspected that your universe and its contents were only dreams, visions, fiction! Strange, because they are so frankly and hysterically insane—like all dreams: a God who could make good children as easily as bad, yet preferred to make bad ones; who could have made every one of them happy, yet never made a single happy one; who made them prize their bitter life, yet stingily cut it short; who gave his angels eternal happiness unearned, yet required his other children to earn it; who gave his angels painless lives, yet cursed his other children with biting miseries and maladies of mind and body; who mouths justice and invented hell—mouths mercy and invented hell—mouths Golden Rules, and forgiveness multiplied by seventy times seven, and invented hell; who mouths morals to other people and has none himself; who frowns upon crimes, yet commits them all; who created man without invitation, then tries to shuffle the responsibility for man's acts upon man, instead of honorably placing it where it belongs, upon himself; and finally, with altogether divine obtuseness, invites this poor, abused slave to worship him![1]

Thus ends Mark Twain's bleak and blistering indictment of Theism, *No. 44, The Mysterious Stranger*. The question here is less whether one can, as theistic thinkers from Augustine to Alvin Plantinga have attempted, show that it is logically consistent to believe that an omniscient, omnipotent, and omnipresent being existing outside space and time Who had created the world ex nihilo could exist, but why would anyone, except perhaps out of fear or awe for the tremendous power of such a being, want to worship such a Tyrant? Mark Twain is among the famous literary rebels, from Voltaire to Camus, who rebelled against such a Being as God. It was not the simple logical incoherence of the idea of God and evil that bothered them. It was the sheer power and "perfection" of a Deity so perfect that no world, no Other, was necessary, and yet He freely chose to fashion a "perfect" creation that required sinners to suffer eternally in hell and creatures to suffer the hell of everyday existence.

Twain's rebellion, most evident in *The Mysterious Stranger* and *Letters from the Earth*, is a powerful example of this literary rebellion against theism that spans nineteenth- and early twentieth-century literature and is found is such diverse works as Mellville's *Moby Dick*, Hugo's *The End of Satan*, Comte de Lautreamont's *Les Chants de Maldoror*, Albert Camus's *The Plague*, and Jean-Paul Sartre's *Saint Genet: Actor and Martyr*, to name a few. Similar critiques are found in movements as diverse as American Personalism and Pragmatism, Process Philosophy, and Existentialism. Edgar Sheffield Brightman, Alfred North Whitehead, William James, and Nicolas Berdyaev are less concerned with the logical problem of evil as proof for the nonexistence of God as they are that the conception of God resembles more a cosmic tyrant than loving parent. Ivan Karamazov says he accepts the existence of God, even accepts the logical proof of God's goodness, but still wishes to return his ticket. In *The Plague*, Dr. Rieux only contends that in practice no one can believe in an omnipotent God; he says if he believed in such a God he would quit curing the sick and leave it to Him.[2] Twain goes further than this in *Letters from the Earth*. Twain's Satan writes home that God always takes credit for whenever a cure is found for a disease, though He had also created the disease in the first place. Satan sarcastically remarks that God had been thinking about curing the disease for several thousand years before the human scientist found the cure but hadn't gotten around to it. Satan concludes, "The poor's only real friend is their fellow man. He is sorry for them, he pities them, and he shows it by his deeds. He does much to relieve their distresses; and in every case their Father in Heaven gets the credit of it."[3] Similarly Camus's Rieux believes that it is better for humans to resist creation as we find it and seek a cure for the plague. "Since the order of the world is shaped by death, mightn't it be better for God if we refuse to believe in Him and struggle with all our might against death, without raising our eyes toward the heaven where he sits in silence."[4] Twain and Camus are both "metaphysical rebels." They are not necessarily atheists, but they are blasphemers. In *The Rebel*, Camus describes "metaphysical rebellion":

The metaphysical rebel is therefore not definitely an atheist, as one might think him, but he is inevitably a blasphemer. Quite simply, he blasphemes primarily in the name of order, denouncing God as the father of death and as the supreme outrage. . . . If the metaphysical rebel ranges himself against a power whose existence he simultaneously affirms, he only admits the existence of this power at the very instant that he calls it into question. *Then he involves this superior being in the same humiliating adventure as mankind's, its ineffectual power being the equivalent of our ineffectual condition.* [author's emphasis][5]

The question of suffering is an old one that isn't going away anytime soon and always merits retelling. There have been many able and subtle defenses of God's omnipotence, omniscience, and omnibenevolence. Suffice it to say since Augustine, the majority position of absolute or creedal theists has mostly answered with some version of an aesthetic defense.[6] Suffering is justified for the greater purpose, the beauty of the whole. For Twain, such a position seems to dismiss the suffering of living beings, and, in its nonuniversalist iterations, it includes the eternal damnation of the majority of the human race because the perfect whole includes hell. Twain's point is what if hell, holocausts, and all the horrors of history don't contribute to the overall beauty of the universe? And even if they do, what makes them worth it? What good are they for those who don't get to enjoy this beauty? Wouldn't it be better to remain loyal to the "poor abused slaves" than to the tyrant artist who creates this grand canvas and demands the "poor abused slave" to worship Him and call Him Father. Twain's rebellion runs through his entire corpus, but I will look to primarily three works, *The Mysterious Stranger Manuscripts, Letters from the Earth,* and the *Dairies of Adam and Eve,* to highlight Twain's commitment to "the damned human race."[7]

A Traditional Statement of the Problem and a Traditional Defense

Usually, the problem of evil is presented to philosophy and theology students in the following way.

1. If God is Omnipotent and Omniscient (All Powerful, Created Everything, and Knows Everything),
2. And God is Omnibenevolent (Completely Good),
3. Then why do suffering and evil exist?

The famous statement of the problem is from Epicurus via David Hume:

> Either God would remove evil out of this world, and cannot; or He can, and will not; or, He has not the power nor will; or, lastly He has both the power and will. If He has the will, and not the power, this shows weakness, which is contrary to the nature of God. If He has the power, and not the will it is malignity, and this is no less contrary to His nature. If He is neither able nor willing, He is both impotent and malignant, and consequently cannot be God. If he is both willing and able (which alone is consonant to the nature of God), whence comes evil, or why does he not prevent it?[8]

This is a simple statement of the problem of evil and has generated a good deal of debate over the years. Recently the Process Theologian David Ray Griffin has explained it thusly,

1. God is a perfect reality.
2. A perfect reality is an omnipotent being.
3. An omnipotent being could unilaterally bring about an actual world without any genuine evil.
4. A perfect reality is a morally perfect being.
5. A morally perfect being would want to bring about an actual world without any genuine evil.
6. If there is genuine evil in the world, then there is no God. (Logical conclusion from 1 through 5)
7. There is genuine evil in the world. (Factual statement)
8. Therefore, there is no God. (Logical conclusion from 6 and 7)[9]

The key term in Griffin's reworking of the problem is "genuine evil." This is the idea that there may be some kinds of evil that serve no higher purpose. This is what years ago Edgar Sheffield Brightman called *dysteleological surds*.[10] Other types of what appears to be evil prima facie may be superseded by development toward a purpose. For example, through suffering a person might develop compassion for others, and the result might be a world filled with compassionate beings rather than simply blissful ones. Or the story of Adam and Eve might be interpreted in such a way that their deepened experience makes love possible for each other and their children: there is thus a purpose to their suffering. But dysteleological surds would be evils that serve no greater purpose. This is the key of many of the debates about the problem of evil: are there "evils" that don't fit into any larger purpose, that serve no greater good, and even if there is such purposive evil, is the suffering of so many beings worth the price? Twain is an empiricist who seeks to show us the variety of such evils infecting "the damned human race" and insists no amount of future joy will atone for them.

This aesthetic defense eliminates the problem by claiming all suffering and evil is only apparently evil, but all suffering serves some greater purpose. For example, many theists will follow the pagan philosopher Plotinus, who, in *The Enneads*, likens creation to a great work of art. When we complain of the suffering of creatures in the world, "We are like people ignorant of painting who complain that the colours are not beautiful everywhere in the picture: but the Artist has laid on the appropriate tint to every spot."[11] Following Plotinus, Augustine emphasizes that from God's point of view there is no evil because everything, including evil and suffering, adds to the fullness and beauty of God's creation. In *The Confessions*, evil does not exist from God's point of view because from the "eternal perspective" it is all good. It is better that there be a great diversity in existence. This would include the lower things, such as hell, suffering, and the damned, as well as the higher, such as heaven and terrestrial beauty. Both the lower and higher add to the overall beauty of the whole. As Augustine explains in *The Confessions*:

> To thee there is no such thing as evil, and even in thy whole creation taken as a whole, there is not; because there is nothing from beyond it that can burst in and destroy the order which thou hast appointed for it. But in the parts of creation, some things, because they do not harmonize with others, are considered evil. Yet, those same things harmonize with others and are good, and in themselves are good. . . . I no longer desired a better world, because my thoughts ranged over all, and with sounder judgment I reflected that the things above were better than those below, yet that all creation together was better than the higher things alone.[12]

In *De Ordine*, Augustine promises us that if we remain faithful, we will receive a vision of beauty that will answer all our questions about the injustice and suffering of this world. "I shall say no more, except that to us is promised a vision of beauty. . . . Whosoever will have glimpsed this beauty . . . that in the intelligible world, every part is as beautiful and perfect as the whole."[13] This is certainly the message of much of theistic writing from Augustine to Rumi, and from Dante to C. S. Lewis.

Thus the eternal necessarily trivializes the import of not only the everyday, but even the most momentous struggles of this life. What happens here has little import. If anything, the purpose of life is to escape the world. No earthly love can compare with the glories of the perfect heavenly realm. It is best to stop up your ears and run as fast as you can from such love toward the eternal beauty. Dante at the end of his journey arrives in paradise and is greeted by his earthly love Beatrice, but when he gets to the highest point in paradise, he turns from her as she turns from him to contemplate the perfect beauty of God. Dante, enraptured by the beatific vision, proclaims: "O light eternal, who alone abidest in Thyself, alone knowest Thyself, and, known to Thyself and knowing, lovest and smilest on Thyself!"[14] In this view, God's eternal perfection is the only thing of ultimate worth. Humans are just Pilgrims in this world, and the sooner we are out of it the better. In John Bunyan's Christian classic *Pilgrim's Progress*, the pilgrim begins his journey by forsaking his family and running toward the eternal city.

> Then said the *Evangelist*, If this be thy condition, why standest thou still? He answered, because I know not wither to go. Then he gave him a *Parchment Roll*, and there was written within, *Fly from the wrath to come*.
>
> So I saw in my Dream, that the Man began to run; now he had not run far from his own door, but his Wife and children perceiving it, began to cry after him to return: but the Man put his Fingers in his Ears, and ran on crying, Life, Life, Eternal Life: so he looked not behind him, but fled towards the middle of the Plain.[15]

Twain gave his 1869 travelogue, *The Innocents Abroad*, the alternate title *The New Pilgrims' Progress*, and in *The Adventures of Huckleberry Finn*, Huck mentions *The Pilgrim's Progress* as he describes the works of literature in the Grangerfords's library as part of a satire of the Protestant southern aristocracy. In a letter to William Dean Howells, Twain once quipped about Henry James: "And as for 'The Bostonians,' I would rather be damned to John Bunyan's heaven than read that."[16] In "Captain Stormfield's Visit to Heaven" and *Letters from the Earth*, Twain deliberately pokes fun at the human ideal of heaven as a place too boring to endure very long. Captain Stormfield discovers that the heavenly chorus is made up of newcomers to the heavenly city who abandon the praise singing after a few hours.[17] Satan describes the hysterical human idea that there is no sex in heaven, which all humans enjoy very much, while they believe Heaven is a continual Sunday worship service, a thing no human can stand on earth.[18]

Twain's Calvinist God

William Dean Howells, who famously dubbed Twain a "Brevet Presbyterian," wrote Twain in 1899, telling him he was a "creature of the Presbyterian

God who did make you."[19] A number of Twain scholars agree that he never escaped his Calvinist upbringing. Twain himself speaks of the importance of childhood training in the creation of the human person. As Clarence tells Hank in A Connecticut Yankee in King Arthur's Court, the gods and superstitions of our youth stay with us forever.[20] Stanley Brodwin, Lawrence Berkove, Joseph Csicsila, Joe B. Fulton, and others have shown Twain offers a "counter-theology" that may evolve through his work but is always an important part of his thinking and art. The God of Twain's youth, against whom he is in constant rebellion, is a hardcore Calvinist God.[21]

The Calvinist God is the epitome of the all-powerful ex nihilo artist of the universe. Even more powerfully than Augustine, Calvin argued that humanity was under the pre-destinating power of God. Augustine had written, "If it were not good that evil things exist, they would certainly not be allowed to exist by the omnipotent God."[22] Calvin goes further in clarifying the position. "Those whom God passes over, he condemns; and this he does for no other reason than that he wills to exclude them for the inheritance which he predestines for his own children."[23] God literally decreed all events to take place. God "foresees future events only by reason of the fact that he decreed they take place."[24] Whence does it happen that Adam's fall irremediably involved so many peoples, together with their infant offspring, in eternal death "because it so pleased God?" Calvin replied, "The decree is dreadful indeed, I confess."[25] But he concludes that "God's will is so much the highest rule of righteousness that whatever he wills, by the very fact that he wills it, must be considered righteous."[26]

Twain does not agree that whatever God does must be good and attacks this God with zeal. Like Voltaire, he argues that the cumulative facts of human existence outweigh the logic of the philosophers and theologians. He hints at this in the "Papers of the Adam Family" in Eve's autobiography. Eve discovers that the Lion is a carnivore by examining its teeth. Adam insists and then shows by logical deduction that this cannot be. There are no carnivores because it is not part of God's plan that any being should eat flesh. Were it so, flesh would have been provided. But Eve then says, "That there is something better than logic." "Indeed?" replies Adam. "What is it?" "Fact," Eve rejoins, and she proceeds to show Adam the Lion's teeth, which are, of course, the teeth of a carnivore.[27] As Voltaire did in Candide, Twain exhibits case after case of human suffering as facts that submerge any logical inference from the perfection of the Supreme Being. The facts demonstrate that dysteleological surds, unjustified sufferings, really do exist.

Satan and Creation

Twain's most sustained characterization of the Christian God is his unpublished novella *Letters from the Earth*. It has been characterized as Twain's final word on God and the "damned human race."[28] The letters are penned by Satan, who is not the Prince of Darkness but an archangel temporarily exiled from heaven for a single "celestial day" of ten thousand years for making remarks that could be read as "sarcasms" about God's creation. Satan, out of curiosity about the place, visits the earth and writes back to his fellow archangels, Michael and Gabriel, about the strange things he observes there.

Before Satan's exile, The Creator, a combination of the Calvinist God, a Deist God, and a curious scientist, creates all beings and places them under automatic law. This is the "LAW OF NATURE," and it is to be followed by all creatures. Satan and the archangels are perplexed by God's activity. The divine being doesn't need the universe but chooses to create it anyway. He creates animals, and Satan is further perplexed and asks The Creator to explain.

"Divine One," said Satan, making obeisance, "what are they for?"

"They are an experiment in Morals and Conduct. Observe them, and be instructed."

There were thousands of them. They were full of activities. Busy, all busy— mainly in persecuting each other. Satan remarked—after examining one of them through a powerful microscope: "This large beast is killing weaker animals, Divine One."[29]

God informs Satan the large beasts have been made to kill the weaker, and they are blameless for doing so. It is the law of his nature. The countless creatures "kill, kill, kill" and are blameless for doing so. It is their nature, and they are part of the experiment. The masterpiece in morals and conduct is man, who is sent to earth as part of the "experiment in morals and conduct." The Creator places in them a variety of characteristics; those containing the fine characteristics will be called good men, and those who have the evil characteristics will be called bad men.

Put into each individual, in differing shades and degrees, all the various Moral Qualities, in mass, that have been distributed, a single distinguishing characteristic at a time, among the non-speaking animal world—courage, cowardice, ferocity, gentleness, fairness, justice, cunning, treachery, magnanimity, cruelty, malice, malignity, lust, mercy, pity, purity, selfishness, sweetness, honor, love, hate, baseness, nobility, loyalty, falsity, veracity, untruthfulness—each human being shall have all of these in him, and they will constitute his nature. In some, there will be high and fine characteristics which will submerge the evil ones, and those will be called good men; in others the evil characteristics will have dominion, and those will be called bad men.[30]

Satan describes a Creator who has the characteristics of the Omnipotent Calvinist God creating beings with all the variety of moral characteristics. This variety contributes to the glory of the creator in the diversity of the work of his hands. They have not chosen their characteristics; God has made them to be what they are and sent them to the insignificant speck called earth as a part of the experiment. The "bad ones" will later be damned, all to the glory of the Creator.

Elsewhere in Twain's story "Captain Stormfield's Visit to Heaven," Stormfield's old friend Sandy explains the creation to the new resident of heaven: how the Creator placed all of the twenty-eight moral characteristics in the first humans. This experiment failed. These beings were all identical and happy but incredibly boring. They are referred to as "the Holy Doughnuts" and are tourist destinations for the bored residents of heaven. The "Holy Doughnuts" are a backhanded slap against the orders of angels perfect without variation and who, in No. 44, The Mysterious Stranger, have eternal happiness and painless lives.[31] The experiment with the "Holy Doughnuts" failed, and so God created humanity, as Sandy further explains:

Certn'ly. There's excursions every week-day. Well, the Authorities started out on the hypotheneuse that the thing to go for in the new race was variety. You see, that's where the Doughnuts failed. Now then, was the Human Race an easy job? Yes, sir, it was. They made rafts of moulds, this time, no two of them alike—so there's your physical differentiations, till you can't rest! Then all they had to do was to take the same old 28 Moral Qualities, and mix them up, helter-skelter, in all sorts of different proportions, and ladle them into the moulds—and there's your dispositional differentiations, b'George! Variety? Oh don't mention it![32]

So the humans are created, and the moral qualities are all mixed up in these mostly unhappy creatures. With their various dispositions they are predestined for salvation or damnation. The omniscient God knows this from eternity. This is a theme throughout Twain's discussions of God's creative act.

Beauty, Suffering, and Love

In "The Chronicle of Young Satan," a group of four young boys meet an Angel named Satan. This is not the famous Satan but only his nephew. Satan is wandering the earth and finds its inhabitants interesting. He has incredible powers, including the ability to change the life paths of human beings. The boy, Theodore, attempts to get the angel Satan to modify the fates of some of the unhappy people of his town. Eventually he stops asking Satan to modify people's lives because there is so little that one can do, and when Satan does anything to their predestined lives, they seem to end up dead or damned. Thus the world created by God is a pretty hopeless one. It seems to be filled with evangelical philosopher and theodicist William Lane Craig's transworld damned.[33] Those poor beings are damned in any possible world created by God, but God created the world anyway, and, of course, it is the best possible world. The fact remains that God made them for damnation, and they add to the variety of being. Twain, following Calvin and his strongly Calvinist mother, says this God damns the majority of humanity. Even in that idyll of Edenic youth, *The Adventures of Tom Sawyer*, the God who damns much of humanity is there. Twain describes the hell of church meeting attendance:

> The minister gave out his text and droned along monotonously through an argument that was so prosy that many a head by and by began to nod and yet it was an argument that dealt in limitless fire and brimstone and thinned the predestined elect down to a company so small as to be hardly worth the saving.[34]

For God and the Angels, time and space have no reality. They live in eternity, and creation is before them like a great painting as the beautiful creation of God. They don't suffer but experience the constant bliss of beauty. In the presence of the angel Satan, the boys and the townspeople forget suffering, and like Dante and Beatrice, they forget each other, preferring the company of the divine being. Like the "Holy Doughnuts," Satan and the other angels didn't eat the fruit and fall. They are ignorant of sin and without blemish. "We cannot do wrong; neither have we any disposition to do it, for we do not know what it is," says Satan after he has just crushed the life out of two of the little people, and proceeds to destroy the entire village of little people he has just created. The Angel mimics God in his creative power and indifference to suffering.[35] The boys are fascinated with the aesthetic visions provided by the beautiful Satan, and this deadens their ethical concerns for the tremendous sufferings that they are also witnessing. They love him for his beauty but are appalled by what he does. His beauty lulls them to a moral sleep. They travel with him to hell and watch the sufferings of the damned but, just like the Aesthetic theodicies that emphasize Divine perfection for philosophers and theologians, Satan's beauty makes them forget the horrors of his indifference to the suffering of the eternally damned creatures.[36]

In *Letters from the Earth*, Satan, presumably the Young Satan's famous uncle, exhibits a fascination with the strange religion of the inhabitants of Earth. In Satan's letters home, Twain launches an all-out attack on Christian theology, the Bible, and the God of his youth, whom he never quite escaped. Satan characterizes the God worshipped on Earth as a malicious being who is unspeakably cruel and unjust. Like Calvin, Satan ascribes to God complete power and complete knowledge of everything that happens. Nothing happens without God's permission. God seems to have created the human race only to make it suffer. They are "suffering machines," as Young Satan says of them in *The Chronicle of the Young Satan*.[37] The elder Satan proclaims that the fact that an author of pain and suffering would be called "Our Father" is the great unconscious sarcasm. The believer enthusiastically calls God the creator of all that is, and says nothing happens without His permission, and yet also calls this Fiend a just, kind, Parent.

> With these facts before you will you now try to guess man's chiefest pet name for this ferocious Commander-in-Chief? I will save you the trouble but you must not laugh. It is Our Father in Heaven!
>
> It is curious—the way the human mind works. The Christian begins with this straight proposition, this definite proposition, this inflexible and uncompromising proposition: *God is all-knowing, and all-powerful.*
>
> This being the case, nothing can happen without his knowing beforehand that it is going to happen; nothing happens without his permission; nothing can happen that he chooses to prevent.
>
> That is definite enough, isn't it? It makes the Creator distinctly responsible for everything that happens, doesn't it?
>
> The Christian concedes it in that italicized sentence. Concedes it with feeling, with enthusiasm.
>
> Then, having thus made the Creator responsible for all those pains and diseases and miseries above enumerated, and which he could have prevented, the gifted Christian blandly calls him Our Father!
>
> It is as I tell you. He equips the Creator with every trait that goes to the making of a fiend, and then arrives at the conclusion that a fiend and a father are the same thing! Yet he would deny that a malevolent lunatic and a Sunday school superintendent are essentially the same. What do you think of the human mind? I mean, in case you think there is a human mind.[38]

Twain concludes that God cannot be omnipotent, omniscient and not be held responsible for the evils and suffering of countless creatures. Adam and Eve discover themselves in the world without direction. They are abandoned children. Their "fall" from the garden is inevitable and indeed foreseen and predestined by the Father. When the prohibition against eating the fruit tells them they will die, they have no idea what that is, and more than this, they have no idea about "good and evil," for that will come only after having eaten the fruit. As Eve describes their situation, "We knew nothing, nothing whatever. We were starting at the very bottom of things at the very beginning; we had to learn the a b c of things. Today the child of four knows things which we were still ignorant of at thirty. *For we were children without nurses and without instructors.* There was no one to tell us anything."[39] It is these two wayfarers who discover love, not God, nor Jesus. In the Bible, these Divinities create a hell of suffering on earth and then pursue the poor "sinners" beyond the grave as the supreme act of vengeance.[40]

As Satan wrote, it is for humans to make a better world. In the midst of suffering it is humanity, in the persons of Adam and Eve, who discover love. And it is after they are expelled from the Garden. Real love seems to be a thing of this world, and as Sophocles claimed, the one thing that makes life bearable. Where Dante and Beatrice lose each other in the contemplation of the ideal, Adam and Eve see each other. Before her death Eve contemplates life after the fall and writes: "The Garden is lost, but I have *him* and am content." At Eve's grave, Adam, now alone, laments: "Wheresoever she was, *there* was Eden."[41]

PART III

MORAL ISSUES

CHAPTER EIGHT

~

The Noble Art of Lying

James Edwin Mahon

"A man is never more truthful than when he acknowledges himself a liar."

–Mark Twain[1]

Mark Twain wrote two essays about lying: "On the Decay of the Art of Lying" and "My First Lie, and How I Got Out of It." They remain among the most original things ever written about lying. Nevertheless, they are seldom included in discussions of lying. This is probably because they are considered too light-hearted.[2] Unlike Oscar Wilde's later, more famous, and similarly titled dialogue "The Decay of Lying: An Observation"—in which, after complaining that politicians, lawyers, and journalists are "unimaginative" in their lies, he proceeds to discuss "Lying in art"[3]—Twain's earlier, largely overlooked essay "On the Decay of the Art of Lying"[4] is devoted to everyday lying. It is said to have been read at a meeting of the "Historical and Antiquarian Club" of Hartford, Connecticut, and offered for the "thirty dollar prize" (which it did not win).[5] Scholars date the reading to April 5, 1880, when Twain delivered it to the Monday Evening Club.[6] It was first published in his collection *The Stolen White Elephant, Etc.*, in 1882.[7] It was in this essay that Twain first discussed the so-called *silent* lie. Twain returned to the silent lie in his somewhat better-known essay "My First Lie, And How I Got Out of It,"[8] which is largely devoted to a discussion of the "lie of silent assertion." This essay was first published in a special Christmas section of *The New York*

World on December 10, 1889, and was reprinted in *The Man That Corrupted Hadleyburg and Other Stories and Essays* in 1890.[9] Taken together, these essays form an important contribution to the philosophical discussion of lying.

Everybody Lies

In "On the Decay of the Art of Lying," Twain says that "Joking aside, there is much need of wise examination into what sorts of lies are best and wholesomest to be indulged, seeing as we *must* all lie and we *do* all lie, and what sorts it may be best to avoid."[10] In order to defend Twain's claim that everyone must and does lie, what Twain means by "lie" should first be explained.

In "On the Decay," Twain makes it clear that lying is anything other than strict candor. The only people who do not lie are people who "*always* speak the truth."[11] That is, the only people who do not lie are people who always volunteer, unbidden, exactly what they are thinking. These are people who are candid all the time. The only people who are candid all the time are "Children and fools"[12]—as well as, we might add, lawyers under the grip of a magic spell,[13] the inhabitants of Earth in an alternate universe,[14] an idealistic boy on a Christmas Day truthful crusade,[15] and the naïve, aptly named Candide of Voltaire's famous novella.[16] The rest of us—"adults and wise persons"[17]—do not always speak the truth. That is, the rest of us do not always volunteer, unbidden, exactly what we are thinking. We either do not say what we are thinking, or we say what we are not thinking. Hence, we are liars. For us, "No fact is more firmly established than that lying is a necessity of our circumstances."[18] Hence, "Lying is universal—we *all* do it."[19] While it is true that "None of us could *live* with a habitual truth-teller," as it happens, "thank goodness none of us has to."[20] This is because "An habitual truth-teller is simply an impossible creature; he does not exist; he never has existed."[21] While it is true that "there are people who think they never lie," as it happens "it is not so—and this ignorance is one of the very things that shame our so-called civilization."[22]

The Silent Lie

According to Twain, you lie whenever you do not share whatever you are thinking. Importantly, lying does not require making an assertion, or even speaking. Twain distinguishes between the spoken lie and the "*silent* lie."[23] The spoken lie, which is what most people understand by a lie, is when you do not say what you are thinking, *and* you say what you are *not* thinking (you speak an untruth). The silent lie, which is more common, is when, simply, *you do not say what you are thinking*. You say *nothing*. Although "Many obstinate truth-mongers indulge in this dissipation, imagining that if they *speak* no lie, they lie not at all,"[24] they fail to appreciate that a person lies "if he keeps his tongue still"[25] and does not say what he is thinking. The silent lie can be "the deception which one conveys by simply keeping still and concealing the truth."[26] This silent lie is the lie of omission, otherwise known as the passive lie.[27] In "My First Lie," Twain says the proportion of the spoken lie to the silent lie is "as 1 to 22,894."[28]

Twain provides an example of a particular kind of silent lie in "On the Decay." Remarking once at a dinner in California that "Yes, *all*—we are all liars. There are no exceptions,"[29] a woman at the table took issue with his claim. "I have made a rule of my life to never tell a lie; and I have never departed from it in a single instance."[30] To this Twain replied that "I don't mean the least harm or disrespect, but really you have been lying like smoke ever since I've been sitting here."[31] She required that he give her a single instance of her lying, and he obliged. She had filled out a form about a sick-nurse who had helped her nephew through his dangerous illness. The form warned the person who filled it out "to be very careful and explicit" in answering the questions, "for the welfare of the service requires that the nurse be promptly fined or otherwise punished for derelictions."[32] She had told Twain that she had been "perfectly delighted with this nurse," and that she had only one fault: "you found that you could never depend on her wrapping Johnny up half sufficiently while he waited in a chilly chair for her to rearrange the warm bed."[33] But in answer to the question on the form, "Was the nurse at any time guilty of a negligence which was likely to result in the patient's taking cold?" she had "*left it blank*."[34] As Twain says, "Just so—you have told a *silent* lie; you have left it to be inferred that you had no fault to find in the matter."[35] Upon hearing this, "that same day . . . she sent a line to the hospital which filled up the neglected blank, and stated the *facts* too, in the squarest possible manner."[36]

The Elephant in the Room Lie

The lie by the aunt who left the section of the form blank was a deceptive silent lie. In addition to saying that lying does not have to involve speaking, however, Twain says that lies do not have to be deceptive to be lies. There can be *nondeceptive* lies, of both the silent and the spoken kind. While certainly not the first to argue that lies do not have to be deceptive,[37] Twain was nevertheless ahead of his time. It is only recently that a number of philosophers have argued that an intention to deceive is not necessary for lying, and that those who make obviously false assertions are still lying even if they do not intend to be believed.[38] Twain goes one step further than these philosophers in holding that keeping silent about something, without intending to deceive anyone, is also lying.

Twain's nondeceptive silent lies include cases of what Thomas Nagel refers to as cases of "non-acknowledgment," where everyone is thinking the same thing, and everyone knows that everyone is thinking the same thing, and no one will say what everyone is thinking.[39] This would be a case of a "the elephant in the room" lie, such as when two people who have been fighting publicly over the Internet about some matter run into each other at a social event and do not acknowledge the fight and talk instead about a neutral topic. Both are silently lying, according to Twain.

Nondeceptive silent lies would also include cases of normal reticence, such as not sharing one's opinions or details about one's life with strangers or people one does not know particularly well. As Nagel says, "The first and most obvious thing to note about many of the most important forms of reticence is that they are not dishonest, because the conventions that govern them are generally known. If I don't tell you everything that I think and feel about you, that is not a case of deception since you don't expect me to do so and would probably be appalled if I did."[40] This kind of lie of the unspoken kind would also include cases of a keeping a secret from friends or family or people you know well, where the person you are keeping a secret from is merely being kept in ignorance of the matter, and has no false belief about the matter.[41] For example, not telling people that you are pregnant is a lie on Twain's account.

The National Lie

Although the silent lie about the sick-nurse is presented as a not very serious silent lie, in the later essay "My First Lie," Twain provides examples of silent lies that are much more serious. Identifying "the lie of silent assertion" as the lie "we can tell . . . without saying a word,"[42] he says that "In the magnitude of its territorial spread it is one of the most majestic lies that the civilizations make it their sacred and anxious care to guard and watch and propagate."[43] The first example he gives is the silent lie across the United States that there was nothing wrong with slavery. This silence about the injustice of slavery was the greatest lie of all:

> For instance, it would not be possible for a humane and intelligent person to invent a rational excuse for slavery; yet you will remember that in the early days of the emancipation agitation in the North the agitators got but small

help or countenance from any one. Argue and plead and pray as they might, they could not break the universal stillness that reigned, from pulpit and press all the way down to the bottom of society—the clammy stillness created and maintained by the lie of silent assertion—the silent assertion that there wasn't anything going on in which humane and intelligent people were interested.[44]

In addition to the silent lie about the injustice of slavery, Twain instances the case of the trial and imprisonment for espionage in France of Captain Alfred Dreyfus, who was scapegoated because he was Jewish: "all France, except a couple of dozen moral paladins, lay under the smother of the silent-assertion lie that no wrong was being done to a persecuted and unoffending man."[45] Twain also instances the silent lie "over England lately"[46] about British imperialism and the immanent second Boer War, where "a good half of the population" were "silently letting on that they were not aware that Mr. Chamberlain was trying to manufacture a war in South Africa and was willing to pay fancy prices for the materials."[47]

These were "three prominent ostensible civilizations working the silent-assertion lie."[48] Twain says that it would be possible to find "a billion"[49] of such lies. The various countries "are working that kind of lie, day in and day out, in thousands and thousands of varieties, without ever resting."[50] The "universal conspiracy of the silent-assertion lie is hard at work always and everywhere."[51] Importantly, the "silent assertion that nothing is going on which fair and intelligent men are aware of and are engaged by their duty to try to stop" is the "most timid and shabby of all lies."[52] It has "mutely labored in the interest of despotisms and aristocracies and chattel slaveries, and military slaveries, and religious slaveries, and has kept them alive."[53] It is the "silent colossal National Lie that is the support and confederate of all the tyrannies and shams and inequalities and unfairnesses that afflict the peoples."[54]

Although he does not say so explicitly, it can be argued that these silent National Lies, such as the silent National Lie in the United States that there was nothing unjust about slavery, were *nondeceptive* silent lies, specifically "the elephant in the room" lies: everyone knew that slavery was unjust, but no one would acknowledge it. Indeed, it is possible to see Twain himself as being complicit in the National Lie about slavery.[55] Twain did not say anything critical about it, at least early on in his life, when he knew, or at least was beginning to understand, that slavery was unjust.[56] At least one commentator has suggested that the "First Lie" of this essay's title, which Twain says he has forgotten, is Twain's own acceptance of slavery.[57] It is also possible to see this silent National Lie about slavery, as well as other silent National Lies, as cases of mass self-deception: people had deceived themselves in believing that there was nothing unjust about slavery.[58] If this were true, of course, then they were *not* silently lying about the injustice of slavery, although they had lied to themselves originally about it.

Twain does not speak about the possibility of silent lies that transcend national boundaries, and that could be classified as "global lies," such as the silent lie that there is nothing unjust about the unequal division of domestic labor between men and women across the world. Nor does he speak about the possibility of silent lies that transcend the boundary between humans and nonhumans, and that could be classified as "human lies," such as the silent lie that there is nothing wrong about killing and eating animals. His analysis of silent lies allows for such silent lies, nevertheless.

Hello, He Lied

Nondeceptive spoken lies are also discussed in some detail by Twain. In "On the Decay," talking about a "far country" (his other essay reveals that he has England in mind), Twain anticipates the title of Hollywood film producer Lynda Obst's memoir, *Hello, He Lied*,[59] when he says that "The men in that far country were liars, every one. Their mere howdy-do was a lie, because *they* didn't care how you did."[60] In response to such a nondeceptive lie, you were obliged to lie in return with your own variation on "Fine, thanks" or "Good, thanks," it would seem: "To the ordinary inquirer you lied in return; for you made no conscientious diagnostic of your case, but answered at random, and usually missed it considerably."[61] Such nondeceptive, polite lying was pervasive. As Twain says, "If a stranger called and interrupted you, you said with your hearty tongue, 'I'm glad to see you,' and said with your heartier soul, 'I wish you were with the cannibals and it was dinner-time.'"[62] Then, "When he went, you said regretfully, '*Must* you go?' and followed it with a 'Call again,'"[63] despite having no wish to see him again. Importantly, in all of these exchanges, "you did no harm, for you did not deceive anybody."[64] Indeed, "all this courteous lying is a sweet and loving art."[65] All politeness and tact, for Twain, is nondeceptive lying: "The highest perfection of politeness is only a beautiful edifice, built, from the base to the dome, of graceful and gilded forms of charitable and unselfish lying."[66] Twain provides, as another example of nondeceptive spoken lying in England, those "ladies who used to go around paying calls, under the humane and kindly pretence of wanting to see each other."[67] When these ladies came home, they said "We made sixteen calls and found fourteen of them out," but "their manner of saying it expressed their lively satisfaction in that fact"[68] that fourteen of the women were not at home to receive them. Their "pretence of wanting to see the fourteen—and the other two whom they had been less lucky with—was that commonest and mildest form of lying which is sufficiently described as a deflection from the truth."[69]

Acts as Lies

In addition to silent lies (both deceptive and nondeceptive), and spoken lies (both deceptive and nondeceptive), Twain considers there to be deceptive nonlinguistic *acts* that are lies. As he notes, it is a "quite commonplace but seldom noticed fact" that "almost all lies are acts, and speech has not part in them."[70] It is possible for a person to "convey deception—and purposely," with "his hands, his feet, his eyes, his attitude."[71] Smiling at a friend's success when one is jealous, waving one's hands in excitement when inwardly one is depressed, appearing downbeat when one is actually elated, etc., all count as lies for Twain. A person lies, he says, "in his joy; in his mourning."[72]

In "My First Lie," Twain says that he remembers his "second lie," which was a nonlinguistic lie that he committed with he was "nine days old."[73] He had noticed that when the pin of his diaper stuck into him, and he "advertised it in the usual fashion," he was "lovingly petted and coddled and pitied in the most agreeable way and got a ration between meals besides."[74] Because "It was human nature to want to get these riches," he "lied about the pin—advertising one when there wasn't any."[75] All babies did, he says. "During the first half of my life I never knew a child that was able to rise above temptation and keep from telling that lie."[76] (Not all children are truth-tellers, it seems). It was not to last: "Up to 1867 all the civilized children that were ever born into the world were liars. . . . Then the safety-pin came in and blocked the game."[77] Twain's nonlinguistic lie as a baby was discovered by his parents: "They found no pin and they realized that another liar had been added to the world's supply."[78] He recollects "that I was reversed and stretched across some one's knee and that something happened" as a result.[79]

Twain provides another example of a nonlinguistic act that is a lie in "My First Lie." Here he tells of an argument he had with an English friend who claimed that "I have never told a lie and I should be very sorry to do such a thing."[80] Twain then describes what his English friend did minutes later: "Just then he lifted his hat and smiled a basketful of surprised and delighted smiles down at a gentleman who was passing in a hansom."[81] Although his friend had no idea who the man was, his friend says that he lifted his hat and smiled at him, "Because I saw that he thought he knew me and was expecting it of me. If I hadn't done it he would have been hurt. I didn't want to embarrass him before the whole street."[82] Twain tells him that "What you did was kindly and courteous and beautiful; I would have done it myself; but it was a lie."[83] Against his friend's protest that "I didn't say a word," Twain replies, "I know you didn't speak, still you said to him very plainly and enthusiastically in dumb show, 'Hello! You in town? Awful glad to see you, old fellow; when did you get back?' Concealed in your actions was what you have called 'a misleading reservation of an explanatory fact—the fact that you had never seen him before. You expressed joy in encountering him—a lie; and you made that reservation—another lie. . . . But don't be troubled—we all do it."[84]

Modified Lies

A final kind of lie that Twain discusses is what he calls a "modified" lie—"a half-breed, a mulatto" lie.[85] A modified lie is an assertion that is truthful but that is intended to deceive—something also known as a palter.[86] He relates the story of how he managed to get "out of an embarrassment in Austria last year"[87] (it is unclear if this story is a lie). He told the police "that I belonged to the same family as the Prince of Wales."[88] After telling them this, "That made everything pleasant and they let me go; and apologized, too, and were ever so kind and obliging and polite, and couldn't do too much for me, and explained how the mistake came to be made, and promised to hang the officer that did it, and hoped I would let bygones be bygones and not say anything about it; and I said they could depend on me."[89]

Twain considered his lie to be merely a modified lie because "I didn't say I belonged to the royal family; I only said that I belonged to the same family as the Prince—meaning the human family, of course; and if those people had had any penetration they would have known it."[90] In other words, Twain did not say something untruthful. He said what was true to the police—that he was a member of the family of humans—but with the intention that the police believe something false—that he belonged to the Royal family. As he said—joking—"of course I was distressed to find out that the police had misunderstood me, but as I had not told any lie I knew that there was no occasion to sit up nights and worry about it."[91]

It should be noted that Twain's English friend, to whom he told this story, refused to agree that he had not told a lie, telling him that "so far as he could see the modification was itself a lie, it being a misleading reservation of an explanatory fact."[92]

Pleasing Lies and Brutal Truths

According to Twain, lies can please others and can cost liars nothing. For example, "You lied to the undertaker, and said your health was failing—a wholly commendable lie, since it cost you nothing and pleased the other man."[93] This way, the undertaker is pleased, and you are pleased by this. By contrast, if you had told the truth, "the truth would have made you both unhappy."[94] In the case of the ladies in London making house calls, these ladies "had a thousand pleasant ways of lying, that grew out of gentle impulses, and were a credit to their intelligence and an honor to their hearts."[95] Their lying "is beautiful, it is noble; for its object is, *not* to reap profit, but to convey a pleasure to the sixteen."[96]

While it is true that, in the case of the silent lie about the sick-nurse, the lie might have endangered the child, and the truth might have led to the sick-nurse's being fired, nevertheless the aunt could have made up the possible harm in telling the truth by adding a harmless "fraudulent compliment."[97] As Twain says, "Almost any little pleasant lie would have taken the sting out of that troublesome but necessary expression of the truth," such as "In one respect this sick-nurse is perfection—when she is on the watch, she never snores."[98] This joke would have counterbalanced the negative report.

In a letter in 1883, Twain said that "I would rather tell seven lies than make one explanation."[99] In contrast to the pleasing results of many lies, the truth can be painful: "What I bemoan is the growing prevalence of the brutal truth. Let us do what we can to eradicate it."[100] Twain invokes the American historian Francis Parkman who said that, "The principle of truth may itself be carried into an absurdity."[101] It is only "imbeciles and nuisances," Parkman says, says, who have a "sick conscience" and who engage in the "habitual violation of the maxim" that "truth should not be spoken at all times."[102] Although Twain admits that this is "strong language,"[103] he believes it to be true. The "iron-souled truth-monger" would "be an ass, and inflict totally unnecessary pain."[104]

Twain says that "an injurious truth" is "an uncommendable thing," and adds that this is "a fact recognized by the law of libel."[105] Twain is correct. In 2009, in *Noonan v Staples Inc.*,[106] a three judge panel of the U.S. Court of Appeals for the First Circuit "issued a ruling that . . . took the 'lie' out of libel law" and made it possible for the truth to be libelous.[107] As the ruling has been summarized, "The three-judge panel wrote, 'under Massachusetts law, even a true statement can form the basis of a libel action if the plaintiff proves that the defendant acted with 'actual malice,' where 'actual malice' is defined as 'actual malevolent intent or ill will.'"[108] The case was one in which Staples management sent a mass e-mail to Staples employees naming an employee, Alan Noonan, who had been fired for violating the company's travel expenses policy. Even though what the e-mail said was true, nevertheless they ruled that the e-mail was sent with ill-will and could be libelous.

The "First Circuit pointed out that the email sender had been employed with Staples for twelve years, yet had never before referred to a fired employee by name in an email. It noted that the sender had failed to send out a similar email with respect to a scandal involving another employee, whom it said had been discovered to be an embezzler. And it pointed out that the massive recipient list to which the email was sent included many employees who never traveled, and thus did not need to be reminded about the travel policy."[109] Overall, the "First Circuit saw enough evidence of ill-will—in the singling-out of Noonan, and the sharing of his fate with over a thousand fellow employees—to send the libel claim to trial."[110] In March the appeals court denied an en banc rehearing of the case, leaving their decision standing. The result is that "the publication of a truth, with nasty intent, can lead to a large damages award."[111] The fact that one's assertions are true, therefore, is no defense. The truth should not always be spoken, for the truth can be harmful, especially if it is told maliciously.

Miseducation about Lies

According to Twain, the first error in his parents' miseducation about lies— and of people's miseducation about lies in general—is that lies must be spoken in order to be lies. The second error is that some people do not lie. If people only understood what silent lies are, they would appreciate that everyone must, and does, lie. In talking about his parents' discovery of his first lie, Twain says that if his parents had "examined a little further" and understood the possibility of the silent lie—"the lie of silent assertion"—then they would have recognized that "all people are liars from the cradle onward, without exception, and that they begin to lie as soon as they wake in the morning, and keep it up without rest or refreshment until they go to sleep at night."[112] If they had recognized this truth, then it would have "grieved them."[113] This grief would have been a mistake on their part. They, like most people, "had been heedlessly and ignorantly educated by their books and teachers"[114] about lying. There is no reason "why should a person grieve over a thing which by the eternal law of his make he cannot help."[115] People who lie—which is all people—"didn't invent the law"; it is merely their "business to obey it and keep still; join the universal conspiracy and keep so still that he shall deceive his fellow-conspirators into imagining that he doesn't know the law exists."[116] The third error of people's miseducation about lies is that the spoken lie is worse than the silent lie. As Twain says, "There is a prejudice against the spoken lie, but none against any other."[117] It is the spoken lie that gets all of the criticism, despite the fact that "by examination and mathematical computation I find that the proportion of the spoken lie to the other varieties is as 1 to 22,894."[118] The truth is that "the spoken lie is of no consequence" by comparison with the silent lie, "and it is not worthwhile to go around fussing about it and trying to make believe that it is an important matter."[119] Rather, "The silent colossal National Lie that is the support and confederate of all the tyrannies and shams and inequalities and unfairnesses that afflict the peoples—that is the one to throw bricks and sermons at."[120] Elsewhere, Twain said that "There are 869 different forms of lying, but only one of them has been squarely forbidden. Thou shalt not bear false witness against thy neighbor."[121] Only deceptive spoken lies, it seems, are condemned. The fourth, and related, error of people's miseducation about lies is that as long as you abstain from telling spoken lies, you are virtuous. Not alone is this an error, but it is an extremely harmful error. People believe that as long as they refrain from telling spoken lies they are doing no harm, when in fact it is their silent lies that cause so much harm, and especially National Lies: "When whole races and people conspire to propagate gigantic mute lies in the interest of tyrannies and shams, why should we care anything about the trifling lies told by individuals? Why should we try to make it appear that abstention from lying is a virtue? Why should we want to beguile ourselves in that way? Why should we without shame help the nation lie, and then be ashamed to do a little lying on our own account? . . . Why should we help the nation lie the whole day long and then object to telling one little individual private lie in our own interest to go to bed on?"[122] This is not to say that people are never instructed to tell lies, of both the silent and spoken kind. As Twain said in another context, "'Speak only good of the dead' is a sentimental way of advising the living to lie—at least as regards the usual run of dead people."[123] Instead of having the view that spoken lies should not be told (at least about the living) but that silent lies are okay, Twain says that one should "be consistent."[124] This means that people should either lie "not at all," which they cannot do, or that people should lie "all the time,"[125] which is precisely what he advocates. That is why people need to learn how to lie.

The Noble Art of Lying

Although Twain believes that people should lie—indeed, they should lie all the time—his "lament"[126] for lying in "On the Decay" is not a lament for the practice of lying. In actuality, he believes that the practice of lying has not declined. His lament is that lying has become "lumbering and slovenly."[127] Lying has been "prostituted."[128] It is important to know that an "awkward, unscientific lie is often as ineffectual as the truth."[129] As he said in "Advice to Youth," a speech to the young women of Boston's Saturday Morning Club on April 15, 1882: "An awkward, feeble, leaky lie is a thing which you ought to make it your unceasing study to avoid; such a lie as that has no more real permanence than an average truth. Why, you might as well tell the truth at once and be done with it."[130] Training is needed, especially with regard to deceptive lying. As he remarked elsewhere: "Anybody can tell lies: there is no merit in a *mere* lie, it must possess *art*, it must exhibit a splendid & plausible & convincing *probability*; that is to say, it must be powerfully calculated to *deceive*."[131]

Given that lies can help to avoid harm, given that they can be a tool for good, what is needed is *better* lying. Lying, he holds, is a "noble art."[132] It is, indeed, "a Virtue."[133] The lie is "a recreation, a solace, a refuge in time of need, the fourth Grace, the tenth Muse, man's best and surest friend, is immortal."[134] It is obvious that "No virtue can reach its highest usefulness without careful and diligent cultivation."[135] The "ignorant, uncultivated liar" has no chance against the "educated expert"[136] when it comes to lying well. Hence, lying "ought to be taught in the public schools."[137] What the world needs is "*judicious* lying."[138] Only when people are experts at lying "shall we be rid of the rank and pestilent truth that is rotting the land; then shall we be great and good and beautiful, and worthy dwellers in a world where even benign Nature habitually lies, except when she promises execrable weather."[139] If "this finest of the finest arts had everywhere received the attention, the encouragement, and conscientious practice and development which this club has devoted to it,"[140] then it would never have declined into the state in which it is in today. Instead, people have been stopped from lying. Often, this is done by simply preventing people from lying. When the safety pin was introduced, which stopped babies from lying about being pricked by pins, such a "reform" was not "worth anything" at all because "it is reform by force and has no virtue in it; it merely stops that form of lying, it doesn't impair the disposition to lie, by a shade. It is a cradle application of conversion by fire and sword, or of the temperance principle through prohibition."[141] This was not true education about lying.

In the case of the aunt who lied by omission about the sick-nurse on the form, "this lady's fault was *not* in lying, but in lying injudiciously. She should have told the truth, *there*, and made it up to the sick-nurse with a fraudulent compliment"[142] in another part of the form. The great problem with liars, such as his friend, was, as he said to her, "your impulse was right, but your judgment was crude; this comes of unintelligent practice. Now observe the results of this inexpert deflection of yours."[143]

The truth is that "Lying is universal—we *all* do it."[144] As we all do it, "the wise thing is for us diligently to train ourselves to lie thoughtfully, judiciously . . . to lie gracefully and graciously, not awkwardly and clumsily; to lie firmly, frankly, squarely, with head erect, not haltingly, tortuously, with pusillanimous mien, as being ashamed of our high calling."[145] Here Twain is repeating something that he said years before, in his speech to young women: "Now as to the matter of lying. . . . Many a young person has injured himself permanently through a single clumsy and ill finished lie, the result of carelessness born of incomplete training. Some authorities hold that the young ought not to lie at all. That of course, is putting it rather stronger than necessary; still while I cannot go quite so far as that, I do maintain, and I believe I am right, that the young ought to be temperate in the use of this great art until practice and experience shall give them that confidence, elegance, and precision which alone can make the accomplishment graceful and profitable. Patience, diligence, painstaking attention to detail—these are requirements; these in time, will make the student perfect; upon these only, may he rely as the sure foundation for future eminence. . . . Begin your practice of this gracious and beautiful art early—begin now. If I had begun earlier, I could have learned how."[146]

Twain claims in "My First Lie" that he is "but a new and feeble student in this gracious art,"[147] which is of course a lie, albeit not a deceptive lie, and that his audience, the "Historical and Antiquarian Club," are "my superiors in this thing,"[148] indeed are "Old Masters"[149] at lying, and that they should receive his lament in the spirit in which it is given, namely, the "spirit of just and appreciative recognition."[150] He thinks that "there is much need of wise examination into what sorts of lies are best and wholesomest to be indulged, seeing we *must* all lie and we *do* all lie, and what sorts it may be best to avoid—and this is a thing which I feel I can confidently put into the hands of this experienced Club."[151] This was not the first or the last time that Twain claimed to be a bad liar. Twain once wrote in a letter to the Reverend Joseph H. Twichell that "I realize that in a sudden emergency I am but a poor clumsy liar, whereas a fine alert and capable emergency-liar is the only sort that is worth anything in a sick-chamber."[152]

The Ethics of Lying

For Twain, the ethics of lying and truth-telling is relatively straightforward. First, he may be said to agree that "The moral reason we have not to lie stems not from the very nature of lying."[153] When lying is wrong, it is wrong because of what it does to others. Twain's first ethical principle is the principle of nonmaleficence, that one should not cause others to suffer. As W. D. Ross has stated it, "No doubt to injure others is incidentally to fail to do them good; but it seems to me clear that non-maleficence is apprehended as a duty distinct from that of beneficence, and as a duty of a more stringent character."[154] One should not injure others—either by telling a lie, or by telling the truth. As between a lie that injures others, and a truth that injures others, there is no ethical difference, Twain insists: "An injurious truth has no merit over an injurious lie. Neither should ever be uttered."[155] However, as between a lie that avoids injuring others, and a truth that injures others, there is a clear ethical difference: the lie is ethically superior. In such a case, it is ethically better to tell the lie: "The man who speaks an injurious truth lest his soul be not saved if he does not do otherwise, should reflect that that sort of a soul is not strictly worth saving."[156]

In addition to appealing to the principle of nonmaleficence to support not telling truths that injure others, and to support telling lies that avoid injuring others, Twain appeals to another ethical principle, the principle of beneficence, to support telling lies that help others. As Ross puts it, some duties "rest on the mere fact that there are other beings in the world whose condition we can make better. . . . These are the duties of beneficence."[157] Importantly, the duty of beneficence is a duty to be *altruistic*, to count one's own well-being as *less important* than that of someone else's, and to make a *sacrifice* for someone else. The duty of beneficence, therefore, is a nonconsequentialist duty: "The utilitarian's ultimate moral principle, let it be remembered, expresses the sentiment *not* of altruism."[158] As between a lie that helps others and a truth that fails to help others, there is a clear ethical difference: the lie is ethically superior. In such a case, it is ethically superior to tell the lie, even if—or because—it comes at a cost to oneself: "the lies I speak of are self-sacrificing ones told for a generous object, not a mean one."[159] The cost to oneself of telling a lie could include losing one's soul, in view of the Biblical commandment against bearing false witness. Twain admits this: "The man who tells a lie to help a poor devil out of trouble, is one of whom the angels doubtless say, 'Lo, here is an heroic soul who casts his own welfare in jeopardy to succor his neighbor's; let us exalt this magnanimous liar.'"[160]

In addition to the pleasing lie that benefitted the undertaker, Twain provides an example of a beneficent lie in "My First Lie." His friend "told of how he happened along once just in the nick of time to do a great service for a family who were old friends of his. The head of it had suddenly died in circumstances and surroundings of a ruinously disgraceful character. If known the facts would break the hearts of the innocent family and put upon them a load of unendurable shame. There was no help but in a giant lie, and he girded up and told it."[161] Twain's response to this story about his friend's lie is to praise him: "the very next man that came along might have been one of these heartless and shameless truth mongers. You have told the truth a million times in your life, G—, but that one golden lie atones for it all."[162] Twain sums up his ethical views on lying when he says to the woman who claimed to have never lied "One ought always to lie, when one can do good by it."[163] Given that we must lie, we should "lie with a good object, and not an evil one," we should "lie for others' advantage, and not our own," we should "lie healingly, charitably, humanely, not cruelly, hurtfully, maliciously."[164]

Lies about Lies

Concerning his ethical views on lying, Twain says that "Some may think me not strict enough in my morals, but that position is hardly tenable. There are many kinds of lying which I do not approve."[165] The first kind of lie that he does not approve is of, of course, "an injurious lie."[166] Into this nonapproved category would fall all three National Lies, as well as other National Lies that he suggests or intimates. All malicious lies, or lies that take advantage of others, would also fall into this category. Twain also says that he does not like "the lie of bravado" nor "the lie of virtuous ecstasy."[167] Both of his examples of these lies are *lies about lies*. As an example of the "lie of bravado," Twain gives essayist Thomas Carlyle's "This gospel is eternal—that a lie shall not live."[168] Twain, however, disagrees with the Scotsman completely.[169] As he wrote elsewhere: "Carlyle said 'a lie cannot live.' It shows that he did not know how to tell them."[170] Because Twain was an admirer of Carlyle's ("I have a reverent affection for Carlyle's books and have read his Revolution eight times"[171]) in his essay, he says that he prefers "to think he was not entirely himself when he told that one."[172] Although Carlyle "was truthful when calm," nevertheless "it is plain that he said it in a moment of excitement, when chasing Americans out of his back yard with brickbats," and "I am quite sure that when he told that large one about a lie not being able to live he had just missed an American and was over-excited."[173] Although Carlyle told this lie "above thirty years ago," it is "alive yet, and very healthy and hearty, and likely to out-live any fact in history."[174]

As an example of the "lie of virtuous ecstasy," Twain gives poet William Cullen Bryant's "Truth crushed to earth will rise again."[175] About this Twain says, "I have taken medals at thirteen world's fairs, and may claim to be not without capacity, but I never told as big a one as that."[176] His excuse, Twain indicates, is that "Mr. Bryant was playing to the gallery; we all do it."[177] Twain himself believes in the efficacy of liars and their lies. As he says in other places, "The most outrageous lies that can be invented will find believers if a man only tells them with all his might,"[178] and "How easy it is to make people believe a lie, and how hard it is to undo that work again!"[179] In his advice to young women in 1882, referencing what seems to be another "lie of virtuous ecstasy"—General Robert E. Lee's "Truth is mighty, & will eventually prevail"[180]—Twain says:

> Think what tedious years of study, thought, practice, experience, went to the equipment of that peerless old master who was able to impose upon the whole world the lofty and sounding maxim that "Truth is mighty and will prevail"— the most majestic compound fracture of fact which any of woman born has yet achieved. For the history of our race, and each individual's experience, are sewn thick with evidences that a truth is not hard to kill, and that a lie well told is immortal. There is in Boston a monument of the man who discovered anesthesia; many people are aware, in these latter days, that that man didn't discover it at all, but stole the discovery from another man. Is this truth mighty, and will it prevail? Ah no, my hearers, the monument is made of hardy material, but the lie it tells will outlast it a million years.[181]

The final lie about lying that Twain discusses is the young George Washington's lie.[182] Washington's claim that he chopped down the cherry tree "was a timely and judicious truth, and I should have told it myself in the circumstances."[183] He says that the future president's telling the truth about cutting down the cherry tree "was not premeditated, but an inspiration. With his fine military mind, he had probably arranged to let his brother Edward in for the cherry-tree results, but by an inspiration he saw his opportunity in time and took advantage of it. But telling the truth he could astonish his father; his father would tell the neighbors; the neighbors would spread it; it would travel to all firesides; in the end it would make him President, and not only that, but first President. He was a far-seeing boy and would be likely to think of these things. Therefore, to my mind, he stands justified for what he did."[184] His truth-telling about the cherry tree can be justified.

Nevertheless, Twain says, "I should have stopped there. It was a stately truth, a lofty truth—a Tower; and I think it was a mistake to go on and distract attention from its sublimity by building another Tower alongside of it fourteen times as high. I refer to his remark that he 'could not lie.'"[185] He says that Washington should have "left it to Carlyle; it is just his style,"[186] implying that Washington's lie may be another example of a "lie of bravado." The "Father of his Country," Twain says, "was excited"[187] when he said that "I cannot tell a lie."[188] This lie that he could not lie was "a mistake."[189] However, as Twain admits, it is that "Tower" of a lie "that makes the other" truth about the cherry true live: "If he hadn't said 'I cannot tell a lie' there would have been no convulsion. That was the earthquake that rocked the planet. That is the kind of statement that lives forever, and a fact barnacled to it as a good chance to share its immortality."[190]

Although Twain distinguishes between injurious lies and these two lies about lies—the lie of bravado and the lie of virtuous ecstasy—it is clear that Twain holds that both of these lies about lies are, ultimately, harmful. If people believe that lies do not live, and that the truth will always win out, they will be harmed. These lies about lies should *not* be told—because they are harmful. Nothing good comes of telling these lies. Lies that can help others, however, *ought* to told. Hence the need for the "high-minded man," the "man of right feeling,"[191] to cultivate the noble art of lying.[192]

~

CHAPTER NINE

Twain's Critique of Human Exceptionalism

"The Descent of Man" and the Antivivisection Movement

EMILY E. VANDETTE

Despite his belief in natural determinism, the author who endowed Huck Finn with free will, allowing the most memorable first-person narrator in American literature to conclude, "All right then, I'll go to hell," clung to his conviction of moral responsibility. An ardent anti-imperialist, Twain railed against social injustice, and his concerns transcended the treatment and subjugation of disempowered members of the human species. As his hope for humanity waned in his later years, nothing provoked the famous satirist's straightforward ire more than when his fellow man abused and exploited nonhuman animals. In his late-career writings, Mark Twain remarkably anticipates posthumanist ideas that mark the "animal turn" in contemporary critical theory. In particular, he depicts animal subjectivity and consciousness, and he calls into question human-centric assumptions about the world. In writings that range from philosopher dogs dialoguing on the nature and worth of mankind to provocative essays that expose the flaws of humanity and revise the Darwinian hierarchy of species, and even a sentimental narrative of a mother dog reflecting on her exploitation by the family who supposedly loved her, Twain upends the anthropocentric premise of human superiority over other animals.

While Twain's writings about and on behalf of animals range stylistically from satirical to sentimental, his philosophical stance is consistent: he challenges the presumption of human supremacy that informed the progressive materialism of his day. In the final decade of his life and career, the first decade of the twentieth century, Twain's sympathy for animals led him to support a cause that was rapidly losing ground in the progressive era: the movement against vivisection. While the practice of experimenting upon live animals was becoming a fixture in medical schools and physiology labs, Twain added his voice to the campaign to put an end to it, aligning himself with the "abolitionist" camp that sought complete eradication, rather than regulation, of vivisection. He rejected outright any scientific progress that depended upon painful experiments on animals. In protesting the practice of vivisection as utterly indefensible regardless of prospective benefit to humans, and in turning the tables on assumptions of human exceptionalism, Twain presents a philosophical stance on animal ethics and the role of the human in relation to other animals that predates by a century animal rights philosophers such as Gary L. Francione, who promote the abolition of human exploitation of animals, and theorists such as Donna Haraway, who question long-standing distinctions between human and nonhuman existence. Whether investing animal characters with voices and empowering them to tell their own stories, or satirically questioning the supreme place of humans in relation to other species, Twain's animal writing poses a philosophical challenge, "a grim suggestion," as he puts it in one instance: "we are not as important, perhaps, as we had all along supposed we were."[1]

Letters from a Dog

A remarkable example of Twain's reversal of human-centered hierarchy takes the form of a classic philosophical epistle—from the point of view of a dog. In "Letters from a Dog," narrator, "Newfoundland Smith," seeks to persuade his reader, "St. Bernard," of the relative worth of humans. "*All things considered*," he maintains, "*a Man is as good as a Dog*."[2] Subverting the usual notion of human superiority to dogs, he satirically explains the differences and similarities between the two species, arguing to a presumably skeptical St. Bernard that humans are nearly as good as dogs: "To speak broadly, one might perhaps say, Give a Man freedom of conscience, freedom of speech, freedom of action, and he is a Dog; take them from a Dog and he is a Man."[3] After establishing that favorable premise for man's nature, Newfoundland Smith develops a series of claims that expose man's shortcomings and failure to evolve "toward the moral heights attained by the other animals."[4] Extending the subversive analogy to nations and breeds, Newfoundland Smith scoffs at the presumption that some groups of "men have imagined close correspondence of character between certain of their groups and certain of ours—a sufficiently humorous idea, truly."[5] The satirical interpretation of breed and nation names suggests the arbitrariness of nationalizing traditions and turns the relationship between nations and dog breeds on its head. If the notion that nations are named after dogs for the particular traits that are intentionally bred into (or, out of) a breed seems absurd, the reverse truth is equally absurd, that the traits of a nation of people are static and determined enough to be applicable to a dog breed.

Considering the worth of humanity from a dog's point of view, Twain asserts animal agency in this comparison of humans and animals. That shift in perspective is especially provocative given that philosophical explorations of the animal-human divide typically privilege the human perspective. For instance, Michel de Montaigne's famous question "When I play with my cat, who knows if I am not a pastime to her more than she is to me?" places human subjectivity at the heart of the question of animal consciousness. "How does [man] know," Montaigne asks, "by the force of his intelligence, the secret internal stirrings of animals? By what comparison between him and us does he infer the stupidity that he attributes to them?"[6] Twain similarly interrogates the presumption of animals' lesser intelligence, but he does so from the provocative point of view of a patronizing canine voice, and he pursues the comparison with the premise of canine superiority, rather than the reverse. By investing the dog's voice with the agency to define the worth of human beings, especially in comparison to a superior nonhuman species, Twain overturns a long history of philosophical perspectives that consider animals' worth from the point of view of humans.

[Hu]Man's Place

Twain's most memorable take-down of human exceptionalism is his essay "Man's Place in the Animal World," arguably his most biting criticism of humanity. In an epigraph, Twain refers to the news of imperialistic atrocities in Crete, including brutal killings of priests, women, and children, as the impetus for his essay. A passionate anti-imperialist, Twain responded to the news with the darkly satiric and misanthropic voice that characterized his late-career writing, knocking humanity from its pedestal by overturning the standard evolutionary hierarchy of species. After "scientifically studying the traits and dispositions of the 'lower animals' (so-called), and contrasting them with the traits and dispositions of man," he proclaims that he must "renounce [his] allegiance to the Darwinian theory" "in favor of a new and truer one to be named the *Descent of Man from the Higher Animals*." Subverting "the scientific method" of evolutionary theory to compare humans to superior species, he concludes that humans are the only animal that is "avaricious and miserly," vengeful, misogynistic, immoral or amoral, prone to "indecency, vulgarity, obscenity," slave-holding, nationalistic, militant, and religious, concluding with the "grim suggestion: that we are not as important, perhaps, as we had all along supposed we were."[7] Given his abolitionist stance against vivisection, Twain's theory of human inferiority to other animals is not merely a rhetorical device in response to the imperialistic events in Crete. His scathing comparison of humans to animals underscores the ideological connections between war, conquest, human subjugation, and the presumption of human exceptionalism. Moreover, read in this context, his philosophical opposition to vivisection parallels his opposition to imperialism, as both modes of progress are materialistic (literally promoting material gains over spiritual and moral considerations), and they involve the exploitative use and abuse of less powerful beings.

While the essay itself does not directly address vivisection and is rather a critique of the depravity of humankind more generally, Twain's satirical inversion of the evolutionary species hierarchy has special salience in the context of the vivisection debate. Opponents of vivisection in Twain's day, as in ours, critiqued the paradox of evolutionary theory as a rhetorical and ideological basis for using animals as laboratory subjects. On one hand, proponents of vivisection drew heavily upon the notion of the shared origins and kinship of species to rationalize the scientific merit of experimenting on live animals to gain knowledge that could benefit humans. On the other hand, vivisectors and their defenders vigorously differentiated human and nonhuman consciousness to defend the ethical propriety of animal experimentation. Animals are deemed to be *like* humans enough to justify using their bodies to gain useful knowledge, but *unlike* us enough to do so without moral concern for their physical or emotional suffering. The same perspective that acknowledges the kinship of animals and humans to justify vivisection denies that animals are as sensitive to pain, capable of feeling emotions, and worthy of compassion as humans.[8] In general, the scientific community relied heavily upon the notion of the evolutionary hierarchy of the species as a justification for vivisection, and it dismissed or downplayed even Darwin's ideas about the emotional similarities between humans and other animals, especially as the practice of vivisection became more common, and the debates surrounding it raged, in the late nineteenth century.[9] Given the popularity of selective aspects of evolutionary theory for the purpose of exploiting animals, even Twain, otherwise an avid follower of Darwin's theories and of natural determinism, would take aim at the more general, and pervasive, campaign of human superiority and exceptionalism that arose from the culture's response to evolutionary science.[10]

Antivivisection Letter

A few years after writing that scathing satirical critique of humanity, Twain delivered an earnest statement of his stance against vivisection. In his letter to the London Anti-Vivisection Society in 1899, Twain asserts his unqualified objection to vivisection for the "pain which it inflicts upon unconsenting animals," regardless of whether the "results are profitable to the human race." The letter, which circulated widely in the United States and Europe, strongly refutes two major tenets argued by proponents of vivisection: (1) the Cartesian notion of animal bodies as mechanistic and insensitive to pain, and (2) the evolutionary defense of human supremacy that justified experimentation on lesser animals as a means to gaining useful knowledge.

In this powerful statement, Twain articulates his abolitionist stance, aligning himself with the shrinking number of antivivisectionists who clung to the goal of completely eradicating the practice of experimenting upon live animals. To that end, he refutes the major claim in defense of vivisection, namely, its prospective benefit to humanity:

> I am not interested to know whether Vivisection produces results that are profitable to the human race or doesn't. To know that the results are profitable to the race would not remove my hostility to it. The pains which it inflicts upon unconsenting animals is the basis of my enmity toward it, & is to me sufficient justification of the enmity without looking further.[11]

Twain directly challenges the notion that gains to humans may be purchased at the cost of the suffering of sentient beings. By dismissing the material value of knowledge produced as a result of vivisection, he refutes the entire premise of the pro-vivisection argument and calls for ethical limitations to the pursuit of knowledge. Regarding vivisection as an injustice toward "unconsenting animals," Twain anticipates the animal rights movement by nearly a century. As for the rhetorical implications of his argument in his own day, his statement profoundly resists the notion that human progress is determined by the accumulation of knowledge that may benefit the species, and he asserts a moral basis for social progress.

Twain's statement against the practice of vivisection emphasizes animal sentience as well as the human suppression of animal expression. Highlighting the most offensive aspects of vivisection, Twain quotes an antivivisection paper's discussion of curare as a particularly sinister method, because, while uses of the drug "effectually prevent any struggle or cry," a "[horrible] feature of curare is that it has no anesthetic effect, but on the contrary it intensifies the sensibility to pain. The animal is perfectly conscious, suffers doubly, and can make no sign."[12] The mechanistic understanding of animal bodies as machines incapable of feeling, an idea infamously maintained by seventeenth-century philosopher Rene Descartes and his followers, was mostly passé by the middle of the nineteenth century, largely thanks to advocates for animal welfare. The basic fact of animal sentience was a widespread premise for the animal protection movement in general, following Utilitarian philosopher Jeremy Bentham's oft-quoted statement, "the question is not Can they reason, nor Can they talk, but Can they suffer?"[13] But the vivisection debate generated a renewed need to assert the notion of animal consciousness and sensitivity, as scientists sought to deny animal sensitivity to pain. The use of curare, which was intended to stifle expressions of pain that animals are supposed not to feel, is paradoxical and dismissive of the evidence of animal suffering. Twain deplored the use of the drug for facilitating painful experiments and suppressing animals' ability to respond to their pain and fear. A later version of the letter, which appeared in print in a pamphlet titled "The Pains of Lowly Life," includes an additional example of a scientist who, in his description of an experiment, notes the shrieking of laboratory animals, and nevertheless insists that animals are insensitive to pain: "Rabbits, we know, are not sensitive, but in this operation they invariably send forth a prolonged shriek."[14] Twain's interest in this example lies in the scientist's failure to recognize a "shriek," "invariably" made in response to a particular operation, as a legitimate expression of pain. In denying the true meaning of a rabbit's shriek, the scientist denies nonhuman agency and communication, exacerbating the violence enacted by the experiment to begin with.

A Dog's Tale

As his letter clearly reveals, Twain objected to the manner in which vivisectors routinely denied animal agency. He eventually responded in a way befitting the author of Huck Finn, the most celebrated subjective narrator in American literary history: he wrote a vivisection story from the perspective of a canine narrator. The short story, "A Dog's Tale," published in 1903 and distributed by antivivisection organizations on both sides of the Atlantic, is told from the surprising point of view of Aileen, a mother dog whose puppy was brutally tortured and killed by her vivisector owner, Dr. Gray, despite her loyalty to his family. While in the past it has been overlooked by Twain scholars who seem mortified that the great satirist contributed a propagandist animal "autobiography," "A Dog's Tale" is a compelling example of Twain's prescient understanding—and critique—of the role of nonhuman animals in society.[15] The story is valuable because it powerfully condemns the culture's acceptance of vivisection, and it argues for a progressive model of compassion across different subject positions. Moreover, as animal studies theorist Erica Fudge suggests, although we may "regard the humanization of animals that takes place in many narratives as sentimental . . . without it the only relation that we can have with animals is a very distant, and perhaps mechanistic one." For Fudge, assigning voices to animals through literature can "serve an ethical function," as, "if we don't believe that in some way we communicate with and understand animals, what is to make us stop and think as we experiment upon them, eat them, put them in cages."[16] By giving narrative voice to a dog, Twain assigns agency and perspective to a figure who otherwise lacks voice in society.

Aileen's narrative perspective makes nonhuman consciousness a central feature of the story. She narrates the history of her role in the Gray family, including her rescue of the baby from a nursery fire, her bonds with the family members and with her own puppy, and, tragically, her master's use of her puppy in a superfluous experiment. Aileen's story exposes her human owner's failure to acknowledge and value her individuality, her consciousness, and her role in the family, as well as his failure to reciprocate her generosity and love. In the end, Dr. Gray's experiment, which he performed in order to prove an already established fact (i.e., that a "certain injury to the brain would produce blindness") in order to impress a circle of pandering colleagues, kills not only the puppy but Aileen, too, as she slowly perishes while waiting for her puppy to "grow" like a plant out of his grave.[17]

In telling a vivisection story from the perspective of a victim's mother, Twain establishes nonhuman agency, subverting vivisection's method of silencing animals. Moreover, Aileen's narrative highlights her subjective emotional experience as a dog belonging to a human family and experiencing love, attachment, happiness, and disappointment. Aileen's individuality is relatable and perfectly in line with conventional sentimental ideals, particularly for motherhood: "By and by came my little puppy," she recalls, "and then my cup was full, my happiness was perfect."[18] By establishing the family dog's experience as a member of the household in terms of her family dynamics and her own sense of personal duty and fulfillment, Twain creates a compelling depiction of a pet as an individual with a subjective experience, making her unjust and inhumane treatment by her human family all the more poignant. As a result, the "heart-breaking bitch," as William Dean Howells referred to Aileen's character in a personal letter to Twain, has the power to move readers to sympathize with the plight of exploited animals and, perhaps, to question the morality of vivisection.[19]

While the cold-hearted Dr. Gray is the clear antagonist of the story, Twain doesn't let the mother and daughter, the kind-hearted representatives of feminine domesticity, entirely off the hook for the injustices Aileen experiences. The faithful canine's role in the family is already circumscribed by her voicelessness, a powerless status that the mother and daughter actively, if mournfully, reinforce. In the scene of Aileen's heroism, when her master finds her dragging the baby out of the burning nursery, he mistakes her rescue for aggression and beats her severely before realizing the nursery is on fire and Aileen has saved the baby from it. In the days after the incident, when curious neighbors visit to hear the fire and rescue story, the daughter, Sadie, and Mrs. Gray withhold the fact that Dr. Gray beat their savior:

A dozen times a day Mrs. Gray and Sadie would tell the tale to newcomers, and say I risked my life to save the baby's, and both of us had burns to prove it, and then the company would pass me around and pet me and exclaim about me, and you could see the pride in the eyes of Sadie and her mother; and when the people wanted to know what made me limp, they looked ashamed and changed the subject, and sometimes when people hunted them this way and that way with questions about it, it looked to me as if they were going to cry.[20]

The Gray women shape their narrative of the event carefully, "proving" their dog's heroism with the physical evidence of her burns but redirecting their guests' notice of the physical proof of her unjust beating. By selectively sharing the romantic aspects of the event while refusing to tell the inconvenient details of Aileen's experience, Sadie and Mrs. Gray affirm her marginalized position in the family. Including the feminized domestic sphere in his indictment of vivisection, Twain reminds us that the lower status of nonhuman animals, even those animals who are regarded as beloved family members, makes such heinous acts as useless experiments upon their bodies possible in the first place. In doing so, he widens the scope of responsibility beyond the laboratory, and suggests the broader implications of a society that endorses the exploitation of those who lack social power, especially those who lack voice.

The story's message of a larger social complicity in animal exploitation notwithstanding, as Aileen's owner, the head of the family, and the esteemed scientist with a professional reputation to affirm, Dr. Gray occupies the most powerful position in "A Dog's Tale" and is the most culpable in violating Aileen's rights. While traditionally, his powerful position as head of a patriarchal family obliges him to protect his less powerful dependents, the desensitized scientist wields power without compassion for the feelings and welfare of his faithful dog or the family who will grieve her loss. Dr. Gray's relationship to Aileen is entirely characterized by his failure to understand and sympathize with this family member from a different species; he mistakes her heroic rescue for aggression, and he fails to reciprocate her protection of his offspring. In contrast to Dr. Gray's lack of awareness or concern for Aileen's feelings, the family servants, powerless to either save her from their master's abuses or redress them in any way, convey compassion and a sense of injustice to the grieving mother dog. Tearfully burying her puppy, the footman pats Aileen's head and laments, "Poor little doggie, you saved *his* child".[21] When the grieving dog remains by the grave night and day, the servants collectively try to intervene and support Aileen: "I cannot eat, though the servants bring me the best of food; and they pet me so, and even come in the night, and cry, and say, 'Poor doggie—do give it up and come home; *don't* break our hearts!'"[22] Especially significant during the absence of the mother and children, who are away on a vacation during Dr. Gray's experiment on Aileen's puppy, the servants collectively perform an important familial function: through touching, feeding, crying, and talking, they acknowledge the dying mother dog's subjectivity, affirm her familial affiliation, and deplore the injustices of her owner, their master. For posthumanist philosopher Donna Haraway, functional animal-human dynamics depend upon "'communication' across irreducible difference" as well as a sense of reciprocity: "If I have a dog, my dog has a human; what that means concretely is at stake."[23] In "A Dog's Tale," Twain presciently portrayed those qualities, and their absence, in the interspecies dynamics of a vivisector's family. Given his inability to understand or reciprocate Aileen's loyalty, Dr. Gray is less refined than his servants, who communicate to Aileen, validate her identity, and reciprocate her love.

If, as advocates of vivisection maintained, emotional sensitivity was deemed a sign of evolutionary superiority, presumably reserved for humans, antivivisectionists were quick to point out that the men who could perform experiments upon live animals must themselves have a deteriorated level of sensitivity. In characterizing Dr. Gray as an emotionally detached scientist capable of coldly killing the puppy of his own faithful dog, Twain subverted the evolutionary logic of vivisection and reinforced a claim from the antivivisection movement that the practice of vivisection had a dangerously desensitizing effect on professional men of science and doctors. "Evolutionary continuities between humans and animals, useful in underwriting practices like vivisection and ethology, could also facilitate claims about the degeneration of 'gentlemen of science,' whose natural sympathies for their human and animal fellows had been deadened by the abstract pursuit of truth."[24]

Dr. Gray's familial affiliation with his laboratory subject especially high-lights the pernicious effect of vivisection. Antivivisectionists feared that "[v] ice would infect society more pervasively as vivisection increased in preva-lence. Before long, those 'ruined' by the practice would intermingle with the innocent, passing on immorality as one passes on a virus."[25] Indeed, Dr. Gray's heartless pursuit of professional glory directly harms his family. Not only does he kill two nonhuman members of his own family with an experi-ment that takes place within his home laboratory, but he hurts the human family members as well: "Those poor creatures! They do not suspect. They will come home in the morning, and eagerly ask for the little doggie that did the brave deed, and who of us will be strong enough to say the truth to them."[26] In this commentary upon the horror of Aileen's death, a grieving family servant remembers the human victims of the atrocity and, in doing so, conflates and reverses species status, as the "poor creatures" are the human family members, the mother and children, who were away during the brutal experiment and its aftermath.

Vivisectionists' insistence upon a natural hierarchy of emotional and physical sensitivity extended to differences within the human species, too, and Twain seized upon the social implications of the evolutionary defense of vivisection. Not only were lesser animals less sensitive than humans, but also, lesser humans were assumed to be less sensitive to pain and emotion than their elite fellow humans. By portraying a stark contrast between the elite-class Dr. Gray's lack of sensitivity and the abundant compassion of his servants, Twain overturns assumptions regarding the natural hierarchies among social classes, a social Darwinism that he was keenly conscious of, and critical of, as an anti-imperialist. In doing so, he not only forges a theo-retical link between the ideologies that inform much social and scientific "progress," but he also makes an important practical point, as many anti-vivisectionists predicted a slippery slope from animals to humans as the subjects of experimentation.[27]

As the last collective voices of the story, the Gray family servants share their heartbreak for Aileen as well as for the human survivors who will mourn her loss, the "poor creatures" who will return home to learn of Ai-leen's death. In doing so, they demonstrate a sense of compassion capacious enough to span species and class difference. Not only, then, does the story overturn assumptions of sensitivity hierarchies, but it also models a progres-sive sense of compassion that encompasses different subject positions. In do-ing so, Twain revises the materialistic and imperialistic definitions of progress of his era to assert the importance of compassion, empathy, and morality in elevating society. He thus joined fellow antivivisectionists in their attempt to restore the role of emotional empathy in society.[28] Moreover, in depicting the servants' empathy for members of other classes and species, Twain is ahead of his time. He anticipates the importance of *difference* in contemporary posthumanist theories that understand compassion as the "capacity, not to know the other, but to pay attention to an otherness in common and to the commonality of otherness."[29]

PART IV

LITERARY DEVICES

CHAPTER TEN

Mark Twain's Serious Humor and That Peculiar Institution

Christianity

Chris A. Kramer

According to Manuel Davenport in his *An Existentialist Philosophy of Humor*, "The best humorists—Mark Twain, Will Rogers, Bob Hope, and Mort Sahl—share [a] mixture of detachment and desire, eagerness to believe, and irreverence concerning the possibility of certainty. And when they become serious about their convictions—as Twain did about colonialism [or slavery, racism, unfettered capitalism, or religion] . . . they cease to be humorous."[1] I like what Davenport has to say in the first part but not the second, as he does not provide examples of Twain's attempts at satire that fail to be humorous. I will examine some of the very serious issues Twain addresses through humor and irony and show how his commentary and argument, though serious, is still funny while not falling into frivolity.

The Laughing Philosopher

The moniker "laughing philosopher" comes from Twain's ability to be humorous without falling into buffoonery.[2] Although he is no fan of titles,[3] he might live with this one given that at least once he admitted he prefers to be considered a philosopher before being seen as a humorist.[4] The title fits because he is capable of deep analysis of serious issues about human suffering while remaining in a playful attitude.[5] He plays with thought not unlike philosophers who present their arguments in the form of thought experiments about serious metaphysical or ethical matters. There is something playful, if not amusing, in mulling over the possibility that we might be nothing but brains in vats, or that a famous violinist has been surreptitiously attached to our back.[6]

The original "laughing philosopher" was Democritus, who was also called the "mocker" as he was prone to laugh at the arrogance and ignorance of his fellow citizens. Democritus and one of his near contemporaries, Xenophanes, were both skeptical of religion and gods created in the images of men (sometimes women), yet their critiques were often lighthearted. Twain's philosophical lineage extends back in their direction, with Schopenhauer, Hume, and Voltaire along the way. Each of these philosophers has critical insights into the religious mind, and each of them had clever rebuttals to theological dogma.[7]

There is a philosophical thread running through Twain's scathing humor that attacks arrogance and a presumed sense of certitude. These two vices, arrogance and certitude, are often found together, and they are a destructive combination that sustains many of the institutions that he confronts: racism, slavery, colonialism, excesses of capitalism, and the often dogmatic, oppressive, and ludicrous nature of a great deal of organized religions.

Twain used humor as an indirect method to at once engage and disarm his audiences when submitting his blistering critiques of serious matters concerning our presuppositions and inconsistencies, which are central foci of philosophers. But the opening quotation from Davenport gives the impression that he could not mix his humor with issues that were important to him. He was either wholly serious, lacking playful humor, or he was funny, but inconsequential in his satire. Twain was aware of this dilemma:

> It's an awful thing to gain a reputation for being witty and humorous. Every time you talk people expect you to tell a story or say something funny. You can't always live up to it. We are all only human beings. . . . What I like about it [a story about him in the London *Chronicle*] is that it takes me just a bit seriously. You see, though I love England from my heart, and I'd go over many seas for the welcome that you've given me, you generally seem to expect a joke if I'm anywhere by. In America I reckon they've got a bit used to my jokes, and they look out for something else now and then.[8]

While Americans might have gotten used to his jokes, it is another thing to say they no longer found them humorous. I think that part of that "something else" they looked for is the serious element of Twain's wit that playfully undermines the feelings of certitude that so many people possess, especially regarding their most cherished but undefended beliefs.

Only the dullest of dullards would proclaim that Mark Twain is not funny. That person, of course, should be prosecuted, then banished. But does Twain deserve to be called a philosopher and can he demonstrate his philosophical convictions and be funny simultaneously? The short answer is yes. Borrowing from Bertrand Russell, "People often make the mistake of thinking that 'humorous' and 'serious' are antonyms. They are wrong. 'Humorous' and 'solemn' are antonyms. I am never more serious than when I am being humorous."[9] Twain had his share of "solemn" occasions, especially later in a life that was rife with tribulations, some brought on himself by foolhardy financial speculations, and others by what he often viewed as a deterministic universe that took away those dearest to him, such as his beloved daughter Susy, his newborn Langdon, his youngest daughter Jean, and his wife Olivia. But his writings on the momentous matters of death and suffering of innocents are not devoid of humor. Twain is serious about these concerns, but not in the *absolutist* sense presumed by Davenport.

Davenport describes the relation between humor and seriousness in this way: "Humor . . . requires a detachment from seriousness. The serious man—the man with undeviating confidence that his values are absolute is no more able to laugh at himself than the serious God."[10] I agree with his general notion that playful humor attacks absolutism. But I think Twain would agree also, and there is no shortage of self-deprecating humor in his writing.[11]

To make sense of this, we can look at one of Twain's unlikely philosophical ancestors, Arthur Schopenhauer: "The opposite of laughing and joking is *seriousness.* Accordingly, it consists in the consciousness of the perfect agreement and congruity of the conception, or thought, with what is perceived, or the reality. *The serious man is convinced that he thinks the things as they are, and that they are as he thinks them.*"[12] The common connotation of seriousness is synonymous with such words as *grave, solemn, somber, severe, sober, stern,* and so on. All of these might be peripherally related to Schopenhauer's conception, but they do not get at its core. This is so for Twain too: he is serious in his humorous appraisals of the type of *seriousness* about which Schopenhauer and Davenport worry. It will be helpful to describe Twain's playful assaults on seriousness through the lens of existentialist thought to further clarify the seriousness *and* playfulness found in Twain's critiques of Christianity and religion in general. "What gets us into trouble is not what we don't know. It's what we know for sure that just ain't so."

This, attributed to Twain,[13] is the sort of certainty and complacent seriousness that his humor attacks. The "just ain't so" bit will be hard to defend epistemologically, so I qualify it: we claim to "know for sure" all sorts of things that we really have no good reason to believe in the first place, and a hefty amount of reason to not believe. This is the negative sort of seriousness that Twain rails against, and it is the same described by Schopenhauer and many later existentialists.

For example, the salient feature in Jean-Paul Sartre's, Simone de Beauvoir's, and Lewis Gordon's descriptions of seriousness, what they refer to as the *spirit of seriousness*, is the absolutist, dogmatic, otherworldliness, and the unquestionable nature of the values and meanings held by serious people. Relating to one peculiar institution, Beauvoir says, "The slave is submissive when one has succeeded in mystifying him in such a way that his situation does not seem to him to be imposed by men, but to be immediately given by nature, by the gods, by the powers against whom revolt has no meaning."[14] Here, seriousness is closer to an attitude that takes reality, with all of its horrors, as inevitable. Slaveholders continually used particular biblical passages in this way to "justify" their peculiar way of life—they could do no other, and any slave attempting to subvert the power structure would be akin to doing battle with a hurricane or any other *natural* disaster. This makes not thinking about such matters easy: there is nothing you can do about it, so "why bother?"[15] This conceit is fortified with the assurances of dogma so often accompanying reverence for an omnipotent deity: the world is the way it is because the God made it so.

Because this God is all good, the world must be as good as it gets; the faithful are humble, and this is *known* with certainty. As Twain notes, when one begins with confidence of this sort, incongruities melt away: "The Christian begins with this straight proposition, this definite proposition, this inflexible and uncompromising proposition: God is all-knowing, and all-powerful . . . [and yet] The poor's most implacable and unwearying enemy is their Father in Heaven."[16] It is comforting to feel certain that there is purpose and structure, and that *everything happens for a reason*. Twain sees this most evidently with the common lot of the poor the world over; to paraphrase the Bible, there will always be the poor among us (so why bother?) and God has His reasons for permitting their suffering. But, Twain points out, God is prone to exacerbate the suffering beyond human moral comprehension.

The spirit of seriousness is an attitude that perpetuates mental inflexibility, or what Lewis Gordon calls *epistemic closure*: "In the act of epistemic closure, one ends a process of inquiry. In effect, it is the judgment 'say no more.' . . . In contrast, epistemological openness is the judgment 'there is always more to be known.'"[17] He writes this in the context of racism and the failure to recognize the complex identities of human beings, but it is also connected to values and meanings associated with power and comfort found in the faithful, who unquestionably hold onto the morals putatively handed down by an omnibenevolent God—a God who, according to Twain, curiously refrains from following his own commandments.[18]

It does sound odd to say that Twain can be serious and humorous at the same time, but that is likely due to an overreliance on a single sense of the term "seriousness." For instance, John Morreall claims that seriousness is different than humorousness in this way: "For us to be serious is to be solemn and given to sustained, narrowly focused thought. It is also for us to be earnest, that is, sincere, in what we say and do. We say only what we believe, and act only according to our real intentions."[19] In contrast, a humorous and playful attitude is one in which we are frivolous, unconcerned with reality in the moment, only interested in "delighting" others.[20] These are the common meanings of these terms, but they do *not* account for the playfulness or seriousness employed by Twain.

Twain is not devious in his insincerity, but he is often explicit that it will be difficult to determine what exactly his "real intentions" are (you might even be shot if you try to divine them, as he warns in the Notice to *Huckleberry Finn*), and he tells us outright in his *Autobiographies*[21] that much of what he writes there is fiction. But as with his humor, it is not *mere* or *pure* fiction. Like the positive image of Socrates, Twain does not really know indubitably what the answers are,[22] and his irony is more of a tool to uncover the ignorance of those who think they do know for sure, including himself, than it is a prideful judgment from above that cannot itself be questioned. Critical reflection does not require absolutism; revealing erroneous thinking in others does not entail you must already have *the* answer.

Twain manages to do what Hume did philosophically against religion but with an unmatched humorous wit. You do not just nod your head in vigorous agreement with Twain's "arguments"; you laugh audibly. I think this is what Twain ultimately desired: to be funny but taken seriously, and to make people laugh about significant issues. He says as much in his *Autobiography*:

> Humorists of the "mere" sort cannot survive. Humor is only a fragrance, a decoration. Often it is merely an odd trick of speech and spelling. . . . There are those who say a novel should be a work of art solely, and you must not preach in it, you must not teach in it. That may be true as regards novels, but it is not true as regards humor. *Humor must not professedly teach, it must not professedly preach; but it must do both if it would live forever.* By forever, I mean thirty years.[23]

Davenport's claim about Twain and seriousness would be supported if he could demonstrate instances of Twain's attempted humor that merely and professedly teaches and preaches. Twain explicitly professes that he intends neither.

His humorous yet serious analysis is open, dynamic, and subject to change upon receipt of counter-evidence and compelling argument. This is so even with his most trenchant criticisms of Mary Baker Eddy. For instance, he is open to learning even from the objects of his irony: "he is careful to explain that he does not condemn Christian Science out and out. There is something in the theory that mind can exert a powerful influence upon the body in conditions of disease."[24] His humor pokes holes in the thin façade of prefabricated presuppositions, but without offering a dogmatic *Truth* to stand in its stead. This does not mean Twain is a nihilist only concerned with removing any and all values, anymore than Socrates was a nihilist, or Sophist, in his ironical disputations with his serious interlocutors who presumed to possess certain knowledge. But it does imply that Twain intends to engage in serious subversion. Bruce Michelson offers a broad conception of humor in his analysis of Twain's satire: "A working definition then, heavily pruned, almost primordial: humor as a *subversion of seriousness*."[25]

> Man is the Religious Animal. He is the only Religious Animal.
>
> He is the only animal that has the True Religion—several of them.[26]

Twain is surely one of the most quotable quippers ever, but these are not simply slogans. Twain takes matters of religion as seriously as he did that other peculiar institution—slavery. He even considered preaching from the pulpit professionally:

> "I never had but two **powerful** ambitions in my life. One was to be a pilot, & the other a preacher of the gospel. I accomplished the one & failed in the other, **because** I could not supply myself with the necessary stock in trade— i.e. religion. . . . But I *have* had a "call" to literature, of a low order—i.e. humorous. It is nothing to be proud of, but it is my strongest suit." He vowed to concentrate his attention on "seriously scribbling to excite the **laughter** of God's creatures."[27]

Self-deprecation aside, Twain possessed a deep understanding of scripture and an insight into the closed dogmatic attitude of many true believers. His failure at theology was not due to a lack of understanding. On the contrary, he understood too well and perhaps thought too deeply to be able to stomach what he saw as the many inconsistencies, or *incongruities*, of religious thinking.

The religious life is meant to be one of holiness, devout worship, and love of God, the very same that *commands* such loving worship. The Christian in particular is to manifest humility before that all-knowing, all-powerful, all-good deity. But many of the very same people are *certain* that they are saved, and they catch no glimpse of the irony that hell for their hubris likely awaits them according to their own theology. Those with a touch less pride are still dead certain that God has all those Omnis, and no matter what, this must be the best of all possible worlds created for us—the "damned human race"! This view is maintained, Twain says, even as the common housefly spreads disease and death upon those created in the image and likeness of God: "The housefly wrecks more human constitutions and destroys more human lives than all God's multitude of misery-messengers and death-agents put together."[28]

He is earnest in his analyses of faith, but his sense of humor does not dissipate in proportion to that sincerity. He even goes so far as to suggest the opposite of humor is religious faith: "I cannot see how a man of any large degree of humorous perception can ever be religious—except he purposely shut the eyes of his mind & keep them shut by force."[29] The concern here is "epistemic closure": the mindset that ignores any hint of cognitive dissonance and only seeks the manufactured comforts in the feelings of certitude. This is willful ignorance, and Twain sees it creep into many facets of American identity both home and abroad.

It is much easier, as a peak into any century of the past will reveal, to torture and kill a person when "God is on your side." This is so even when those slaughtered are women and children, an event that occurred in the Philippines that Twain discusses at considerable length. Here is one example that is apropos given current events:

> When a country is invaded it is because it has done some wrong to another country—some wrong like the United States did in taking the Philippines—a stain upon our flag that can never be effaced. Yet today in the public schools we teach our children to salute the flag, and this is our idea of instilling in them patriotism. And this so-called patriotism we mistake for citizenship; but if there is a stain on that flag it ought not to be honored, even if it is our flag. The true citizenship is to protect the flag from dishonor—to make it the emblem of a nation that is known to all nations as true and honest and honorable. And we should forever forget that old phrase—"My country, right or wrong, my country."[30]

I think this is the sort of commentary that Davenport felt was bereft of humor, and this is not surprising as there is not much to laugh about when a U.S. regiment of well-armed soldiers is shooting down at a band of "savages" trapped in a crater who are poorly armed, or not at all. To echo Twain, we should not expect even the greatest comedians to never have a moment of solemnity. The subject of analysis is not in itself amusing, and admittedly, Twain is not intending to *merely* delight his readers on this occasion. But he is also not merely preaching, condemning, or ridiculing from an absolutist perch.

This is primarily political critique, but Twain rarely dissociates the political from the religious because the two were seldom detached in American public life at the time. The reports from the battlefield and the newspaper headlines laud the "heroism" and "gallantry" of the "Christian soldiers." Twain juxtaposes these plaudits with the facts mentioned above—that the majority of the enemy was poorly armed and already trapped—but also in contrast with the horrifying casualties *on both sides* during the American Civil War. He satirically describes the Philippine incursion this way: "*This is incomparably the greatest victory that was ever achieved by Christian soldiers of the United States.*"[31] There is irony in this illustration of incongruity between American ideals, morals, and values and the reality of governmental actions driven by a globalized "manifest destiny." He knows, as would anyone else who could see beyond their patriotic-religious fervor, that such a massacre "would not have been a brilliant feat of arms even if Christian America, represented by its salaried soldiers, had shot them down with Bibles and the Golden Rule instead of bullets."[32] Twain brandishes the Golden Rule like a weapon to crack open the spirit of seriousness that permeates and perpetuates the "my country right or wrong" attitude.[33] In contrast to Davenport's assessment, Twain cleverly and amusingly exposes the seriousness, arrogance, and complacent sense of certitude embedded in religious nationalism.

Twain does the same with more straightforwardly theological matters. For instance, consider how Twain puts his scorching irony into the mouth of a toddler in his short story "Little Bessie." Bessie relentlessly questions her mother about the natures of Christ, God, and human suffering: "Mamma, is Christ God? Yes, my child. Mamma, how can He be Himself and Somebody Else at the same time? He isn't, my darling. It is like the Siamese twins—two persons, one born ahead of the other, but equal in authority, equal in power."[34] From this, Bessie reasons: "I understand it, now, mamma, and it is quite simple. One twin has sexual intercourse with his mother, and begets himself and his brother; and next he has sexual intercourse with his grandmother and begets his mother. I should think it would be difficult, mamma, though interesting."[35] Admittedly, the particulars offered by Mamma might not be the most nuanced view in Christendom, but the mysteries of the Trinity, Incarnation, and of course, Immaculate Conception, require an impressive degree of mental acrobatics to avoid little Bessie's absurd description. Apparently, Bessie has pondered these matters more so than many of the zealously faithful—and she does not stop with Christology.

Bessie, like Twain after the loss of so many of his own family members, worries about the suffering of the most vulnerable and innocent of God's creatures: "Did [God] give Billy Norris the typhus? Yes. What for? Why, to discipline him and make him good. But he died, mamma, and so it *couldn't* make him good. Well, then, I suppose it was for some other reason. We know it was a *good* reason, whatever it was."[36] Bessie continues: "What do you think it was, mamma? Oh, you ask so many questions! I think; it was to discipline his parents. Well, then, it wasn't fair, mamma. Why should *his* life be taken away for their sake, when he wasn't doing anything? Oh, I don't know! I only know it was for a good and wise and merciful reason. . . . He does nothing that isn't right and wise and merciful. You can't understand these things now, dear, but when you are grown up you will understand them, and then you will see that they are just and wise."[37]

Mamma denies that humans are capable of knowing the whys and wherefores of an infinite being such as God: so shut up already! I call this *Ad Hoc Mysterianism*. This where no conceivable counter-evidence will ever suffice because we always have the phrase "for all we know" that evades any potential inconsistencies. "Mysterianism" typically applies to complex religious notions in a positive sense. For example, a central conception like the Trinity is to be revered but not fully unraveled as if it were a problem. I use the term in a negative sense, coupled with ad hoc, to imply an all-too convenient tactic to sustain the internal coherence of an idea in the face of otherwise compelling counter-evidence. Twain calls this attitude "insane, rotten, and irrational."[38]

Mamma, finally growing weary of coming up with adequate answers to her three-year-old's inquiries, ultimately gives up, unable to *protect* "an innocent child's holy belief": "There, now, go along with you, and don't come near me again until you can interest yourself in some subject of a lower grade and less awful than theology. Bessie, (disappearing.) Mr. Hollister says there *ain't* any."[39]

The secret source of Humor itself is not joy but sorrow.

There is no humor in heaven.[40]

What of Heaven and salvation in the end for all of those who followed the commands of God? Recall that this is the very same God who designed humanity with a specific nature, namely, one that makes us really enjoy sex, but it is a nature we are constantly ordered to deny,[41] as Twain has Satan inform us in *Letters from the Earth*: "To wit, that the human being, like the immortals, naturally places sexual intercourse far and away above all other joys—yet he has left it out of his heaven!" [42] The vast majority of Twain's Christian contemporaries proclaimed the desire for salvation and heaven, yet it is unclear what that actually meant; they just knew it's going to be good. Satan's letter continues: "The very thought of [intercourse] excites him; opportunity sets him wild; in this state he will risk life, reputation, everything—even his queer heaven itself—to make good that opportunity and ride it to the overwhelming climax. From youth to middle age all men and all women prize copulation above all other pleasures combined, yet it is actually as I have said: it is not in their heaven; prayer takes its place." [43] Not only do we lose a good, we gain a negative in prayer, along with other unpleasantries Twain catalogues, like group singing—eternally. Can we really be the same people in heaven that we are on Earth if our desires seem to be so vastly changed? Are we even the same *type* of beings in heaven? If not, why, Twain implicitly asks, do we constrain ourselves with the Lord's unbending commands here and now for rewards that somebody else might receive?

What are some of these Godly commands that must be obeyed to permit entrance into Heaven, where there is only praying, singing, and absolutely no sex? "'Thou shalt not commit adultery' is a command which makes no distinction between the following persons. They are all required to obey it: Children at birth. Children in the cradle. School children. Youths and maidens. Fresh adults. Older ones. Men and women of [forty]. Of [fifty]. Of [sixty]. Of [seventy]. Of [eighty]. Of [ninety]. Of [one hundred]." [44] Again, most Christians simply follow the commands of an all-knowing being without giving them much thought. This is because if you start with certainty that God is, and is all the Omnis, complacency quickly sets in. But even a brief rumination on just this one command, Twain shows, uncovers a range of absurdities:

> The command does not distribute its burden equally, and cannot. It is not hard upon the three sets of children. It is hard—harder—still harder upon the next three sets—cruelly hard. It is *blessedly softened* to the next three sets. It has now done all the damage it can, and might as well be put out of commission. Yet with *comical imbecility* it is continued, and the four remaining estates are put under its crushing ban. Poor old wrecks, they couldn't disobey if they tried. And think—because they holily refrain from adulterating each other, they get praise for it! [45]

Admittedly, with the advent of Viagra and other remedies for "blessed softening," disobeying the command is not entirely impossible today, so there could still be a stiff penalty for it.

Man is the Animal that Blushes.

He is the only one that does it—or has occasion to.[46]

It seems Twain is a bit embarrassed about humanity, or a large portion of it at least. He might wish that more of his fellow creatures would in fact blush, and more often than they do. Twain sees much to blush about related to religious doctrines and indoctrinations. There is so much that is funny in the "Huh, that's strange" sense, and that is significant because the beliefs about these issues have actual consequences in the real world. Twain is able to take these "funny-strange" cases, and maintain their seriousness but add to them a "funny-ha-ha" element.[47] This humor can offer a relief for himself and his readers, but that is not the only goal of his satire.

According to Michelson, "It goes without saying that talk of God's absence and the general nastiness of the human condition can be serious business. But it also can be a way of blowing off steam about things solidly mundane: family trouble, business downturns, old age and failing health."[48] Perhaps we have a different notion of "mundane." Death of family members, bankruptcy, aging, and imminent death of self, while they happen all-too often (and this might be all that Michelson means here), do not meet my understanding of mundane. These are all serious matters that have deep religious, theological, philosophical, and ethical implications that Twain views as worthy of our sincere contemplation.

Twain does not shy away from them in his writing, nor is he simply hiding behind his humor as a release from the pressures that everyday suffering imposes, suffering for which, if God of the Bible existed,[49] God would ultimately be responsible. He is making the case that this is not a God worthy of worship. Rather, it is an idea invented by a few humans who have failed to recognize that the "moral sense" the deity is supposed to have imparted to us is nowhere found in Him:

Our Bible reveals to us the character of our God with minute and remorseless exactness. The portrait is substantially that of a man—if one can imagine a man charged and overcharged with evil impulses far beyond the human limit; a personage whom no one, perhaps, would desire to associate with, now that Nero and Caligula are dead. . . . To Adam is forbidden the fruit of a certain tree—and he is gravely informed that if he disobeys he shall die. How could that be expected to impress Adam? Adam was merely a man in stature; in knowledge and experience he was in no way the superior of a baby of two years of age . . . he had never heard of a dead thing before. The word meant nothing to him. If the Adam child had been warned that if he ate of the apples he would be transformed into a meridian of longitude, that threat would have been the equivalent of the other, since neither of them could mean anything to him.[50]

And yet, men toil to provide food, women suffer childbirth and often die from it, and children die of disease because of the Adam-child's single transgression. Serious indeed, but Twain is not so dogmatic that he cannot find a humorous and enlightening analogy in it.

Back to Davenport's partly insightful conception of humor as a "mixture of detachment and desire, eagerness to believe, and irreverence concerning the possibility of certainty."[51] Morreall would agree with Davenport that we fall out of the playful mode when we are too close emotionally to the content of our potential humor. In such cases, we fail to achieve the appropriate distance to think humorously about the issue, and worse, we lose the critical perspective as well. Twain maintains both of these in his discerning humor.

Twain's seriousness is not the closed-minded dogmatic seriousness that his humor attacks; instead, it is an attitude toward a given issue that he views as consequential. With his humor, he is able to step back enough to retain a critical eye and play with the significant beliefs in the way well-trained philosophers can often do. The philosopher needs *some* degree of emotional attachment to the subject matter, or else there would be no motivation to even think about it. But this does not preclude her from finding the right degree of detachment to see a problem for what it is. Twain seems to have found that emotive and cognitive sweet spot that enables both humorous and critical reflection. It is not coincidental that these two virtues often go hand in hand in the process of recognizing the incongruities between professed ideals and reality that so often falls short of them, or scrutinizing purported Truths about the cosmos. With Twain, we can laugh while we think. The reverse is true too.

~

CHAPTER ELEVEN

Socratic Irony in Twain's Skeptical Religious Jeremiads[1]

DALE JACQUETTE

Mark Twain in his novels, short fiction, journalism, and travel literature is often described as America's great ironist. That frequently encountered pronouncement, even if true, is of limited value unless it can be explained what is meant by irony generally and by Twain's distinctive ironic outlook and ironic literary voice in particular.

All too often, talk of Twain's irony is bandied about without pausing to attempt a critical explanation of his colorful development of comic and caustic irony. Different commentators can mean very different things in labeling a writer like Twain an ironist, and they owe it to potential readers to make their respective definitions clear. Richard K. Barksdale, illustrative of the trend toward calling attention to Twain's irony without saying very precisely what this means, writes in his otherwise insightful *Mark Twain Journal* article, "History, Slavery, and Thematic Irony in *Huckleberry Finn*":

> By bringing black runaway Jim into close association with white runaway Huck, Twain obviously desired to explore the *ironic* implications of such an association in a "sivilisation" riddled by racial division and prejudice. The *irony* employed here is similar to that used in Pudd'nhead Wilson's story in which Twain recounts the comi-tragic consequences of a situation in which a light-skinned "colored" baby is substituted for a white baby. In the Huck story, however, Twain's *ironic conclusion* is that two human beings, however

different their backgrounds and "previous condition of servitude" will, if far enough removed from the corrupting influence of "sivilisation," become friends. (emphases added)[2]

What is all this talk of irony, ironic implications, and ironic conclusion supposed to mean? How should it be interpreted? The word "irony" is sprinkled profusely throughout popular commentary on Twain, but the concept is seldom carefully explained and never adequately analyzed either essentialistically or as a family resemblance relation. Without giving explicit meaning to the irony cognate cluster, Barksdale forges fearlessly ahead as though "ironist" and now "ironic forethought" were words whose meanings were universally transparently understood. He uses them freely as a widely spoken univocal nomenclature in which we can speak and be understood with confidence concerning an author's qualities. When in truth without meticulous disambiguation the irony cluster terms are heavily laden with equivocations to trip up deductively valid inference. Barksdale only compounds the problem when a few paragraphs later he adds to his attributions:

> Twain, the *ironist* who doubted that social and/or moral benefits could accrue from a civilization beleaguered by greed and prejudice, concluded that, given the nature of slave-time America, a friendship of that kind [between Huck and Tom] could develop only outside the normal areas of civil and social discourse. . . . But Twain the *ironist* did not stop there. He developed with careful *ironic forethought*, an interracial friendship between two outcasts who, under civilization's auspices, were normally inveterate enemies. (emphases added)[3]

Something more positive needs to be said about the general concept of irony if the category in Twain is to have any cachet, and more especially if it is to accomplish any respectable conceptual work in literary criticism when predicated of a writer like Twain. He is understood in the analysis to follow as developing and taking strategic advantage of many rhetorical devices in his writing, irony being only one of them, from solid investigative journalism and factual reportage to hilarious burlesque and everything in between. As Vic Doyno recognizes in his "Foreword" to his recent edition of Twain's (1907) *Christian Science*, Twain's devices are complex. "Over the years," he observes, "Twain honed his skills of sarcasm, irony, humor, verbal thrusts, humane reasoning, and concise flashing phrases."[4] Irony is but one of Twain's effects that if Doyno is right must be somehow set apart from Twain's darts of similar-sounding sarcasm and homespun humor.

Twain's Irony Aimed at Religious Pretense

A reasonable survey of rhetorical expedients makes it imperative in studying Twain's irony to distinguish the effect from the other pigments on his panel. His irony is easily confused with his wry commonsense humor. These are not always the same. Irony, Twain's especially, is often but not inherently comic. It is not merely that Twain's irony can sometimes be bitterly or sardonically comic, but on the contrary that it is sometimes entirely sober in at least two ways excluding the comic that are designated in this analysis tragic and historical. It is possible to identify and illustrate from Twain's substantial body of work both what this study distinguishes as comic and sober irony; the latter subcategory of which includes historical and tragic irony. Twain weaves a tapestry of literary devices, including but not limited to irony local and global, comic and sober, tragic and historical. To understand Twain's irony is to know something of these variations of saying the opposite of what is intended on which he plays.

They are seen especially in Twain's responses to religion. Part of the message seems to be that none of this business is to be taken too seriously in the first place because it all touches on subjects about which human knowledge is virtually nonexistent. Twain's reactions are uniquely and distinctively Twain-like, but his conclusions coincide to a remarkable extent with those of Voltaire in the previous century, a wit known also for irony and religious skepticism in deferent respect for what cannot be known. We focus as illustrative of the general theme on Twain's responses to the preservation and veneration of religious relics and surrounding folklore of the gullible faithful in *The Innocents Abroad* (1869) and Twain's (1896) historical novel *Personal Recollections of Joan of Arc*.

The later work enables Twain to portray from an aide-de-camp's imagined perspective the heroic rise and even more tragic fall of Jean d'Arc at the hypocritical paranoid self-serving hands of the church and state that Jean ironically enough had nobly fought to help preserve. The bishops who signed her execution warrant to be burned at the stake as a witch and unrepentant apostate may have thought it was their Catholic Christian duty to prevent Jean from becoming too popular, too powerful, more revered than Mary or even Christ, had she been allowed to continue.

Irony for Twain and all is not so much a foodstuff in its own right but a spice that adds memorable pique flavor to more substantial ingredients in a literary composition. When played against his other literary talents at reportage, sarcasm, deadpan humor, again not to be confused with irony in its proper technical sense, and occasional sermonizing, Twain's irony in its measure serves a specific psychological purpose in delivering moral messages when he chooses with a mule's kick. If we look for a single category of irony in Twain, we are bound to be disappointed—which is to say delighted at the wealth of different modes of irony at his command to be discovered and explicated. Nevertheless, the varieties are always there to be found, however subtle or hidden away in a target text of Twain's œuvre. The expectation that such an exposition of Twain's thinking and writing choices can be given encourages critics to look at aspects of Twain's work that might otherwise be overlooked.

That Twain is an ironist is not up for dispute. The question is exactly what kind of ironist he makes of himself. What exactly does it mean to say of Twain or any other thinker or writer that the individual is ironic, that they engage or indulge in irony? What is irony? In what ways are Twain's writings ironic? How can they be characterized and categorized as instantiating irony as distinct from other thought and literary qualities? The question for literary critical-philosophical inquiry is therefore twofold: What is irony generally? What is Twain's irony specifically? Twain is master of several kinds and subcategories of irony, making his classification a complex branching configuration of types. Twain occupies these nodes of the sprawling irony tree, making similar uses of opposite expression instances of Twain-like irony. Twain's irony, correctly isolated from other complementary rhetorical effects, is further characterized as a signature style of specifically *Socratic irony* as unique to Twain as it is to Twain's ancient Greek predecessor. The completed picture offers a sense of irony as practiced specifically by Twain in terms of other more recognizable categories.

Vlastos on Quintilian's Concept of Irony

Appropriately, the general concept of irony on which the interpretation of Twain's irony as Socratic faithfully relies is unimprovably explained by Gregory Vlastos in the opening sentences of his essay-chapter on "Socratic Irony" in his collection, *Socrates: Ironist and Moral Philosopher*. Vlastos cites and approves a respected late classical authority:

> "Irony," says Quintilian [Marcus Fabius Quintilianus (AD 35-100)], is that figure of speech or trope "in which something contrary to what is said is to be understood" (*contrarium ei quod dicitur intelligendum est*) [citing the *Institutio Oratorica* 9.22.44]. His formula has stood the test of time. It passes intact in Dr Johnson's dictionary ("mode of speech in which the meaning is contrary

to the words" [1755]), and survives virtually intact in ours: "Irony is the use of words to express something other than, and especially the opposite of, [their] literal meaning" (*Webster's*).[5]

Irony, generally, is saying the opposite or contrary of what is meant in such a way that the real intended meaning is recoverable. The characterization works fine for ironic expressions in thought and language. An ironic perspective or ironic outlook on life can then be interpreted as a psychological disposition toward ironic expression. Vlastos proceeds from the general concept of irony to those traits he finds distinctive of Socrates's irony. There are other things to say about Socratic irony, and we shall not deliberately follow Vlastos in defining his specific brand. There are innumerable ways to say the opposite of what is actually meant with a wink and nod to the knowing, and hence there are as many types of irony. These in turn present countless opportunities for different ironists to develop their own unique styles of ironic expression, to be blended with humor, pathos, or flatfooted categorical propositional historical matter of fact. Socrates and Twain are ironists in this sense with many similarities in common.

There are innumerable ways in which a thinker can say the contrary of what could otherwise be literally maintained. Often irony is resorted to when polite indirect expression is required rather than blunt confrontation of opinion. No guarantee of success or appealing turn of phrase is given merely by satisfying the definition of "irony." Clearly, saying "It is raining" when manifestly it is not the case that it is raining is not ordinarily judged ironic. The deception must be more clever than that, more subtle. There must be a trickle of information by which the wary can discern that the opposite of what has been said is actually intended. Twain's established character as ironist in his own writing does much of the work for him by the time the reader has reached the end of the first chapter. Twain does not mean and expects not to be understood as expressing his literal opinion relatively late in *The Innocents Abroad* when he remarks "I was more interested" in the presentation of another chunk of the true cross than some of the other rarities exhibited. Twain crafts a brilliant gradually built up sense of scorn cast on the European relics racket and his travel group's subjection to a credibility-straining barrage of pieces of the true cross, Roman nails thereof, crowns of thorns, scurges, spears, robes, and related religiously significant historical paraphernalia. When he says that he was more interested in being exhibited another professed piece of the true cross than the other relics he may have been making a relative pronouncement as to how little he was interested in the cathedral's holdings. To say that he was more interested in the true cross splinter is classically Twain ironic on any interpretation. Twain explains deadpan that at the Cathedral Notre Dame de Paris the group was shown "some nails of the true cross, a fragment of the cross itself, a part of the crown of thorns. We had already seen a large piece of the true cross in a church in the Azores, but no nails."[6]

Context may not be everything, but it is indispensable in understanding whether literal or ironic meaning is intended. One imagines circumstances for colonists on Mars, to take an extreme but suggestive example, in which even the blunt negation of well-known fact "It is raining" could be considered ironic, even fall-down funny. A masterful use of irony must say the opposite of what is intended while remaining in character, yet managing to let the mask slip just enough for audience or readers to congratulate themselves on seeing through the deception and penetrating to the thinker's real meaning. Otherwise every bald-faced lie would be ironic. The ironic expression must somehow manage to convey that the opposite of its literal meaning is actually intended. There are unlimitedly many heedless and ingenious ways in which this can be done in what comprises a wide-open field of opportunities for distinctive styles of spicing up meaningful discourse with irony. Twain's public persona, like Socrates, is imbued with irony, and the reader quickly comes to understand that Twain is often pulling someone's leg.

When this happens, the opposite intention often makes and is anyway usually intended to make a more powerful impact than would the flat statement of fact expressed as its contrary without irony. That is arguably all the mystery of irony's rhetorical and polemical force when it is effective. Part of the fun is the fact that ironic expression as the opposite of what is intended often leaves it open as to exactly what the opposite meaning literally expressed is supposed to imply. Two differently oriented thinkers can come away from encountering the same ironic expression, recognize alike that the statement is ironically intended, and build in the empty space of the undetermined opposite meaning to that ironically expressed a variety of contrary propositions opposed to the original in literal sense, reference, and connotation. The reader or listener is encouraged to do this, to personally discover the opposite meanings that are likely to have been intended, and in the process to a degree make them their own.

Comic and Sober, Local and Global Irony

We are disposed to imagine the ironist as wearing a smirk, seeing the world as we suppose an ironist to do as a better-knowing smart aleck walking the stage. It might as well be a scowl, however. There is nothing essentially humorous or comic about irony, if with Vlastos we hold that irony in itself is saying or being disposed to say the opposite of what is supposed to be understood as meant. We find Twain making brilliant use of tragic and historical sober irony as well as comic irony in his writings, clearly marking the distinction in his probably untheorized de facto authorial practice.

To appreciate the difference between sober and comic irony, a further distinction proves useful. Twain is master of two main categories of irony to be emphasized in this analysis of his work as *local* and *global*. Roughly, local irony is irony typically contained in the form of a sentence or short tale of several paragraphs inserted into a larger context of generally expository text or fictional narration. Global irony is irony where an entire published work or analogous public presentation is made ironic by declaring of itself the opposite of what is to be understood as true. If Socrates's life is interpreted as his large-scale philosophical work, a concept-object, then its global irony is assured by his ironically distancing interpretation of the sybil's Delphic assertion that he is the wisest man in Athens in knowing that he is unwise.

Twain's (1896) historical novel, *Personal Recollections of Joan of Arc*, and his (1913) *Monist* article authored under his birth name Samuel L. Clemens on "The Philosophy of Mark Twain" are two examples of Twain's global sober seldom comic irony. The entire book *Personal Recollections of Joan of Arc* is fraudulently presented. Its frontmatter, unless very closely scrutinized, does not reveal that the work is a contemporary historical fictional account of Jean d'Arc, Maid of Orleans. It purports to be a record kept by Joan's own "Page and Secretary," the Sieur Louis de Conte, and translated "out of the Ancient French into Modern English from the Original Unpublished Manuscript in the National Archives of France by Jean François Alden, the latter of whom is none other than Twain, which is to say Clemens, the true author of the *Personal Recollections*. We are not the first to remark the coincidence that 'Sieur Louis de Conte' contain the same initials S.L.C. in that order as 'Samuel Longhorne Clemens.'"[7]

If irony is to express the opposite of what is intended, then Twain's *Personal Recollections of Joan of Arc* is globally ironic, saying of itself the opposite of what is true, adopting the ironic distance that is a prime motivation for engaging or indulging in irony. Motivations abound, but one reason for Twain to do so is in order to avoid making high-handed criticism of the church and monarchy of France in his own voice, even as Twain rather than Clemens, from the contemporary perspective at the time of someone who is neither religious nor French. The *Personal Recollections* purport to be written by Jean d'Arc's page, a contemporary long dead who was both religiously devout and bona fide distant relative of the aristocracy of fifteenth-century

France. He could say what he wanted more than four hundred years ago, and the Translator (also Twain, Clemens) does the scholarly and educated world a favor by making available what was written about the Maid of Orleans so long ago. Clemens has two grades of ironic distance in *Personal Recollections*, separated from both imaginary author and translator. The book is none of the things it professes to be, for which a further clue is provided in the list of historical sources, "Authorities examined in verification of the truthfulness of this narrative" that appears en face the Translator's Preface. What is true is presumably that Twain's imaginative history of an unconscionably ideal-ized Joan of Arc is largely based in the "Authorities" Twain mentions on the original court documents of indictment and court records of Jean d'Arc's trial and execution, and what responsible historians rather than novelists have said about it since. There is poetic license and significant ironic distance nonetheless between the legal briefs and statements Jean and many witnesses left behind as a trail of breadcrumbs for future historians and Twain's *Personal Recollections of Joan of Arc*.

Late in the novel, Twain (Clemens) testifies as though in de Conte's voice what again is not true: "I was present on most of these occasions."[8] Twain has the unmitigated audacity to preface the contents with "A Peculiarity of Joan of Arc's History" with the bald-faced untruth: "The details of the life of Joan of Arc form a biography which is unique among the world's biographies in one respect: *It is the only story of a human life which comes to us under oath*, the only one which comes to us from the witness-stand. . . . The Sieur Louis de Conte is faithful to her [Jean] in his Personal Recollections, and thus far his trustworthiness is unimpeachable; but his mass of added particulars [Twain's fictional spinning] must depend for credit upon his own word alone. THE TRANSLATOR."[9] We are to believe no such thing beyond what Twain truthfully remarks concerning the extant documents of Jean's trial, all the church and state machinery directed against a young person barely at the doorstep of womanhood.

Local irony in Twain is exemplified in many ways, typified here, although we shall consider several examples, by the choice of remark in his (1869) *The Innocents Abroad*, when he says in the course of a factual report of the sights visited on the Grand Tour of Europe and the Holy Land: "They also showed us a portrait of the Madonna which was painted by St. Luke, and it did not look half as old and smoky as some of the pictures by Rubens. We could not help admiring the Apostle's modesty in never once mentioning in his writ-ings that he could paint."[10] The Madonna was not painted by St. Luke, and St. Luke was not so modest as to conceal his nonexistent painting abilities. The opposite of these statements in Twain's travelogue are true. It is all

Twain's local irony embedded in the general account of his travels in Europe, here in Genoa. The opposite of what is meant is said. It is irony, although the entire work of generally humorous factual reportage in *The Innocents Abroad*, unlike *Personal Recollections of Joan of Arc* or "The Philosophy of Mark Twain," is not globally ironic. The irony is confined to an incident in a larger matrix of factual recounting of the treasures the traveling group from America was asked to admire in church after cathedral. Twain is ironic about the presumption of the gullibility of his fellow visitors to the sanctuary where the painting was housed. There is plenty of naïve credulity to spare and share between hosts and guests as the Americans struggle to recover some part of their lost European heritage on tour.

Twain and Socratic Irony

A further final classification is now ventured. Twain embodies a distinctively *Socratic* irony in major works, especially where the popular dogmatic teaching, preaching, and practice of organized religion is concerned. Twain's comic and sober local and global irony appears in several ways to be like that of the great first Western ancient Greek philosopher, Socrates. The suggestion is not that Twain deliberately cultivated a specifically Socratic irony, nor indeed that he was aware of any similarities.

Like Socrates, Twain directs most of his ironic barbs at the pretensions of "experts" to know things that no one knows or can know. A large part of Twain's appeal is his arriving at an integrated scoffing of snake oil religious malarkey, saying things even if only ironically that many of his readers believe but do not dare to say. Again in *The Innocents Abroad*, pursuing the theme of disregard for keepsakes of dead religious figures, Twain invites the reader to reflect with him on the preposterous trade in holy relics:

> But isn't this relic matter a little overdone? We find a piece of the true cross in every old church we go into, and some of the nails that held it together. I would not like to be positive, but I think we have seen as much as a keg of these nails. Then there is the crown of thorns; they have part of one in Sainte Chapelle, in Paris, and part of one also in Notre Dame. And as for the bones of St. Denis, I feel certain we have seen enough of them to duplicate him if necessary.[11]

The display does not end there for the American culture pilgrims. Ten pages later in *The Innocents Abroad*, we progress from Paris to Milan in a pattern that by repetition also lends an ironic touch as Twain explains the treasures shown the weary travelers trudging in and out of yet another cathedral. Now Twain narrates:

The priests showed us two of St. Paul's fingers and one of St. Peter's; a bone of Judas Iscariot (it was black) and also bones of all the other disciples; a handkerchief in which the Saviour had left the impression of his face. Among the most precious of the relics were a stone from the Holy Sepulchre, part of the crown of thorns (they have a whole one at Notre Dame), a fragment of the purple robe worn by the Saviour, a nail from the Cross, and a picture of the Virgin and Child painted by the veritable hand of St. Luke. This is the second of St. Luke's Virgins we have seen. Once a year all these holy relics are carried in procession through the streets of Milan.[12]

Later at St. Peter's Basilica in the Vatican, Rome, Twain crisply remarks in guidebook-writing mode: "They have twelve small pillars in St. Peter's, which came from Solomon's Temple. They have also—which was far more interesting to me—a piece of the true Cross, and some nails, and a part of the crown of thorns."[13] The humor in situ of these passages is lost when they are extracted and embedded in commentary as we have had to do here. The effect Twain achieves requires the slow mounting of repeated experiences of such similar kinds, calling up the isolation of these cathedrals with their relic treasures who think that they must be amazing the visitors to their tabernacles. It happens again. Then it happens again. We add up for ourselves the fragments of the true cross, the nails therefrom, crowns of thorns, robe, diapers of Jesus (in Aachen), not to mention what is left over from their Earth's sojourn of all the saints and apostles and martyrs with all their memorabilia of special importance to the faith. Twain reports on a similar episode during the group's ecclesiastical tourism in Genoa:

The main point about the cathedral [of San Lorenzo] is the little Chapel of St. John the Baptist. They only allow women to enter it on one day in the year, on account of the animosity they still cherish against the sex because of the murder of the saint to gratify a caprice of Herodias. In this chapel is a marble chest, in which, they told us, were the ashes of St. John; and around it was wound a chain, which, they said, had confined him when he was in prison. We did not desire to disbelieve these statements, and yet we could not feel certain that they were correct—partly because we could have broken that chain, and so could St. John, and partly because we had seen St. John's ashes before, in another church. We could not bring ourselves to think St. John had two sets of ashes.[14]

Twain's practiced eye readily detects a scam. If there are enough purported pieces of the true cross on which Christ was crucified as someone in this era remarks to build a good-sized schooner with enough left over to crucify the crew, then it will prove practically impossible to distinguish genuine from sham pieces of the true cross. That is perfect; no disappointment at all. It implies that any particular putative relics we might be viewing in any particular location could after all be the actual article. The multiplication of relics does nothing whatsoever to diminish their value spiritually and in other categories. That is something more literally like Twain's intended meaning, ironically expressed as sober explication of what he and his fellow culture seekers were earnestly advised by their Italian cathedral tour guides. Despite the farce, the faithful need and want something to which they can cling under any circumstances. If the object of faith starts out as patently false, then there is not much the critic can do to defame or discredit the belief by citing logic or facts. Twain chooses comic irony in *The Innocents Abroad* to cast commonsense reactions against religious pretenses that mystify and demand acceptance or banishment, rather than enlighten.

Twain voices skeptical attitudes concerning both the truth and social compassion of received religious belief. More pointedly, he evinces heartfelt scorn for the hypocrisy of religious practice when it is not in accord with an individual's profession of faith. Twain's ironic distance enables him to convey his moral epistemic disregard for religious dogma that is out of step with the same intuitive reasoning that the wretched human race has relied on throughout its improbable historical progression and refined in Twain's day as the beginnings of a respectable Science. Twain's point throughout appears to lament the foolishness of individuals no smarter on average than anyone else who pretend to know what no one knows or can know, who have no hesitation nonetheless in bringing fire and sword to reinforce irrational commitment to the great unknowns of creation, moral answerability, and the afterlife.

How in comparison now does Socrates manage to say the opposite of what he means? Often in playful fun in Plato's dialogues, Socrates ironically asserts superiority by deferring to an authority who eventually evinces no grasp of the speciality's basic concepts or ability to define essential derived terminology. Socrates's global irony is established by the Delphic oracle's pronouncement that Socrates is the wisest man in Athens, interpreted by Socrates ironically as meaning that his wisdom consists in knowing that he is not wise, that he does not have superior knowledge. Paradoxically, global Socratic irony makes Socrates's greatest wisdom his acknowledgment that he lacks wisdom. Socrates is wise when and only when he acknowledges that he is not wise but lacks wisdom. As Vlastos in the final sentences of his previously cited essay avows: "Socrates doesn't say that the knowledge by which he and we must live is utterly different from what anyone has ever understood or even imagined moral knowledge could be. He just says he has no knowledge, though without it he is damned, and lets us puzzle it out for ourselves what that could mean."[15]

Socrates and Twain use irony for the same basic reason. When the interlocutor or readers understand the irony, *if* that moment dawns, then the opposed meaning ironically expressed can make a greater more profound polemical impact than if categorically expressed without irony. When we grasp what is not being said we feel freely autonomous in completing the argument in what appears to be our uncoerced way, even when we have been given few, if any, alternatives. We are unguided in our conclusions after we learn without editorial comment as a plain matter of fact that a monastery boasts *three* skulls of John the Baptist—one as an infant, another as a young man, and a third after death. That cannot be, you may find yourself wanting to say, even if the author accepted these facts at face value.

Twain, again like Socrates, exhibits an ironic wisdom especially about Christian religion that makes an epistemic and moral virtue out of respecting the limitations of what we can and cannot reasonably know about the creation of the universe, the human moral relation to a hypothetical divine personality, the nature of sin, the prospect of an afterlife, and most articles of specific religious cults and belief systems, sparing none in its critical comprehension. If we cannot know about such things, then Twain believes it is a moral offense to pretend that we have answers to life's questions where no presumptive beliefs are warranted one way or the other. If there is a God, he implies ironically whenever given the opportunity, then let us exercise our God-given common sense especially in matters of religious belief.[16]

PART V

COMPARISON TO OTHER PHILOSOPHERS

CHAPTER TWELVE

~

The American Diogenes

Mark Twain's Sacred Profanity

BRIAN EARL JOHNSON

> I warmed to that butcher the moment he began to swear. There is more than one way of praying, and I like the butcher's way because the petitioner is so apt to be in earnest.

> –Mark Twain[1]

In 1867, Mark Twain set off for the Mediterranean on a tour organized by the Plymouth Church of Brooklyn, New York. There was initially some doubt about whether Twain's application to join their excursion to the Holy Lands would be accepted because he surely did not meet their puritan standards for such a pilgrimage. A decade later, the details of his interview for the expedition generated a bit of controversy and prompted Twain to "defend" himself in a letter to the editor to the *New York World*. Twain cheerfully concedes to the charge that he had been falsely represented as a "Baptist minister cruising after health," but he spends most of his letter on the allegation that he smelled of bad whiskey. He replies that he could not afford the good whiskey and then scoffs, "How could I know that the 'captain' was so particular about the quality of a man's liquor?"[2]

Despite this hiccup, Twain was permitted to join, yielding a series of reports about the journey for a newspaper and later compiled into his travelogue, *The Innocents Abroad, or The New Pilgrims' Progress*, published in 1869.

While it is difficult to summarize any of Twain's travelogues, Mark Twain's official biographer, Albert Bigelow Paine, puts it this way:

> It was the most daring book of its day. Passages of it were calculated to take the breath of the orthodox reader; only, somehow, it made him smile, too. It was all so good-natured, so openly sincere. Without doubt it preached heresy—the heresy of viewing revered landmarks and relics joyously, rather than lugubriously; reverentially, when they inspired reverence; satirically, when they invited ridicule, and with kindness always.[3]

Twain's own presence on the journey did not, however, always provoke smiles. "Doctor [William] Church was a deacon with orthodox views and did not approve of Mark Twain; he thought [Twain] sinful, irreverent, profane. '[Twain] was the worst man I ever knew,' Church said; then he added, 'And the *best*.'"[4] And Twain was quite capable of barbs about his fellow passengers. "They never romped, they talked but little, they never sang, save in the nightly prayer-meeting. The pleasure ship was a synagogue, and the pleasure trip was a funeral excursion without a corpse. (There is nothing exhilarating about a funeral excursion without a corpse.)"[5]

Key for our understanding of Mark Twain's persona concerning religion is the following moment from their visit to Athens: "We walked out into the grass-grown, fragment-strewn court beyond the Parthenon. . . . As we turned and moved again through the temple, I wished that the illustrious men who had sat in it in the remote ages could visit it again and reveal themselves to our curious eyes. . . . But more than all, I wished that old Diogenes [the Cynic], groping so patiently with his lantern, searching so zealously for one solitary honest man in all the world, might meander along and stumble on our party. I ought not to say it, may be, but still I suppose he would have put out his light."[6] Twain's wish to be recognized by Diogenes as an honest man is especially significant in light of Twain's own humorously tall estimate of himself from an 1885 notebook entry: "When a merely *honest* man appears, he is a comet—his fame is eternal—needs no genius, no talent—mere honesty—Luther, Christ, & maybe God has made [two] others—or one—besides me."[7]

Mark Twain thus invites us as readers to understand him as linked with the mission of Diogenes the Cynic. And, as I shall argue, Twain's characterization of himself is especially apt. Early American thinkers and writers have often been compared to figures from classical Greece—Benjamin Franklin, for example, having been dubbed the American Socrates. In contrast, Mark Twain's thought, especially his treatment of religion, has much in common with the Classical example of Diogenes the Cynic (404–323 B.C.). Diogenes's words and antics were so outlandish that Plato called him "Socrates gone crazy."[8] While Socrates asked questions with religious implications, such as "What is piety?" lending support to fears that he was a skeptic of the gods of the city, Diogenes directly satirized religious and moral customs that he found repugnant. And yet, while both Socrates and Diogenes had support of the sacred oracle for their missions, Socrates was executed for impiety, whereas Diogenes was voted a brand new bathtub when a rowdy schoolboy broke the one that served as his home in the agora.[9] Diogenes found a way to engage in a scorching critique that hit its mark with the Athenian people.

The present chapter will explore how Twain operated in the spirit of Cynicism, rather than Socratic skepticism. For Diogenes, moral hypocrisy was truly profane, while natural honesty was genuinely sacred; the irreverent takedown of phony religious sentiments therefore constituted a sacred profanity. Twain, too, found a way to be profane in the very dangerous arena of the sacred, and, like Diogenes, his stories and antics were met with public acclaim. I aim to show that Twain was not a skeptic of religion; rather, he was a Cynic of Christianity as practiced in his day. Just as Diogenes was appalled by the pretensions of powerful Greeks, which he deflated with hilarious stunts and one-liners, so Twain humorously took down creationists, self-important ministers, and slavery apologists who cited the Bible. At the same time, much like Diogenes the Cynic, Twain was unafraid of confronting human misery and did not fantasize about a happy afterlife as a way to assuage the fear of misery and death. Finally, in their avoidance of systematic theology, Diogenes and Twain remain fluid and vital in their respective cognitions of religious ideas, and thus evade easy categorization.

Coins, Customs, and the Uses of Sacred Profanity

According to ancient reports, Diogenes the Cynic got himself into trouble for defacing the coinage of his native town, Sinope (now in modern-day Turkey), and thus fled to Athens. It was this story, more than the one about the lantern, that stuck in the minds of ancient admirers and emulators because it worked on two levels. On its face, the story is a political one about the legitimacy of a city-state's coinage (each Greek city-state having its own currency). Even in the ancient world, coins were counterfeited, most often by covering a disc of cheap metal with a valuable metal. To ensure that a coin was real, a banker could weigh the coin, listen to the sound it made upon tapping, or cut into the coin, exposing its core. If a coin turned out to be counterfeit, the banker would give it a deep gash in order to ensure that it was removed from the currency. Thus, Diogenes may have challenged the legitimacy of Sinope's coins, or wilder still, he was actively debasing the currency by producing his own counterfeit coins.

And yet, under the surface of this story happens to be its precious metal. In ancient Greek, the same word *nomisma* is used for a "coin" as it is for a "custom." Diogenes the Cynic was thus understood in the ancient world as one who tested *customs* in order to determine which ones should be removed from circulation. He did not invent new customs; instead, he was concerned to eliminate our counterfeit practices. In order to remove false customs, Diogenes adopted many personae, the most famous was that of a dog. "Once Alexander the Great came and stood by him, and said, 'I am Alexander, the great king.' 'And I,' said he, 'am Diogenes the Cynic.'"[10] Literally, he declared "I am Diogenes the Dog," from whence the term Cynic (*kuôn*) is derived. Diogenes went on to explain the epithet: "And when [Diogenes] was asked to what actions of his it was owing that he was called a dog, he said, 'Because I fawn upon those who give me anything, and bark at those who give me nothing, and bite the scoundrels.'"[11]

While his canine persona seemed to prompt some of his wilder exploits, from sleeping wherever he could (outside or in a tub) to his scandalous belief that anything could be done in public (such as sexual acts),[12] Diogenes did not advocate becoming feral, nor was he against being human. "On one occasion he was eating his dinner in the marketplace, and the bystanders kept constantly calling out 'Dog;' but he said, 'It is you who are the dogs, who stand around me while I am at dinner.'"[13] Similarly, "He used to say that he was a dog of the kind that were praised; but that none of those who praised them dared to go out hunting with him."[14] Indeed, what disappointed Diogenes was the fact that most people were unworthy of the epithet "human being," so his quest to find a (real) human being was apparently in vain[15]; instead, most people were "scoundrels"[16] who "contended with one another in punching and kicking, but that no one showed any striving in the pursuit of virtue."[17]

Furthermore, Diogenes embraced human reason (*logos*) and it was human *logos* that led him to challenge superstition as well as any counterfeit customs in relation to piety. "Another of his sayings was that he thought humans ought oftener to provide themselves with reason (*logon*) than with a belt (*brochon*)."[18] Thus, for example, he utilized reason to explain to a superstitious woman the mistake of prostrating oneself before the gods: "Once he saw a woman falling down before the gods in an unbecoming attitude; wishing to cure her of her superstition, . . . he came up to her, and said, 'Are you not afraid, O woman, to be in such an indecent attitude, when some God may be behind you, for every place is full of him?'"[19] Similarly, Diogenes challenged food taboos, arguing that "according to right reason, everything was a combination of all things. For in bread there was meat, and in vegetables there was bread, and so there were some particles of all other bodies in everything."[20] Through his various personae, Diogenes utilized quips, sarcasm, and puckish antics as his way of putting a gash in any counterfeit cultural coins and thus removing them from circulation.

Mark Twain, for his part, shared the general approach of Diogenes, although Twain was more restrained. In a notebook entry, he wonders why there were not more books about "the vile and contemptible human race— books that laugh at the whole paltry scheme and deride it. . . . Why don't I write such a book? Because I have a family. There is no other reason."[21] In a similar vein, he surely would not have joined Diogenes, for example, in suggesting that love-making could be done in public.[22] Twain was certainly annoyed with the constrictive modesty of missionaries and Victorians in their horror at nudity,[23] and he admired women for their capacity to be sexually active throughout their entire lives[24]; he could also be quite bawdy (see his "Conversation, as It Was by the Social Fireside in the Time of the Tudors"). But I am sure he would have regarded public fornication as a crude nuisance to bystanders.

Nevertheless, Twain's own personae (author, speaker, and the narrative voices in his stories) have much of Diogenes's Cynicism in them. Twain was open to the image of a dog as a way to highlight human hypocrisy. "If you pick up a starving dog and make him prosperous," he wrote, "he will not bite you. This is the principal difference between a dog and a man."[25] Moreover, he took up one authorial voice that allowed him his most dangerous and profane reflections on the sacred: the voice of a Satanic figure. He tries out this voice in two story lines published posthumously precisely because he understood that he was turning the Bible on its head. As he explained to a friend about one of the works, "it would be felony to soil the mails with it, for it has much Holy Scripture in it of the kind that . . . can't properly be read aloud."[26]

The first story line is The Mysterious Stranger Manuscripts. The work exists in the form of incomplete manuscripts describing a visit to Earth by Satan, or at least a close relative of Satan; he is given the moniker the "mysterious stranger" or "Number 44." In one version, Number 44 visits St. Petersburg of an indeterminate era; in two versions, he visits Austria of a bygone era; and in the shortest version, Number 44 visits the schoolhouse of Tom Sawyer and Huckleberry Finn. The incomplete story lines of each unfold differently, but the Satanic figure, Number 44, is fairly consistent throughout. Number 44 has supernatural powers, a frightful indifference to human life, and a forceful disdain for human pretensions (including their claim to be elevated by their "moral sense" or "conscience"). Additionally, as Number 44 intervenes in human affairs at the pleading of the humans who befriend him, it sets off catastrophic consequences that cannot be avoided, thus challenging providence. Number 44 is both terrifying and darkly funny, while he shows us the base metal underneath the shiny coatings of our counterfeit coins.

The second unfinished and posthumously published story line, titled *Letters from the Earth*, is the funnier of the two. It presents itself as a series of letters written by Satan to God, in which Satan acts as an anthropologist, commenting on the "experiment" of creation, morality, the flood, and human theological beliefs. Throughout, Twain displays a deep knowledge of the Bible and uses it to comic effect much in the same way Diogenes comically utilizes a deep knowledge of Homer.[27]

By means of the Satanic figure, Twain is able to write with acerbic candor, and this honesty again links him with the Cynic tradition. As above, he explicitly hopes that he would answer Diogenes's quest for the (elusive) honest human being. Twain's fixation upon honesty is significant because it not only provides a way for us to understand his own project, but it allows us to characterize Cynicism in Twainian terms as well as locate their respective use of sacred profanity.

Twain seems to understand honesty to mean reporting the world exactly as he sees it, an honesty that makes us laugh. This firsthand perspective is especially brought out by his biting remarks concerning his fellow pilgrims in *Innocents Abroad*. "Our pilgrims have brought their verdicts with them. . . . I can almost tell, in set phrase," he complains, "what they will say when they see Tabor, Nazareth, Jericho and Jerusalem—because I have the books they will 'smouch' their ideas from. These authors write pictures and frame rhapsodies, and [these] lesser men follow and see with the author's eyes instead of their own, and speak with his tongue."[28] In turn, Twain's truth-telling can be downright funny. Likewise, Diogenes not only spoke his mind without fear but was funny in doing so. "Once, while [Diogenes] was sitting in the sun . . . Alexander [the Great] stood over him, and said, 'Ask any favor you choose of me.' [Diogenes] replied, 'Get out of my light.'"[29]

This provocation of laughter by telling the truth is the basis of sacred profanity. For both Diogenes and Twain, truth-telling requires not only unvarnished speech but profane speech. Diogenes was once asked "what was the most excellent thing among humans; and he said, 'Outspokenness.'"[30] His one-word answer, *parrhesia*, is a little difficult to capture, as it principally entails the kind of frank speech only permitted to a free-standing Athenian, so it is often translated as "freedom of speech," but it can also mean "freedom of action." Interestingly, Diogenes, a resident foreigner of Athens, is claiming such freedom for himself. Diogenes's own profanity took the form of action, such as pointing out a famous oratorical demagogue by giving him the finger.[31] Twain adds to Diogenes's notion of free speech by explicitly connecting free expression with profanity, when he angrily declares "what a lie it is to call this [*viz.* the United States] a free country, where none but the unworthy and undeserving may swear."[32] He also asserts that profanity is perfectly consonant with the divine. "I have often used profane language in the presence of God. As he has always put up with it, I had an idea that maybe a damned theatre manager could stand it."[33] He did jokingly concede, however, that if he could not swear in heaven, "I shall not stay there."[34]

Twain's conception of laughter was intermingled with his understanding of his own career and the power of humor for removing counterfeit customs from circulation. Of himself, he said, "I never had but two powerful ambitions in my life. One was to be a pilot and the other a preacher of the gospel. I accomplished the one and failed in the other, *because* I could not supply myself with the necessary trade—i.e. religion. I have given it up forever. . . . I was by nature unfitted and turned my attention to seriously scribbling to excite *laughter* of God's creatures."[35] Indeed, he often turned laughter back to the trade of religion. "No god or religion can survive ridicule. No church, no nobility, no royalty or other fraud, can face ridicule in a fair field and live."[36] In the *Mysterious Stranger*, Twain has the Satanic figure declare that when other implements fail, only laughter will do. "Power, Money, Persuasion, Supplication, Persecution—these can lift at a colossal humbug—push it a little—weaken it a little, century by century, but only laughter can blow it to rags and atoms at a blast. Against the assault of Laughter nothing can stand."[37]

But, it is imperative to see that neither Twain nor Diogenes had a project of destroying what they regarded as legitimately sacred. Twain's respect for the sacred is best brought out in a letter he wrote to his brother, Orion: "Neither [my friend William] Howells nor I believe in hell or the divinity of the Savior but no matter, the Savior is none the less a sacred Personage, and a man should have no desire or disposition to refer to him lightly, profanely or otherwise than with the profoundest reverence."[38] Diogenes, too, respected what was genuinely sacred and provides a very literal version of sacred profanity. "When [Diogenes] was eating dinner in a temple, some dirty loaves were set before him, he picked them up and threw them out, saying that nothing impure ought to come into a temple."[39]

Accordingly, we may define sacred profanity as either (1) to profane the pseudo-sacred but also (2) to make profanity into its own form of sacredness. In this latter case, one takes up the speech or actions regarded as profane by one's culture (e.g., Twain's cursing) and declares it sacred precisely because it is honest (e.g., Twain's butcher). In the remainder of this chapter, I will examine four counterfeit coins that both Diogenes and Mark Twain sought to remove from circulation: superstition, hypocrisy, artificial morality, and heavenly rewards.

Superstition

He used likewise to say that when, in the course of his life, he beheld pilots, physicians, and philosophers, he thought humans the wisest of all animals; but when again he beheld interpreters of dreams, and soothsayers, and those who listened to them . . . then he thought that there was not a more foolish animal than a human.[40]

A certain person was admiring the offerings in the temple at Samothrace [for surviving a shipwreck], and [Diogenes] said to him, "They would have been much more numerous, if those who were lost had offered them instead of those who were saved."[41]

Twain's own treatment of superstition exemplifies the boundaries and the positive uses of his sacred profanity. As above, he regarded Jesus as a sacred figure because he regarded him as a truly honest person; thus one should not profane Jesus himself. However, Twain poked fun at the Biblical claim that Jesus was born of a virgin and he attacked the idea of special, divine providence.

Mark Twain's send up of the virgin birth of Jesus appears in chapters 4 and 5 of his short tale, "Little Bessie." Twain utilizes the voice of a young girl in order to bring out how he finds the doctrine senseless.[42] The story unfolds as a conversation between a devout mother and her forthright daughter, Little Bessie, "a good child, and not shallow, not frivolous, but meditative and thoughtful, and much give to thinking out the reasons of things and trying to make them harmonise [sic] with the results."[43] Regarding the virgin birth, Twain has Bessie say that, if a virgin birth was alleged under any other circumstance, reasonable minds would conclude that it was a fabrication to cover for premarital sex.[44] Twain is at his most profane when Bessie takes up Mary's continued title as a virgin, given that Mary had more children after Jesus. He targets what he sees as the counterfeit assumption behind the virgin birth, namely that sex is impure and cheapens women, such that the Gospel authors invented the story that Mary was a virgin.[45] If Mary remained a virgin after "a lot of child-bearing, spread over years and years and years," Little Bessie declares, it "would ultimately wear a virgin's virginity so thin that even Wall street would consider the stock too lavishly watered and you couldn't place it there at any discount you could name, because the Board would say it was wildcat, and wouldn't list it."[46] Not surprisingly, Bessie's mother exclaims, "Go to the nursery, instantly! Go!"

Still, of all human beliefs that most irked Twain as superstition, it was surely the Calvinistic idea of special providence. He practically shouts into his notebook, "Special Providence! That phrase nauseates me—with its implied importance of mankind and triviality of God."[47] In the 1880s, he wrote down a kind of credo for himself stating, "I do not believe in special providences. I believe that the universe is governed by strict and immutable laws: If one man's family is swept away by a pestilence and another man's spared it is only the law working: God is not interfering in that small matter, either against the one man or in favor of the other."[48]

Twain subjected the idea of special providence to both biting satire and lighthearted comedy. One of his sharpest satires on special providence appears in a darkly comic 1905 letter of congratulations to a friend lucky enough to survive a railroad accident. "I am once more glad that there is an Ever-watchful Providence . . . to save our friends. The Government's Official report, showing that our railways killed twelve hundred persons last year and injured sixty thousand convinces me that under present conditions one Providence is not enough to properly and efficiently take care of our railroad business."[49] As Diogenes did before him, Twain was astounded by those who thank Providence for being saved without recognizing how many more lives were not spared.

His exasperation at the idea of special providence crops up in many places in his corpus, but his funniest and most light-hearted send-up is the twin burlesques, "The Story of the Good Little Boy Who Did Not Prosper" and "The Story of the Bad Little Boy That Bore a Charmed Life." These stories were evidently modeled on the Sunday school stories of boys who met with a terrible fate for skipping Sunday services or of angelic boys who were amply rewarded for their do-gooder ways. In "The Story of the Good Little Boy," Jacob "always had a hard time of it." Jacob assists a blind man, for example, who had been pushed over by a group of bad boys. Jacob is greeted not with gratitude but a crack on his head by the cane of the blind man. Twain ends the tale by explaining, in a mock serious tone, that Jacob "did the best he could, but didn't come out according to the [Sunday school] books. . . . His case is truly remarkable. It will probably never be accounted for."[50] By contrast, in "The Story of the Bad Little Boy," a boy named Jim engages in all manner of wickedness (and which, I think, Twain delights in chronicling) but meets only with success. Twain even deliberately chooses the name Jim because "bad little boys are nearly always called James in your Sunday-school books."[51] The tale of the bad little boy ends on a similarly ironical note as that of the good boy. "So you see there never was a bad James in the Sunday-school books that had such a streak of luck as this sinful Jim with the charmed life."[52]

Behind the doctrine of special providence, as Twain indicates, is a belief that human beings are so magnificent that God anxiously watches our every movement, just as a parent might a newborn child. This view is subject to rather scorching satire in the version of the mysterious stranger story titled "The Chronicles of Young Satan." Number 44 explains to a group of awed boys with whom he had become friendly:

> Here is a red spider, not so big as a pin's head; can you imagine an elephant be-ing interested in him; caring for whether he is happy or isn't; or whether he is wealthy or poor; or whether his sweetheart returns his love or not; or whether his mother is sick or well; or whether he is looked up to in society or not. . . . These things can never be important to the elephant, they are nothing to him. . . . The elephant has nothing against the spider, he cannot get down to that remote level. . . . The elephant is indifferent. . . . The elephant would not take the trouble to do the spider an ill turn. . . . The elephant lives a century, the red spider a day; in power, intellect and dignity, the one creature is separated from the other by a distance which is simply astronomical.[53]

At an earlier moment in the same story line, one of the boys objects to Number 44's minimization of humanity as a case of bad manners. Number 44 defends himself in a way reminiscent of Diogenes's frankness (*parrhesia*): "Manners! . . . [W]hy it is merely the truth, and truth is good manners; manners are a fiction."[54]

Hypocrisy

> [Diogenes] used to say, "That musicians fitted the strings to the lyre properly, but left all the habits of their soul ill-arranged. . . .That orators were anxious to speak justly, but not at all about acting so."[55]

> And to those who were excited at their dreams, he said that they did not pay attention to what they do while they are awake but instead make a great fuss about what they fancy they see while they are asleep.[56]

> On one occasion, when he had seen the religious officials leading off one of the stewards who had stolen a goblet, he said, "The great thieves are carrying off the little thief."[57]

Neither Diogenes nor Twain rejected ethics; both of them, for example, admired generosity as a virtue.[58] And, owing to their commitment to virtue, both men detested hypocrisy. For his part, Twain was ready enough to accept hypocrisy as the normal condition of humanity. "I have been reading the morning paper . . . knowing well that I shall find in it the usual depravities and basenesses and hypocrisies and cruelties that make up civilization," he wrote to his friend, William Dean Howells.[59] But, when hypocrisy become the foundation of unfairness or cruelty, Twain railed against it. He found this kind of hypocrisy both in how Christians treated those less fortunate but also in the very character of the Biblical God.[60]

Concerning cruel hypocrisy in human behavior, Twain was at his most fiery around the turn of the century. He saluted the end of the year 1900 with a short, handwritten note to the *New York Herald*, which it published on December 30. In it, he comments on the behavior of Christian Powers abroad: "I bring you the stately matron named Christendom, returning bedraggled, besmirched, and dishonored, from pirate-raids in Kiao-chou, Manchuria, South Africa, and the Philippines, with her soul full of meanness, her pocket full of boodle, and her mouth full of pious hypocrisies. Give her soap and towel, but hide the looking glass."[61] Twain's anger is palpable, but so is his fierce sense of irony. It is hard not to laugh at the "stately matron" who needs a good bath, but who also could not bear to see herself honestly, so that we shall not allow her a mirror.[62]

Twain found grim irony not just in the aggrandizement of Christian powers, but in the willingness to torture or kill those who do not believe in the Christian gospel of compassion. In *Innocents Abroad*, he makes us laugh through our tears when he writes about the use of torture to convert the pagan barbarians:

> when the holy Mother Church became mistress of the barbarians, she taught them the error of their ways . . . and pointed to the Blessed Redeemer [viz. Jesus], who was so gentle and so merciful toward all men, and they urged the barbarians to love him; and they did all they could to persuade them to love and honor him—first by twisting their thumbs out of joint with a screw; then by nipping their flesh with pincers—red-hot ones, because they are the most comfortable in cold weather; then by skinning them alive a little, and finally by roasting them in public. They always convinced those barbarians. The true religion, properly administered, as the good Mother Church used to administer it, is very, very soothing. It is wonderfully persuasive, also.[63]

To point out the hypocrisy of humanity was a safe bet for Twain and still likely to provoke laughter even as it forces us to admit that we are far from perfect. But he enters more dangerous territory when he tackles the hypocrisy he locates in the God of the Bible. He describes this God as "irascible, vindictive, fierce and ever fickle,"[64] and he quips that "God's inhumanity to man makes countless thousands mourn."[65] God makes "one moral law for man and another for Himself."[66] Twain particularly felt that the Biblical God was hypocritical about the fall of Adam and Eve. He was fascinated by the tale of Adam and Eve, and he returned to it many times, treating it from many angles but always showing particular empathy for Eve. In one telling of the tale, he attributes the fall to Eve's curiosity rather than to temptation.[67] He also defends Adam, saying that God "was unfair in Adam's case. He commanded Adam not to eat of the tree of the knowledge of good and evil; To disobey could not be a sin, because Adam could not comprehend a sin *until* eating the fruit should reveal to him the difference between right and wrong. So he was unfair in punishing Adam for doing wrong when he could not know it was wrong."[68] Twain even muses on the question of why Satan got involved with the forbidden fruit in the first place and suggests that it was an erroneous misunderstanding on his part.[69]

Twain's most profane reflections on the fall of Adam were among his dictations that he requested be set aside for a century because they would "get my heirs & assigns burnt alive if they venture to print it this side of 2006 A.D."[70] And yet, while he terms his reflections "fearful things," he exhibits a rapier wit. He says, "It was decreed that all of Adam's descendants, to the latest day should be punished for the baby's trespass against a law of his nursery fulminated against him before he was out of his diapers. For thousands and thousands of years his posterity, individual by individual, has been unceasingly hunted and harried with afflictions in punishment of the juvenile misdemeanor which is grandiloquently called Adam's Sin."[71]

False or Artificial Morality

> [Diogenes] used to show in practice, really altering people's habits, and deferring in all things rather to the principles of nature than to those of custom; saying that he was adopting the same [free-ranging] fashion of life as Hercules had, preferring nothing in the world to liberty.[72]

Both Diogenes and Mark Twain found human customs to entail numerous artificial constraints; while they set their sights on different customs, they both earmarked their share of counterfeit coins. While Diogenes utilized the Classical language of nature versus (artificial) custom, Twain utilized the nineteenth-century language of compassion and the Golden Rule versus conscience and the moral sense. For Twain, conscience is not morality; it is "the creature of *training*; it is whatever one's mother and Bible and comrades and laws and system of government and habitat and heredities have made it."[73]

Even though the term "conscience" is a post-Classical one, Twain's campaign against it aligns him with the spirit of Cynicism. When Diogenes embraced the title of "dog" (or "Cynic"), his followers understood that to entail a campaign against shame (*aidôs*), the closest Greek equivalent to "conscience." Hence, the later Cynics took up "shamelessness" as a sort of rallying cry.[74] The Cynics held that there was something unnatural about shame and artificial norms for decency. In a very similar spirit, Twain's notebooks contain many Cynic reflections on the subject. "Nature knows no indecencies; man invents them."[75] Similarly, "Man is merely and exclusively the Immodest Animal, for he is the only one who covers his nakedness, the only one with a soiled mind, the only one under the dominion of a false shame."[76] He also humorously notes the impious irony of conscience when he writes, "The first thing a missionary teaches a savage is indecency. He makes him put clothes on. He is as innocent and clean-minded up to that time as were our first parents when they walked naked before the Lord [in the garden of Eden] and were not ashamed. He hid the knowledge of indecency from them; the missionary doesn't."[77]

Twain brings out these Cynic themes and deliberately profanes (allegedly sacred) conscience in hair-raising exhibition offered up by Number 44 in the "The Chronicle of Young Satan."[78] The exhibition begins when one of the boys, who has befriended Number 44, wonders what it is like to be inside a jail. In a flash, Number 44 has transported them inside a prison, and they watch (while invisible) the beginnings of a torture session upon an accused heretic. The young boy finds it inhuman, but Number 44 grimly explains that it is precisely "a *human* thing."[79] He adds that, "It is like your paltry race—always lying, always claiming virtues which it hasn't got, always denying them to the Higher Animals, which alone possess them. No brute ever does a cruel thing—that is the monopoly of the snob with the Moral Sense."[80] The Satanic figure then teleports them to a sweatshop and sardonically explains that "It is some more Moral Sense. The proprietors are rich, and very holy; but the wage they pay to these poor . . . is only enough to keep them from dropping dead of hunger."[81] Number 44 completes the factory exhibition by saying that the owners "think themselves better than dogs. Ah, you are such an illogical, unreasoning race!"[82]

Afterward, the Satanic figure returns them to the village, and they are joined by another local boy. The three begin to discuss a town drunkard who beats his dog viciously. Number 44 takes the opportunity to remind the boys that not only is it human to behave that way, but it is "slander" to call animals "brutes" because it is humans who are the real brutes. "None of the Higher Animals is minted with the disease called the Moral Sense," he adds; "Purify your language . . . drop those lying phrases out of it." The Satanic figure then heals the dog and communicates with it in dog mutters and moans. Number 44 learns from the dog that its cruel master has fallen off a cliff, and yet the dog still seeks help for its master. Number 44 bluntly says to the two boys, "What do you think of your race? Is heaven reserved for *it*, and this dog ruled out, as your teachers tell you? Can your race add anything to this dog's stock of morals and magnanimities?"[83]

Death and the Afterlife

When [Diogenes] was asked whether death was an evil, he replied, "How can that be an evil which we do not feel when it is present?"[84]

When the Athenians entreated him to be initiated in the Eleusinian mysteries [an Athenian religion promising rewards for initiates in the underworld], and said that in the underworld the initiated had the best seats; "It will," he replied, "be an absurd thing if Agesilaus and Epaminondas [two Greek heroes] are to live in the mud, and some miserable wretches, who have been initiated, are to be in the islands of the blest."[85]

Twain was uncertain whether he believed in an afterlife, at times indicating belief and at others disbelief; at one time, he declares himself indifferent about whether we survive death, and at another he says that he is "vexed to find that I more believe in the immortality of the soul than disbelieve it."[86]

If death amounts to a total cessation of the self, or "annihilation" as Twain terms it, he held exactly the same view as Diogenes, namely, "If annihilation is to follow death, I shall not be aware of the annihilation, and therefore shall not care a straw about it."[87] Twain elsewhere adds that annihilation should be regarded as peaceful. "Annihilation has no terrors for me, because I have already tried it before I was born. . . . There was a peace, a serenity, an absence of all sense of responsibility, and absence of worry, an absence of care, grief, perplexity; and the presence of a deep content and unbroken satisfaction in that hundred million years of holiday which I look back upon with a tender longing and with a grateful desire to resume, when the opportunity comes."[88]

Twain's conviction that death is not an evil for the deceased remained firm even though he recognized the deep loss for those still living. He treats this duality in heart-breaking detail, both in nonfiction ("The Death of

Jean") and in fiction ("Passage from Eve's Diary"). In nonfiction, he takes up his pen to process the unexpected death of his daughter, Jean, who died on Christmas Eve, 1909. He writes "I have never wanted any released friend of mine restored to life since I reached manhood. I felt in this way when [my daughter] Susy passed away; and later my wife, and later Mr. Rogers. When Clara met me at the station in New York and told me Mr. Rogers had died suddenly that morning, my thought was, Oh, favorite of fortune—fortunate all his long and lovely life—fortunate to his latest moment! The reporters said there were tears of sorrow in my eyes. True—but they were for ME, not for him. He had suffered no loss."[89]

In fiction, Twain treats the subject of death through its discovery by Eve in "Passage from Eve's Diary," one of his many treatments of the garden of Eden story in *Genesis*. This version of Eve's story shows how Eve struggles to comprehend the death of her son, Abel. She waits by his body for many days thinking that he is asleep; she watches him with a mother's care—kissing his cold cheek and wishing he would awake—though she is grateful that he gets rest. Finally, she begins to grasp what has happened. "Oh, is it that long sleep—is it Death? And will he wake no more?" Twain appends to this diary a note from Satan. "Death has entered the world . . . the product of the Moral Sense [gained from eating the 'forbidden fruit'] is complete. The Family think ill of Death—they will change their mind."[90]

If, however, we survive death, Twain says, "I feel sure it will be for some more sane and useful purpose than to flounder about for ages in a lake of fire and brimstone for having violated a confusion of ill-defined and contradictory rules said (but not evidenced) to be of divine institution."[91] Twain asserted that hell was one of the "superstitions in which I was born and mis-trained."[92] He equally rejected the idea that having orthodox beliefs was necessary for entry into heaven. "I am not able to believe one's religion can affect his hereafter one way or the other, no matter what that religion may be."[93] For these reasons, he faulted Jesus for inventing hell, an idea he clearly found unfair and lacking in mercy.[94] He outright mocked the idea of unbaptized babies "roasting in the red fires."[95] Accordingly, he would only entertain the idea of hell for comic purposes; he teased, for example, that he hoped to see all in heaven "except the inventor of the telephone."[96]

Why, then, invent hell? Twain supplies no answer where Jesus is concerned, but he believes hell was taken up as a weapon of control by later followers. His second travelogue, *Roughing It*, brings out this very point in its concluding account of his adventures in Hawaii. He makes fun of the missionary efforts to end public nudity, and he satirizes, the missionaries [who] braved a thousand privations to come and make them permanently miserable by telling them how beautiful and how blissful a place heaven is, and how nearly impossible it is to get there; and showed the poor native how dreary a place perdition is and what unnecessarily liberal facilities there are for going to it; showed him how, in his ignorance he had gone and fooled away all his kinfolks to no purpose; showed him what rapture it is to work all day long for fifty cents to buy food for next day with, as compared with fishing for pastime and lolling in the shade through eternal Summer, and eating of the bounty that nobody labored to provide but Nature. How sad it is to think of the multitudes who have gone to their graves in this beautiful island and never knew there was a hell![97]

In light of Twain's love of Hawaii, this passage gives us the sense that it is the missionaries who have committed an impious profanity against what is truly sacred.

Should there be a heaven, Twain had no positive account to offer,[98] but he was at his Cynic-best in striking down Victorian ideas about the afterlife. In *Letters from the Earth*, Satan marvels:

It [viz. humanity] has invented a heaven out of its own head, all by itself: guess what it is like! In fifteen hundred eternities you couldn't do it. The ablest mind known to you or me in fifty million aeons couldn't do it. Very well, I will tell you about it.

1. First of all, I recall to your attention the extraordinary fact with which I began. To wit, that the human being, like the immortals, naturally places sexual intercourse far and away above all other joys—yet he has left it out of his heaven! . . .
2. In man's heaven *everybody sings*! . . . it goes on, all day long, and every day, during a stretch of twelve hours. . . .
3. Meantime, *every person* is playing on a harp—those millions and millions!—whereas not more than twenty in the thousand of them could play an instrument in the earth, or ever *wanted* to. . . .

Make a note of it: in man's heaven there are no exercises for the intellect, nothing for it to live upon. It would rot there in a year—rot and stink. Rot and stink—and at that stage become holy. A blessed thing: for only the holy can stand the joys of that bedlam.[99]

Twain also satirized Victorian and Biblical notions of heaven in his story, "Captain Stormfield's Visit to Heaven." It is difficult to do this rollicking story justice, but a few key moments will hopefully suffice. After dying, Stormfield (who believes he is headed for hell) hurdles across empty space for thirty years before arriving at heaven. But, as he unwittingly veered slightly off course, he arrives at the wrong gate for heaven, one intended for sentient beings from another part of the cosmos. After a fair amount of confusion between Stormfield and a heavenly administrator who has never heard of Earth, it comes out that Earth is known as "The Wart." When Stormfield is teleported to his proper gate, he is outfitted with a "harp and a hymn-book, pair of wings and a halo, size No. 13."[100] He soon realizes that these items are provided simply because Christians expect them even though they are of no use, so he says "I just quietly dumped my extra cargo."[101] Soon he begins to worry that he has eternity ahead of him. "This *ain't* just as near my idea of bliss as I thought it was going to be," he confides, "when I used to go to church."[102]

The satire heats up when he becomes a spectator to all the new arrivals to heaven and the ironies their entrances entail.

> For instance, there's a Brooklyn preacher by the name of [Thomas De Witt] Talmage, who is laying up a considerable disappointment for himself. He says every now and then in his sermons, that the first thing he does when he gets to heaven, will be to fling his arms around Abraham, Isaac and Jacob, and kiss them and weep on them. There's millions of people down there on earth that are promising themselves the same thing. . . . If they [Abraham, Isaac and Jacob] were of a mind to allow it, they wouldn't ever have anything to do, year in and year out, but stand up and be hugged and wept on thirty-two hours in the twenty-four.[103]

By contrast, pride of place was given to "a common tailor from Tennessee, by the name of Billings" because he "wrote poetry that Homer and Shakspere [sic] couldn't begin to come up to; but nobody would print it . . . and they laughed at it."[104]

In the last month of his life, Twain penned his final parody of heaven, a hilarious short piece composed for his biographer, Albert Paine, "Etiquette for the Afterlife: Advice to Paine." It includes many gems, from advice against taking St. Peter's photograph since "Hell is full of people who have made that mistake," to "Play no jokes—it isn't the place for humor."[105] It includes, fittingly enough, the recommendation: "Leave your dog outside. Heaven goes by favor. If it went by merit, you would stay out and the dog would go in."[106]

Mark Twain, Cynic, and Humanist

When Mark Twain invoked the spirit of Diogenes in *Innocents Abroad*, he reports the tale as it has often been repeated—that Diogenes is carrying a lantern in daylight while looking for an honest man. As I have argued, honesty or frankness (*parrhesia*) provides the foundation of their sacred profanity. However, unbeknownst to Twain, the Greek text about the episode merely says that Diogenes is searching for a human being (*anthropon*),[107] presumably meaning that he is looking for a real human being.[108] And yet, even when translated this way, Twain has good grounds to hope that Diogenes would still recognize in him the answer to his quest. "I do not represent a country myself," Twain wrote, "but am merely Member at Large for the Human Race."[109] In one sentence, he identifies himself as a real human being and implies that that makes him a citizen of the world. Here, too, he seems connected to Diogenes across the ages, as Diogenes the Cynic appears to be the origin of the word "cosmopolitan." "The question was put to [Diogenes] what countryman he was, and he replied, 'A citizen of the world [*kosmopolitês*].'"[110]

This re-translation of Diogenes brings out one core difference between him and Mark Twain, one that has been lurking in the background—their use of the concept "human." While Diogenes used the term "human being" aspirationally in the sense that most of us do not measure up, Twain used the term critically in the sense that we are far worse than we humans think we are. Nevertheless, even with Twain's satirical view that humanity has devolved rather than evolved, as expressed in his curmudgeonly essay, "The Damned Human Race," he targets the same sort of vices as Diogenes would. In that essay, Twain faults us for being irrational (i.e., being superstitious), for believing we have the "True Religion, several of them" (i.e., hypocrisy), and for our erroneous pride in our "Moral Sense" (i.e., false morality). Plus, he mocks us for being "the only animal who loves his neighbor as himself and cuts his throat if his theology is not straight. He has made a graveyard of the earth in trying to smooth his brother's path to happiness and heaven."[111]

Both men find many vices among us that they wish to eliminate. Diogenes carried a lantern, Twain a looking glass. By the light of Diogenes's lantern, we see that we are not what we believe ourselves to be (human), and by the reflection of Twain's mirror, we likewise see that we are not what we believe ourselves to be (inhuman). In either case, we find that we are in need of purification. But, Diogenes held, ritual purification does not erase vice[112]; Twain would surely agree.[113] For Diogenes and for Twain, only sacred profanity can cleanse us.

CHAPTER THIRTEEN

~

An Epicurean Consideration of Superstitions in Mark Twain and in the Good Life

Jennifer Baker

Pretty soon a spider went crawling up my shoulder, and I flipped it off
and it lit in the candle; and before I could budge it was all shriveled up. I
didn't need anybody to tell me that that was an awful bad sign and would
fetch me some bad luck, so I was scared and most shook the clothes off
of me. I got up and turned around in my tracks three times and crossed
my breast every time; and then I tied up a little lock of my hair with a
thread to keep witches away. But I hadn't no confidence. You do that
when you've lost a horseshoe that you've found, instead of nailing it up
over the door, but I hadn't ever heard anybody say it was any way to keep
off bad luck when you'd killed a spider.

–*Huckleberry Finn*, chapter 1[1]

Mark Twain is not the only writer of a good ghost story. Edgar Allen Poe,
Stephen King, and even Neil Gaiman might edge him out in a contest. But
among our great tellers of spooky tales, it is Twain who deploys them critically. What I want to explore in this chapter is whether Twain, our greatest
satirist, is concerned about tales of superstition in just the way the ancient
Epicureans were. Ghost stories are not the most typical target of social
critics, but surely not even religious critics, trying to keep only approved
ghost stories current, were ever as clear and confident as the Epicureans on
the subject of superstitions. Though we will see that Twain can be found

articulating the Epicurean view in a way that is nearly indistinguishable from its ancient formulation, there is still this large tension in how close he seems to come to their position. He spreads the stories, told rather effectively, himself. At least, if we do not become believers, we take great joy in his telling. It is possible, that by Epicurean lights, Twain may have done more harm than good through his rollicking reports of the haunted houses, ghosts, and the various uses of dead cats.

Our Strange Interest in Frights

To be sure, ethicists do not tend to occupy themselves with the topic of ghost stories these days. On the other hand, psychologists have done ample work on the impact of horror films. *Jaws* is studied far more than Jim's boo hags. Researchers have taken great care in determining that for a portion of us, frightening depictions in media, seen when young, can have long-term impacts. Joanne Cantor and colleagues have surveyed college students, 90 percent of whom report having been very frightened, to the extent the fear lasted longer than the source media. A fourth of these students suggested that they are still experiencing the effects of fear at the time of the survey. (Consequential effects of the fear included things such as needing to sleep with the light on).[2]

And that frights can be consequential for some of us is not the same as knowing why we find ourselves so attracted to them in the first place. And this question seems simpler than one just as relevant to Twain: why we find ourselves so attracted to scaring others. In the rare occasion that questions like these are taken up, the answers on offer seem a bit breezy. The Nobel Prize–winning poet Szymborska, in a review of Hans Christian Andersen, praises Andersen's ability to scare children because it takes "children seriously." She writes that, "his fairy tales, peopled with fantastic creatures, are more realistic than whole tons of today's stories for children, which fret about verisimilitude and avoid wonders like the plague. Andersen had the courage to write stories with unhappy endings. He didn't believe that you should try to be good because it pays (as today's moral tales insistently advertise, though it doesn't necessarily turn out that way in real life), but because evil stems from intellectual and emotional stuntedness and is the one form of poverty that should be shunned."[3]

I don't think Twain could be sold on this explanation. To begin, we certainly are not going to consider the ghost stories in Twain's books as "more realistic" than anything else he describes. No, the stories Jim, Tom, and Huck believe are *unrealistic*. Twain teasingly sets them alongside Aunt Polly's belief in quack medications, but also the teachings of the Bible. (In a letter Twain is said to have sent to a critic he explained that yes his books were too frightening for children, but that he was certain they were not more terrifying than what he had learned in Sunday School.) It's childishness that he associates with religion and ghost stories, not any kind of sophistication or truth-telling.

And Twain's characters, like us, also make various practical uses of superstitions. A supernatural explanation sometimes generates the comfort of a ready explanation, when no other explanation is at hand or when it revises the fewest beliefs. (No matter how many times it takes to find a marble; the trick is said to work once it is found.) A supernatural explanation, similarly, can remove the sting of our own culpability, by turning the focus to a matter of simply failing to abide by easily neglected spirit-world rules. (When tired of treasure-hunting, one might blame witches and ghosts rather than admit to fatigue.) At other times, we frighten others to control them. Tom certainly seems to pull out stories that suit his purposes. (Huck should stay, Tom thinks, and finds his reason: Injun Joe's ghost can't get them if there is a cross nearby!) But our involvement is not just practical and manipulative; we do not just stand outside these particular fears and susceptibilities. Twain makes sure his characters can be seen paying a costly sort of allegiance to superstitions (such as Tom Sawyer deciding he cannot swim, having lost his rattlesnake bracelet). And finally, it is undeniable, and Twain's own work reflects this, a certain pleasure is experienced as we perpetuate scary stories. These are all odd behaviors. Twain knows it. So is he just having a bit of fun along with us, or is he offering a critique of our gullibility?

I cannot answer that particular question authoritatively, but I can investigate whether Twain can be usefully aligned with the anti-ghost story views of some ancient philosophers, virtue ethicists called the Epicureans. The Epicureans focused on the harm done by spooking ourselves and others. They were committed to the idea that ghost stories (and the like) are bad news: bad for society, bad for moral development in particular. Would Twain think they go too far? Or is Epicureanism a decent accompaniment to the Tom Sawyer, Jim, and Huck Finn stories we've learned so well?

To get us started, here is Twain, in his *Autobiography*, providing what can only be called an Epicurean line on death:

> Annihilation has no terrors for me, because I have already tried it
> before I was born—a hundred million years—and I have suffered more in an
> hour, in this life, than I remember to have suffered in the whole
> hundred million years put together. There was a peace, a serenity, an
> absence of all sense of responsibility, an absence of worry, an absence
> of care, grief, perplexity; and the presence of a deep content and
> unbroken satisfaction in that hundred million years of holiday which I
> look back upon with a tender longing and with a grateful desire to
> resume, when the opportunity comes.[4]

Virtue Ethics: Good Sense and Good Morals

Epicureanism is a form a virtue ethics. According to some ancient and contemporary philosophers, virtue is the best way to frame a discussion of ethics. Virtue, philosopher Julia Annas explains, is not a mere inclination. The generous person, if virtuous, "is reliably and habitually generous." Virtue is not a mere habit, however. Not "in the sense in which habits can be mindless." It is instead "a disposition to act, exercised through the agent's practical reasoning. It is a disposition built up as a result of making choices."[5] Virtue is a way a person's character can be developed so that doing the right thing seems like the obvious choice among options. People who manage to be consistently ethical are likely to have developed virtue to some degree. Those who perpetuate actions they know to be immoral and those unwilling to live up to their own stated ideals are likely to have experienced a truncated moral development.

In the loosest sense, Mark Twain is certainly writing about "virtue." As we will see, for us to follow Huck's deliberations as he determines whether to turn in Jim is to see how moral development goes. But it is not likely the author is working with the theoretical account of virtue offered by philosophers.

Virtue ethics is the theoretical explanation of how the right thing to do is determined. A "virtue ethic" tends to account for right action by reference to a description of the virtuous person's psychology. These descriptions are frequently original to each philosopher writing up her view, however. This can make it difficult to generalize about "virtue ethics." To narrow the category down, we can describe the ancient theories of virtue (or traditional accounts of virtue). These accounts can be called "eudaimonist" (in Attic Greek the word means "happiness"; to distinguish it from other senses of happiness we may think of it as "flourishing") as they suggest that we pursue virtue for the sake of being (truly) happy. Such accounts are still being developed today, and of course the original version serves as the source of inspiration for all manner of contemporary virtue ethics.[6]

The ancient tradition in ethics was committed to an understanding of flourishing being our highest good. Many things followed from this determination. We were, as a result, best off if we organized our aims around our longest-term goal: the happiness of our lives as a whole. Yet this would be to react against what we are encouraged to do, which is to focus on shorter-term goals. Power, wealth, fame: these were, the ancients argued, shorter-term goals. They are not resources that could reliably guarantee happiness and so could not, despite what common sense suggested, be candidates for what it is we, ultimately, live for. This was both a matter of our psychology, which would not be satisfied, they found, with any level of, for example, fame, but also a matter of the nature of these goods themselves. They can so easily be taken away. Their care can easily consume us with worry and attention. Once attained, to levels even beyond our expectations, they do not satisfy.

The remedy to this problem was to recognize that there was indeed a most final goal on which we could focus that could help us to include, in a satisfying way, pursuit of other less long-term goods in our lives. If we focused on our most comprehensive and long-term goal, then our commitments to lesser goals would be transformed. We would no longer expect satisfaction to come from just power, wealth, or fame. And this, then, makes their pursuit and attainment less vexing. Once we discover for ourselves this most final end, we will come to understand what true happiness is, and common sense accounts of happiness would be capable of being revised and recognized to be poorly developed. But where does morality come into this description of how we ought to organize our lives?

The ancients determined that our immoral impulses were the result of having goals other than the happiness of our lives as a whole. When we lie, when we steal, when we neglect others: the explanation will be that we were calculating the benefits of doing these things from a less than comprehensive perspective on our lives. The conclusion eudaimonist philosophers came to was that a life lived for the sake of being moral was the best candidate for achieving our most comprehensive and long-term goal: human happiness. Such a life was something with the potential to satisfy one psychologically— once the hard work of becoming committed to such a life is over, at least. And only a life lived for the sake of being moral would transform us in the right ways to make the pursuit of other, and conflicting, goods easier to put into their proper context and to make inevitable losses of any lesser goods easier to bear. The consequence of committing one's self to such a life would be the development of the virtues.

Virtue and Huck

So what *is* a virtue? The ancient virtue theorists we're considering maintained: virtue is the psychological condition we develop and require in order to make choices that are in accord with the value scheme we commit to when in pursuit of our most final end. To give a simple example, think of being left alone before a till of money at the checkout counter, and it being obvious that you could grab a handful of bills without the absent clerk being any the wiser. Many of us might consider taking the money and begin to weigh the consequences of doing so. Others would not even consider taking the money. Those who would not consider taking the money have attained something of virtue. Evidence for this comes from what would happen once the clerk returns, but shortchanges you on your purchase. You would then ask for the correct amount of change back. This shows that money never lost value to you—indeed you will argue with a clerk and pursue your change a moment after you have failed to consider taking money from the till. But money that is stolen has lost value to you. This would be an effect of a commitment to a far longer-term goal than the accumulation of money.

If we practice our commitment to being moral, we will get better at recognizing which norms apply in a moral situation. Furthermore, to make the process of being good easier, it is required that a person have uncomplicated motivation sets. To develop virtue requires that your motivations do not include contradictions that you may not even be aware of. A person who struggles to not steal, though she desperately wants to avoid doing it, has an overly complicated set of motivations with which to contend. Virtue is not assisted by such a condition. In order to function as a virtuous person, one has to attempt to figure out which motivations interfere with doing what one has been able to determine one should do.

As Jonathan Bennett has pointed out in "The Conscience of Huckleberry Finn," Finn is used by Twain to illustrate a predictable conflict we encounter. In Finn's case, when deliberating over whether to turn his friend Jim in, poor social mores conflict with Finn's own concern and sympathy for Jim. Here is how Twain describes this overly complicated set of motivations. Huck has lied to Jim about going to scout around but is actually planning to turn Jim in:

> As I shoved off, [Jim] says: "Pooty soon I'll be a-shout'n for joy, en I'll say, it's all on accounts o' Huck I's a free man. . . . Jim won't ever forget you, Huck; you's de bes' fren' Jim ever had; en you's de only fren' old Jim's got now." I was paddling off, all in a sweat to tell on him; but when he says this, it seemed to kind of take the tuck all out of me. I went along slow then, and I warn't right down certain whether I was glad I started or whether I warn't. When I was fifty yards off, Jim says: "Dah you goes, de ole true Huck; de on'y white genlman dat ever kep' his promise to ole Jim." Well, I just felt sick. But I says, I got to do it—I can't get out of it.[7]

When asked if the person on the raft is white or black, Finn explains "I didn't answer up prompt. I tried to, but the words wouldn't come. I tried, for a second or two, to brace up and out with it, but I warn't man enough—hadn't the spunk of a rabbit. I see I was weakening; so I just give up trying, and up and says: 'He's white.'"[8]

Bennett points out that some explanations of this episode are too strong. It is not the case that "Huck suffers 'excruciating moments of wavering between honesty and respectability.'" Bennett says, "that is hopelessly wrong" and instead maintains that "The conflict waged in Huck is much more serious: he scarcely cares for respectability and never hesitates to relinquish it, but he does care for honesty and gratitude—and both honesty and gratitude require that he should give Jim up."[9]

Bennett insists (quoting another scholar) that instead it is the following that is "precisely correct": "It is not, in Huck, honesty at war with respectability but love and compassion for Jim struggling against his conscience. His decision is for Jim and hell; a right decision made in the mental chains that Huck never breaks. His concern for Jim is and remains irrational. Huck finds many reasons for giving Jim up and none for stealing him. To the end Huck sees his compassion for Jim as a weak, ignorant, and wicked felony."[10] The "reasons" Huck has are only on "one side of the conflict.—'It hadn't ever come home to me before what I was doing'—'I tried to make out that I warn't to blame'—'Conscience said "But you knowed . . . "'—I couldn't get around that'—'What had poor Miss Watson done to you?'—'This is what comes of my not thinking'—'. . . children that belonged to a man I didn't even know.'" Bennett explains that "On the other side, the side of feeling, we get nothing like that. When Jim rejoices in Huck as his only friend, Huck doesn't consider the claims of friendship or have the situation 'come home' to him in a different light."[11]

Bennett applauds Huck's "checking of one's principles in the light of one's sympathies. This is sometimes a pretty straightforward matter. It can happen that a certain moral principle becomes untenable—meaning literally that one cannot hold it any longer—because it conflicts intolerably with the pity or revulsion or whatever that one feels when one sees what the principle leads to. One's experience may play a large part here: experiences evoke feelings, and feelings force one to modify principles."[12]

Yet Bennett himself is not a virtue ethicist, and virtue ethicists would have an additional diagnosis and would also predict the moral malaise that Huck confesses to. Virtue ethicists would argue that Huck is bound to be confused by conventional morality because he has not been told that virtue requires us to endorse only parts of what we pick up from the culture, and it requires that parts be soundly rejected.

In other words, in a slave-holding culture, Huck is on the path to virtue for recognizing that, "It don't make no difference whether you do right or wrong, a person's conscience ain't got no sense, and just goes for him anyway. If I had a yaller dog that didn't know no more than a person's conscience does, I would pison him. It takes up more room than all the rest of a person's insides, and yet ain't no good, nohow."[13] Without virtue, it *don't* make no difference.

Eudaimonists argue that virtue has an intellectual, a dispositional, and an affective component.[14] When these components are described separately, virtue can seem an abstract and theoretical ideal, but we can recognize the effect of the conjunction of these components in the example I have given. The intellectual component of virtue is a matter of knowing the money is not yours, that you do not yourself expect to be taken advantage of, and perhaps that the economic system as it exists tends to function well enough to warrant your endorsement. You would, in other words, be able to explain why stealing is wrong. Virtue ethics does not require that your explanation be technical. Instead, it could be just as I have described it. Of course, Huck, not seeing any good reason to pay for a circus ticket if it can be avoided, is not there yet.

Huck does, however, display signs of having developed dispositions that might count as contributing to some future virtue. The dispositional component of virtue is a matter of how a propensity not to steal has become second nature to you. You tend not to steal. If you steal in other contexts, and not taking the money in this case was an exception, then your character is not virtuous. In order to develop a virtuous disposition you must work on developing the intellectual and affective components of virtue. You must attempt to relate your beliefs about stealing being wrong to your other claims and understanding about ethics, and you must work at internalizing the coherent account that emerges so that you no longer find yourself attracted to bad behavior. Huck, of course, has the disposition to steal but lacks the disposition to turn in Jim.

There is one last component of virtue: the affective. This is a matter of your not thinking that, when you act rightly, you have given up on some guaranteed pleasure. People who have made themselves good do not regret money they have not stolen, for example, and they do not see vicious people as having made choices of which they could be envious. Huck shows signs of this kind of independence. For example, Twain is teasing us when writing that Huck lacks the courage of a rabbit for betraying his slave-owning society. Huck is not weak for doing the right thing, even though he thinks it is the wrong thing and he's going to hell for it. A virtue ethicist would see the culture's morality as a sham and his resoluteness as a strength.

You must be wondering when we will get back to the ghosts? Right now, then.

Ghosts and False Beliefs

Here is Twain addressing the impact of superstition directly:

> When even the brightest mind in our world has been trained up from child-
> hood in a superstition of any kind, it will never be possible for that mind, in
> its maturity, to examine sincerely, dispassionately, and conscientiously any evi-
> dence or any circumstance which shall seem to cast a doubt upon the validity
> of that superstition. I doubt if I could do it myself.[15]

There is one type of virtue ethics that would strenuously recommend against
telling any child—or any adult primed to be afraid—a ghost story. This
would be the Epicureans.[16] The Epicureans believed that we can never come
to be happy (or have virtue) until we remove false beliefs. This is so crucial
because with false beliefs come false desires, and these distract us from aiming
for what would actually satisfy us. Of course Epicureans do not focus equally
on all false beliefs. They focus on the main ones, or the ones that are going to
interfere with happiness (the proper human end) most of all. The main false
belief we nourish and maintain? The one with the harshest consequences?
The one that we pass on to every child we tell a ghost story to? It is that we
should be terrified of death. That we should be terrified is, the Epicureans are
going to argue, false. Importantly false. We should feel no terror at death nor
at anything else that is inevitable.

This falseness of this belief—that death requires great fear—has an impact the Epicureans regard as painful. We long for immortality and suspect
boo hags are hiding in closets. None of this is the proper way to live nor the
proper kind of pleasure. Epicurus in the *Letter to Menoeceus* explains that we
need philosophy to "drive out those beliefs from which the greatest upheaval
seizes the soul."[17] The Epicurean poet Lucretius insists that the "fear which
shakes human life at its very foundations, covering everything over with the
blackness of death, and which does not leave any pleasure fluid and pure"
must be "hurled out headlong."[18]

What the Epicureans think signals mental distress are what can be regarded as rather conventional behaviors, it is true. To an Epicurean, people
rushing about after all sorts of objects of desire—wealth, luxury, power, love,
and, above all, immortal life—are frantic not because these ends are so
valuable. They are frantic as a result of the irrational fears they have been
brought up believing. The central cause of unhappiness is the idea that we
must constantly struggle to pursue ends that are in no way final. In Twain,
the Shepherdsons and the Grangerfords, feuding for no reason and going to

church with their guns, well illustrates the syndrome. This might be the best-known Epicurean description: "Here's a man who often goes outside, leaving his house, because he's tired of being home. Just as suddenly he turns back, since he feels no better outdoors. He rushes off in haste to his country house, bringing his slaves, as if the house were burning down and he had to bring help; he turns back again, as soon as he touches the threshold; or, heavy, he seeks forgetfulness in sleep; or, full of haste, he charges back to the city. Thus each person flees himself. But in spite of all his efforts he clings to that self, which we know he never can succeed in escaping, and hates it all because he is sick and does not know the cause of his sickness."[19] As Martha Nussbaum puts it in her magisterial *The Therapy of Desire: Theory and Practice in Hellenistic Ethics* (on the Stoics and the Epicureans), "The greedy accumulation of wealth makes its possessor feel further from death, since poverty seems to be a slipping toward death. The same can be said for the 'blind lust for honors and power' in which people pursue an immortality of reputation. These two passions, in their turn, cause many criminal acts, ruptures in families, enviousness of others, betrayals of friendship, betrayals of civic duty. This bad behavior is in many cases not accompanied by a subjective awareness of fear." She continues to explain that another result of not being Epicurean in one's outlook is "a kind of aimless and restless frenetic activity that has no point at all, other than the avoidance of one's own self and one's own finite condition: If only human beings, just as they seem to feel a weight in their minds that wears them out with its heaviness, could also grasp the causes of this and know from what origin such a great mountain of ill stands on their chest, they would hardly lead their lives as we now often see them do, ignorant of what they really want, and always seeking a change of place as if they could put down their burden."[20]

And yet there is an Epicurean solution: remove the false beliefs and one's desires will become natural and easily satisfied. Life will become full of pleasures: the simple ones. Some desires the Epicureans count as natural. We need food and drink and shelter. Friends matter. The challenge is to reject the desires that are empty, the results of just our upbringing. Superstitions are the very most dangerous of these. The Epicureans have many reasons for thinking so. They seem to be certain that we get softened up for later irrationality and mental subservience by being fed tall tales as youngsters. We get accustomed to reacting to imaginary things and get ourselves into tizzies. Or as Twain illustrates:

'Fraid to live!—why, I was that scared I dasn't hardly go to bed, or get up, or lay down, or set down, Sister Ridgeway. Why, they'd steal the very—why, goodness sakes, you can guess what kind of a fluster I was in by the time midnight come last night. I hope to gracious if I warn't afraid they'd steal some o' the family! I was just to that pass I didn't have no reasoning faculties no more. It looks foolish enough now, in the daytime; but I says to myself, there's my two poor boys asleep, 'way up stairs in that lonesome room, and I declare to goodness I was that uneasy 't I crep' up there and locked 'em in! I did. And anybody would. Because, you know, when you get scared that way, and it keeps running on, and getting worse and worse all the time, and your wits gets to addling, and you get to doing all sorts o' wild things, and by and by you think to yourself, spos'n I was a boy, and was away up there, and the door ain't locked, and you—[21]

We also get accustomed to *others'* reactions to imaginary things. Seeing the power of a false story gives us the wrong kinds of incentives. Think of how cruel it was for Huck to trick Jim with the snake, or of Huck and Tom making a witch-pie-making game out of Jim's freedom, or of Tom's general insensitivity due to his ability to stay a bit removed from the tales he tells. The Epicureans insist, instead, that ethics is not consistent with manipulation. Life is simple, too simple for such machinations to be necessary. And to refine the thesis: nothing good, the Epicureans and (often enough) Twain, too, insist, can come from the master-manipulation those in the religion business provide.

Do the complaints sound familiar? We may be unable to detect Twain's own final view, unsure as we are where the satire ends, but Finn himself seems to hew to a philosophy we could call "Epicurean." Begging Tom to keep the money from him, Finn explains why he is not going to be happy living like everyone else does:

I ain't everybody, and I can't *stand* it. It's awful to be tied up so. And grub comes too easy—I don't take no interest in vittles, that way. I got to ask to go a-fishing; I got to ask to go in a-swimming—dern'd if I hain't got to ask to do everything. Well, I'd got to talk so nice it wasn't no comfort—I'd got to go up in the attic and rip out awhile, every day, to git a taste in my mouth, or I'd a died, Tom. The widder wouldn't let me smoke; she wouldn't let me yell, she wouldn't let me gape, nor stretch, nor scratch, before folks—[Then with a spasm of special irritation and injury]—And dad fetch it, she prayed all the time! I never see such a woman! I *had* to shove, Tom—I just had to. And besides, that school's going to open, and I'd a had to go to it—well, I wouldn't stand *that*, Tom. Looky-here, Tom, being rich ain't what it's cracked up to be. It's just worry and worry, and sweat and sweat, and a-wishing you was dead all the time. Now these clothes suits me, and this bar'l suits me, and I ain't ever going to shake 'em any more. Tom, I wouldn't ever got into all this trouble if it hadn't 'a' ben for that money; now you just take my sheer of it along with your'n, and gimme a ten-center sometimes—not many times, becuz I don't give a dern for a thing 'thout it's tollable hard to git—and you go and beg off for me with the widder.[22]

Can't we imagine Finn pondering over an Epicurean thought like this? Thanks to blessed Nature, because she has made the necessary things easy to procure, and the things difficult to procure she has made unnecessary! And to the extent Huck is a rather sympathetic character, we might at least be able to recognize that Twain has a certain sympathy for the Epicureans themselves.

As Finn puzzles over the rationale for the trickery of the Duke and King and the heated vengeance of those who punish them, as he refuses to succumb to the "civilized" manners of the day, he represents an Epicurean fairly well. Even his final note of regret for ever getting involved in this book-writing project in the first place is pitch-perfect, as the Epicureans told us that, preferable to getting involved in the back and forth of politics, we should "stay home and wear a warm hat." Huck won't want to stay home of course, but we get the sense that for Huck, post-story, the simple pleasures are what he will pursue and appreciate—at least for a while until that civilization catches up to him.

Mark Twain's Culpability in Scaring Children

There is one last tension to note. If Twain has such friendly feelings toward the Epicurean view, why would he be writing as he does? Other historical writers, like Tom Paine, for example, have been committed to dispelling myths and encouraging rationality in all things—you won't find that he authored a set of ghost stories. It is the nature of satire to promote what it also critiques, it seems. Though you would think Epicureans might be good at taking a joke, I think in this case they would not. It is a lot of trouble to write a book, as Finn attests, and you want it to be for the good. Twain makes tall tale-telling and Sunday School–shirking seem so enviously glamorous and high-falutin, his stories are just so darn enjoyable, that I believe the Epicureans would accuse him of working at cross-purposes. He gets us to enjoy the wrong things, and it just isn't natural.

~

CHAPTER FOURTEEN

Moral Value and Moral Psychology in Twain's "Carnival of Crime"

Frank Boardman

Mark Twain's short story "The Facts Concerning the Recent Carnival of Crime in Connecticut" (hereafter "Carnival") is, above all, funny. In a moment, we'll be probing the work for its philosophical significance. But as the humor of the story is integral to this project, and because our conversation will drain some of the fun out of the story, I have to insist that—if you have not already done so—you put down this volume and read "Carnival" for yourself.

The "Facts"

The story itself has five crucial movements that fit together like an unfolding joke:

1. *The title:* A good deal of the humor of the story comes from the seeming incongruity of the title and the main body of the text. It is not until the very end that we come to understand how it is that we're reading a description of "facts concerning" a "recent carnival of crime."
2. *The set-up:* A New England writer of some renown—Twain very likely had himself in mind—happily looks forward to a favorite aunt's arrival. The narrator mentions how happy he is to no longer be pained by his conscience over his smoking habit, even when this favorite aunt brings it up.

3. *The abrupt introduction of the fantastic:* He's so happy that he says to himself, "If my most pitiless enemy could appear before me at this moment, I would freely right any wrongs I may have done him." And so his "most pitiless enemy" appears at his door. It is his conscience made manifest. We learn later that the better (i.e., the more noble, virtuous, moral and given to pangs of guilt) a person is, the larger and more robust a person's conscience will be. The narrator's conscience is "a shabby dwarf" with "a vague, general, evenly blended, nicely adjusted deformity." The narrator tries right away to kill his conscience, but being too light (following our "light conscience" expression) he is too quick and nimble to be caught. The conscience preys upon the narrator, taking great pleasure in reminding him of his past moral crimes. We learn in the process that the conscience has overplayed his hand on a few vices (like smoking) to which the narrator has become callous and unmoved by reproach. When the narrator thinks about these vices or someone upbraids him for them, the conscience becomes drowsy and falls asleep.

4. *The resolution:* The aunt arrives and quickly chastises the narrator for some broken promises and failures to help others in need. These things still have the power to arouse the narrator's guilt, and his conscience (which is invisible to the aunt) grows heavy and falls from his perch. The narrator sees his chance and lunges at his conscience. When his behavior frightens his aunt, he attributes it to his smoking. Thus, the aunt berates him for smoking, he feels nothing, and his conscience falls asleep. He then kills his conscience and joyously casts out his aunt.

5. *The punch line:* The narrator describes killing thirty-eight people in two weeks, settling old scores, burning buildings, cheating widows and orphans, and killing "assorted tramps" to sell their bodies to medical colleges. We thus finally come to the "carnival of crime" this whole story has been explaining.

A few more details of the story will be especially pertinent to our discussion later on. First, the narrator's conscience is presented as a tormentor and oppressor even before it is made flesh. He is happy and free to the extent that he can overcome it. And his conscience is not something he can control, either physically or psychologically. Once he realizes that a heavy heart would make the conscience heavy as well—and therefore catchable—he laments that he cannot lament his desire to kill in that moment. "I could no more be heavy-hearted over such a desire," he says to himself, "than I could have sorrowed over its accomplishment. So I could only look longingly up at my master, and rave at the ill luck that denied me a heavy conscience the one only time that I had ever wanted such a thing in my life."[1]

Second, pangs of conscience are unavoidable. When discussing his various responses to begging "tramps" at his door, it is clear that his conscience bothers him no matter what he does. It may well be that there are circumstances that compel us to choose among a number of bad actions, and so our consciences *should* be aroused no matter what. But these situations are the exceptions. If a conscience is to be at all useful, it should help us learn from our moral errors. And we cannot learn what is an error and what isn't if we are punished for vice and virtue alike. Yet in "Carnival", a painful conscience doesn't track vice, nor does its absence track virtue. It just assaults us. In one significant passage, the narrator asks his conscience why they torture us over and over, well after we've likely learned whatever lesson we need. The Conscience replies:

"Well, WE like it; that suffices."

"Do you do it with the honest intent to improve a man?"

That question produced a sarcastic smile and this reply:

"No, sir. Excuse me. We do it simply because it is 'business.' It is our trade. The purpose of it is to improve the man, but we are merely disinterested agents. We are appointed by authority, and haven't anything to say in the matter."[2]

Nothing substantive is asked or offered about this "authority." We are left to imagine, if we like, who or what is meant by it.

Third (and finally), recall the recurring discussion of "tramps" and the narrator's treatment of them. The first thing the conscience uses (once it has taken physical form) to attack the narrator is the fact that the narrator had lied to a vagrant that morning, telling him that he had no food to offer and his cook was away. Before his liberation, the narrator laments his guilt over every response to vagrants. Afterward, they become his primary—or at least most numerous—victims. Twain wrote and first presented "Carnival" early in 1876, in the very middle of the "long depression" following the Panic of 1873. Unemployment was extraordinarily high and vagrancy common, especially in Twain's New England. These issues were a constant concern of Twain's. Generally, the plight of the poor (which he himself was occasionally in danger of becoming) was for Twain of enormous moral and political significance.

The "Exasperating Metaphysical Question"

Twain wrote "Carnival" for *The Atlantic Monthly*, which was edited at the time by W. D. Howells, a friend with whom Twain frequently corresponded. Twain first mentioned "Carnival" in a letter to Howells on January 11, 1876, where he described his intention to read a draft of it to The Monday Evening Club, a group that met regularly in Hartford to hear one another's works. It is worth noting that the usual fare at these meetings was political or philosophical nonfiction. Even Twain's contributions to that point had been tracts on press freedoms and universal suffrage. To Howells, Twain wrote of "Carnival": "I shall put in one more day's polishing on it, & then read it before our Club, which is to meet at our house Monday evening the 24th inst. I think it will bring out considerable discussion among the gentlemen of the Club—though the title of the article will not give them much notion of what is to follow—this title being 'The *Facts* Concerning the Recent Carnival of Crime in Connecticut.'"[3] By the eighteenth, Twain was feeling even more ebullient about "Carnival", and wrote Howells again to invite him to attend the club meeting. In that letter, he writes "I can always work after I've been to your house; & if you will come to mine, now, & hear the club toot their various horns over the exasperating metaphysical question which I mean to lay before them in the disguise of a literary extravaganza, it would just brace you up like a cordial."[4]

Howells was unable to attend, but the club, according to Twain biographer Albert Bigelow Paine, "was deeply impressed by the little fictional sermon. One of its ministerial members offered his pulpit for the next Sunday if Mark Twain would deliver it to his congregation."[5] It was published in the *Atlantic* and was generally well-received and regarded at the time, though it has not found its way into the canon of Twain's most well-known works. Howells himself became something of a champion of it and years later wrote that it "ought to have won popular recognition of the ethical intelligence underlying [Twain's] humor. It was, of course, funny; but under the fun it was an impassioned study of the human conscience."[6]

Perhaps "Carnival" has not achieved the long-lasting fame of some of Twain's other works in part because of the intensity of that "ethical intelligence" and the difficulty the reader has in working through that "exasperating metaphysical question." There is clearly something significant going on in "Carnival", though it is very difficult to pin down.

So what exactly is the question that "Carnival" presents? Whatever it is, it's a question about morality, and specifically our feelings and attitudes toward it—as these are what is principally at stake in the story. But the question is not about which actions are right and which wrong or about which things tend to arouse our consciences. With this fantastic little tale, Twain is attempting to say something about the nature of morality or about the nature of our feelings about our own moral worth—perhaps both. Whatever the case, there is clearly a substantive philosophical issue in play here. Let's then turn to two plausible candidates for the kind of thing Twain has in mind.

Moral Value and Psychology: Nietzsche and Hume

Moral theories come in many varieties. Some seek to identify the principles by which we ought to act. These theories may proclaim that actions are right or wrong depending on their propensity to promote happiness, inculcate virtue, or respect persons. These theories are often denoted as normative ethical theories. Other theories, which are often called "metaethical" theories, instead dig deeper, inquiring about the very meaning of moral terms and whether there can be such a thing as moral truths. Regardless, nearly all of these approaches grant that morality—whatever it is—is a good thing. But one can reasonably ask, "Is morality a good thing for us?" or "Are the commands of morality something we ought to respect?" We might call theories that address these types of questions "valuation" theories. Finally, we might note that some theories don't concern themselves with moral values at all but instead look to the psychological processes by which we discover or create them. These theories more or less fall under what we call "moral psychology." Of course, any robust moral theory will address these various questions to some extent, but it is worth noting that an inquiry into morality and moral values can lead down several paths. These divisions are not always very distinct. It is often difficult (and perhaps not all that necessary) to say which category or categories a given theory fits into. And the answer to one set of questions will often have implications for answers to others. Still, it will be valuable to have these broad categories in mind when we consider just exactly what is going on in "Carnival".

The first theory we should consider falls squarely into the "valuation" category and perhaps secondarily into metaethics and moral psychology. This is the famous—perhaps infamous—moral theory of Friedrich Nietzsche. Nietzsche often wrote in a bold, literary style, often aphoristically, and sometimes through allegorical fictions. Interpretations of Nietzsche are as various as they are plentiful. We'll focus here on one of his clearer statements, found in his *On the Genealogy of Morality*. In the *Genealogy*, Nietzsche has a clear project, method, and purpose. The project is a critique of moral values—specifically to provide a negative valuation of those values. The method is genealogical, a kind of history in the form of the conditions that must have been necessary for the emergence and acceptance of these moral values. The purpose is to lay the foundation for a revaluation of all values and the emergence of a new kind of person, an "Overman" who is (to borrow the title of another of Nietzsche's works) *beyond good and evil.*

On Nietzsche's telling, a pre-moral order privileged strength and power. Those who had them preyed on the weak according to their whims and desires. As they were in this position of power, they took the right to name themselves "good" and the others (the weak) "bad." Morality, then, is what emerges from the inversion of these values wherein the "bad" become the "good" and the "good" become "evil." This for Nietzsche is "the beginning, the true *deed* in the conception of a slave morality."[7] Under this "slave morality," the strength that once proved the goodness of the powerful was seen as vicious, and the weakness of the other perceived as virtuous. No longer was strength revered. Instead it was moral to be humble and meek. One key to this inversion of values, Nietzsche thinks, is the lie that power could be latent and unexpressed. Under the sway of this lie, not expressing power, which was once a weakness, can now be taken as a form of strength, a *moral* goodness. The leading idea for us seems to be that the lie can fall away once we see it for what it is and recognize it in its many forms (religion, democracy, and moralism, to name a few).

The second position comes from Hume, and is (for our purposes anyway) best thought of foremost as a theory in moral psychology, though it has clear metaethical implications as well. On Hume's account, morality comes from—in a sense just *is*—our moral feelings or sentiments rather than something we discover through reason. Two of Hume's arguments for this claim deserve particular attention here. We can summarize the first one this way:

1. Reason alone cannot influence actions and affections.
2. Morals have a direct influence on actions and affections.

Therefore,

3. Reason alone cannot distinguish between good and evil.[8]

The two premises require a bit more discussion. First, reason is of itself inert regarding our actions and affections. Reason can alert us to the existence of something that then arouses a passion, as when we come to desire French fries once we learn that a particular restaurant has them. And reason can guide us toward an end by discovering series of causes and effects, as when we order French fries in order to receive them. But reason alone does not have the power to make us want the fries or to order them. Only our sentiments can actually drive us in these ways. Second, morality alone influences our actions and affections. We sometimes act or fail to act just because we think it the right thing to do, and we readily judge others and their actions only on moral grounds.

The second argument is a bit simpler and perhaps a bit stronger. This is the key premise: "If the thought and understanding were alone capable of fixing the boundaries of right and wrong, the character of virtuous and vicious either must lie in some relations of objects, or must be a matter of fact, which is discovered by our reasoning."[9] Hume's argument for this claim is that discovering relations and discovering matters of fact (i.e., facts of the world independent of our ideas) are the only two functions of the understanding. So if he can show that right and wrong are not determined strictly in either of these ways, then he will have shown that they are not determined through the understanding.

To accomplish this, Hume provides two cases: the oak tree and the willful murder. We can all agree that except in extraordinary circumstances, killing a parent is among the worst things a person can do. Hume thinks of this as an extreme form or manifestation of ingratitude, but this seems hardly to cover the evil of it. So think of the relations involved in this act: *x gives life to y* and *y ends the life of x* seem to be the critical ones. And yet these relations are satisfied equally well by oak trees in the normal course of things. An oak tree drops an acorn which becomes another oak that eventually overshadows and therefore kills the first tree. True, there is nothing willful about what the oak tree does, but (at least in Hume's view) the will of the human parent-murderer only *explains* the critical relations entered into but does not *determine* a new relation. So virtue and vice do not lie in particular relations, nor does making a moral judgment amount to recognizing such relations.

The willful murder case, then, demonstrates that virtue and vice cannot be discovered by attending strictly to matters of fact. Imagine the description of a killing from the perspective of pure science. An examination of all of the physical facts will show at one level of observation the motions of bodies and the ending of certain anatomical processes. On another sort of observation, we just have the interactions of atoms. But at no point does a dispassionate observation of matters of fact yield anything like a judgment of the wrongness or viciousness of the act of killing.

So Hume concludes that virtue and vice, good and evil are not discovered by reason but are instead the products of our feelings. Ultimately, to say "such and such was wrong" is to express our negative attitude toward it, and this attitude is born of the pain or discomfort it causes us. As Hume says, "when you pronounce any action or character to be vicious, you mean nothing, but that from the constitution of your nature you have a feeling or sentiment of blame from the contemplation of it."[10] Crucially, this is not to say that morality is somehow counterfeit or moral judgments ill-formed or incorrect. Indeed, some virtues (benevolence, generosity, sympathy) are "natural" in the sense that they are simply part of our constitution, and their lack is a significant defect of feeling to which we're naturally inclined. Other virtues (justice, for instance) are more artificial, but still their lack may speak to a kind of social failing.

Nietzsche and Hume in "Carnival"

The descriptions in the last section of Nietzsche's and Hume's positions were cursory and short on any number of important nuances and details. But they will suffice, I hope, to allow us to reconsider "Carnival" and its "exasperating metaphysical question."

In the Nietzschean interpretation, "Carnival" is a story about the birth of the Overman, at least insofar as he shrugs off the shackles of our given morality and rises above good and evil. By subduing, conquering, and ultimately killing his conscience, the narrator takes for himself the right to revalue all values. His new valuation of moral values is not merely negative but entirely dismissive. The narrator is free, finally, to act solely on whim and desire.

Just as Nietzsche hopes that the key moment in re-valuing moral values will be recognizing their duplicitous and untoward origins, the key moment for the narrator is seeing his conscience made flesh. In that moment, he sees it for what it is, not a worthy guide to his improvement but a sadistic encumbrance and an enemy to his freedom. In fact, the story itself is a continuous re-valuation of values, slowly undoing the psychological bonds built by the kind of "slave revolt in morality" that Nietzsche describes. Morally oriented members of the community are degraded to pathetic victims of their mighty consciences. The once-lauded aunt is reduced to a hysterical relic of an antiquated moral age. And horrific moral crimes are reduced to joyful expressions of freedom and entrepreneurship.

In the Humean interpretation: "Carnival" is akin to a narrative restatement of the two main arguments Hume makes for the claim that morality is ultimately a product of our emotions. First, at no point does the conscience appeal to the narrator's reason in order to compel him to be moral. More to the point, once the conscience is destroyed, nothing is lost to the narrator in the way of understanding or rational capacity. What is lost is a particular source of feeling and with it all motivation to act morally. What's more, there cease to be any moral facts for the narrator once he no longer feels pain at doing what was wrong or pleasure at doing what was right. Once he'd divested of moral feeling, he is incapable of acting morally. Especially in his final speech to his aunt, it is clear that he is able to reason to what the moral thing *would* be, but that reason is causally inert vis-à-vis his actions once he's freed himself from the moral feeling his conscience once provided.

Second, "Carnival" provides lessons similar to those of Hume's oak tree and willful murder cases. The relations between the narrator and his aunt when he verbally abuses her are the same as those that hold between his conscience and him. The killing of local enemies and vagrants looks just like the killing of his conscience. And—at least from his unfeeling perspective—there is no wrongness to be found just in the act of verbal abuse or even killing. If we the readers are outraged by the narrator's treatment of the aunt or by his killing other people, it is only because we're still given to the sorts of feelings from which the narrator freed himself.

Neither and Both

"Carnival" predates Nietzsche's *Genealogy* by a decade, and there is no evidence (that I know of) that Twain ever read Hume. But no one is claiming or should claim that Twain had the entirety of either philosopher's views in mind here. The question is rather to what extent "Carnival" presents a fundamentally Nietzchean and/or Humean view, or even is able to provide insight into these different approaches to moral theory.

In order to better evaluate these interpretations, let's consider a few criteria. First, a good philosophical interpretation of "Carnival" must account for the moral, psychological, and metaphysical significance of the story—taking into account both the content of the story itself and the scant comments we have from Twain about it. One way to do that is to treat "Carnival" as contributing to both metaethics and moral psychology. The Nietzschean interpretation achieves this by connecting both the metaethical and psychological questions to the question of the value of moral values. Morality turns out to be a set of values imposed upon us in part via our psychologically internalizing them and from which we can escape by conquering and doing away with those psychological bonds. On the Humean interpretation, moral psychology is primary, and while we may not get anything like a complete account here of what morality is, we can rule out theories on which moral values attach to actions regardless of our attitudes toward them.

A second criterion for a good interpretation is that it helps explain the three important details of the story that we discussed earlier. The Nietzschean interpretation quite easily explains the fact that conscience is for the narrator always a bad thing and never under his control: Conscience is a bad thing for us because morality is a bad thing for us, and it is as uncontrollable as any lie with which we live. In the Humean interpretation, the conscience provides feelings, and feelings are not given to direction and command the way that reason at least can be. And his conscience is an enemy to the narrator from the beginning because he lacks a strong moral feeling—recall how dwarfish and malformed his conscience is. Perhaps, were he a better person, he would achieve some pleasure from doing the morally right thing, a pleasure that would at least balance the pain inflicted by his conscience.

Next, there is the fact that pangs of conscience are unavoidable for the narrator—they seem to come no matter what he does. In both interpretations, this can be read as a point about the location of moral value. Pangs of conscience do not track particular actions or action-types because morality is not determined solely by actions or action-types. There will be slightly different answers, however, to the related question of just who or what is the "authority" on which the conscience carries out his tortures. In the Nietzschean view, it is the authority invested in the great lie of moral values. In the Humean view, it is that function of human nature that determines moral feeling. So according to the former, killing the conscience is the final step in seeing morality for what it is. And in the latter, that killing is a final step toward a very odd (and perhaps deviant) way of feeling.

Lastly, we should step back a bit and ask how these interpretations would handle the apparent disparity between the narrator and Twain himself, especially in their attitudes toward the victims of the long depression. Now of course, we don't always (or even usually) have to ask about the differences between narrators and authors of fictions. Lots of stories are written first-personally from the perspective of fictional characters obviously not meant to be the author. But that is not so obvious in "Carnival". The narrator shares with Twain a number of important characteristics. They are both well-known New England writers, for instance. Paine goes so far as to call "Carnival" "autobiographical, a setting-down of the author's daily self-chidings."[11] This may be a bit of an exaggeration, but there is clearly good reason to think that the narrator is a fictionalized version of Twain. So why, then, doesn't this fictionalized version share Twain's attitudes toward the vagrants with whom he comes into contact? And why would Twain choose an issue about which he had such deep feeling and concern? In the Nietzschean interpretation, the story is a kind of wish fulfilment fantasy. Twain writes about an issue of deep moral concern to him because it is just that sort of concern from which he would like to be free. In the Humean interpretation, Twain makes these choices to most starkly bring out the significance of his own feelings to his moral judgments. If he would, once his moral feeling is gone, do the sorts of things he could least imagine doing now, then it must be those feelings that are determinative of the fact that he shouldn't and wouldn't actually do them.

So both interpretations satisfy some key criteria. Still, there are plenty of reasons to doubt them both. Chief among these may be that both interpretations assume too much about how we are supposed to think and feel about the narrator throughout and especially by the end of the story. That is to say, it is far from clear how Twain means to value morality here, even if the Nietzschean interpretation is correct that such values are in question. That is to say, even if Twain gives us—or fictionally makes of himself——a kind of Overman, is he actually advocating for such a creation? Similarly, even if "Carnival" presents a kind of Humean point via the narrator's moral obligations evaporating along with his moral feeling, is such a view being endorsed or lampooned? We should notice, for instance, just how outrageous his moral crimes seem to us at the end. It is, in fact, largely our horror at them that makes the whole thing funny. It is most likely that that Twain had both of these sorts of questions in mind. What remains remarkable about "Carnival"—in addition to its humor—is what a nuanced and sophisticated treatment of these "exasperating metaphysical" questions it contains.

∾

CHAPTER FIFTEEN

Making the Heart Grow Fonder

Twain, Psychical Distance, and Aesthetic Experience

Jeffrey Dueck

While Mark Twain is most well-known for novels like *Adventures of Huckleberry Finn* and *The Adventures of Tom Sawyer*, his 1883 travelogue *Life on the Mississippi* provides rich insight into his extraliterary background and the events and experiences that shaped his view of the world. In the middle of his prodigious writing career, Twain published *Life on the Mississippi* as a reflection on his lifetime love affair with the river and his work as a steamboat pilot. While the book serves primarily as a memoir, Twain's writing also reveals important philosophical issues along the way. The significance of memory and history, the meaning and interpretation of nature, and his observations about the development of American society are all treated with wit and insight. And one of the most personal—and simultaneously philosophical—concepts that rises to the surface of the work is the challenge we face in maintaining awe and wonder in the midst of our day-to-day experiences.

Throughout *Life on the Mississippi*, Twain reflects on the evolution of his experience with the river. From times of enchantment and wonder, to observations of flora and fauna, to the river's place amid the unfolding of home and country after the Civil War, Twain artfully reveals the tensions inherent in the relationship between description and interpretation. In doing so, he provides a glimpse into the very nature and value of aesthetic experience. In one passage in particular, Twain raises a poignant example that confronts this important philosophical theme, as he muses about his experience of the river and its significance to him as he transitions from awe and wonder to professional and practical concern. While he celebrates the knowledge he has gained in navigating the river as a pilot, he pines for the days when its beauty and majesty entranced him in aesthetic wonder:

> The face of the water, in time, became a wonderful book—a book that was a dead language to the uneducated passenger, but which told its mind to me without reserve, delivering its most cherished secrets as clearly as if it uttered them with a voice. . . . In truth, the passenger who could not read this book saw nothing but all manner of pretty pictures in it painted by the sun and shaded by the clouds, whereas to the trained eye these were not pictures at all, but the grimmest and most dead-earnest of reading-matter. . . . Now when I had mastered the language of this water and had come to know every trifling feature that bordered the great river as familiarly as I knew the letters of the alphabet, I had made a valuable acquisition. But I had lost something, too. I had lost something which could never be restored to me while I lived. All the grace, the beauty, the poetry had gone out of the majestic river![1]

Later in the same passage, Twain ponders the life of the physician whose professional path has led him beyond the beauty and charm of a woman's face and, instead, to consider her as a case for medical treatment. Romance, attraction, and amazement are trodden under the practical considerations of an occupation. He concludes, "And doesn't he sometimes wonder whether he has gained most or lost most by learning his trade?"[2]

This powerful observation strikes at the core of our humanity and our experience of the world. What makes an experience "aesthetic" or "moving"? How should we approach events and circumstances when they can be interpreted in myriad ways, from bearing practical importance, to posing a threat to our well-being, to being beautiful or inspiring, or even as opportunities of emotive maturation? Twain opens us to the question of aesthetic experience itself: what is it that makes an experience "aesthetic," as opposed to something else? In light of his words from *Life on the Mississippi*, it seems clear that whatever is aesthetic about our interaction with the world, Twain feels it is threatened by the tyranny of the urgent and our constant concerns over means and ends. In some philosophical approaches to the aesthetic, the search for its character focuses on qualities the objects of our experience must have in order to trigger such experience. Beauty, symmetry, provocativeness, contextual meaningfulness . . . all are potential candidates for this objective approach. But Twain puts the onus on the viewer, the subject, when it comes to aesthetic experience. How we are stationed in our perspective on the world makes all the difference—though it also seems there is a push and pull from environmental factors beyond our volition. How can we navigate such a winding river? Twain's struggle with aesthetic experience would later be developed in an influential essay entitled "'Psychical Distance' as a Factor in Art and as an Aesthetic Principle" by the Cambridge aesthetician Edward Bullough.[3] We now turn to his proposal for preserving awe and wonder in our daily lives.

Distance and Aesthetic Experience

"Psychical distance" (not to be confused with "physical" distance) refers to our mental engagement with the world around us and, for Bullough, is the identifiable feature of genuine aesthetic experience. His insightful case for artistic engagement argues that a balanced tension is required in order to authentically experience a work of art or a situation of aesthetic quality. We must find an appropriately composed perspective in our interaction with the world if there is to be anything substantive about the term "aesthetic." This balance is to be found in resisting the tendency to collapse into the practical requirements of experience while also resisting the abstract intellectualizing or aloof indifference that we sometimes slip into. Rather than making the aesthetic about the objects or circumstances that we engage, Bullough (like Twain) places the emphasis on the perspective that we bring to our experiences. It is at least to some degree within our power to determine if our experiences will be aesthetic in nature. When we are able to resist the extremes of underdistancing and overdistancing, we open ourselves to the possibility of aesthetic appreciation.

If we are underdistanced to a work or an experience, we will be engaged by practical concerns and pressing immediacies. We might focus on how we could use an artifact or circumstance to deal with our experiences, or we might be consumed by emotional, physical, and psychological concerns such as embarrassment or pleasure. For example, if a person treats a painting as merely something to cover a hole they have in their wall, or to hide a wall-safe, they are not experiencing the painting as art but rather as a decorative tool. Or, if one is psychologically unprepared to view a nude sculpture, there is a chance that aesthetic appreciation of its beauty and form will be overwhelmed by feelings of awkwardness, bashfulness, or even erotic excitement. While we may want to avoid entirely disconnecting these types of feelings from what goes into an aesthetic experience, there is something about appreciating art that goes beyond its practical use or those associated feelings connected to reputation, self-image, or pleasure. Underdistancing compromises aesthetic experience because, as in the case of Twain and the river, it draws us out of an appreciative reflective perspective and into the necessities and pressures of the moment. Indeed, this is often our normal approach to life, rooted in instincts of survival, management, and stability. But when we switch into an aesthetic mode because of an appropriate distancing from the "normal," we experience a depth of experience that awakens us to beauty and significance. Bullough writes:

> The working of Distance is, accordingly, not simple, but highly complex. It has a *negative*, inhibitory aspect—the cutting-out of the practical sides of things and of our practical attitude to them—and a *positive side*—the elaboration of the experience on the new basis created by the inhibitory action of Distance.
>
> Consequently, this distanced view of things is not, and cannot be, our normal outlook. As a rule, experiences constantly turn the same side towards us, namely, that which has the strongest practical force of appeal. We are not ordinarily aware of those aspects of things which do not touch us immediately and practically, nor are we generally conscious of impressions apart from our own self which is impressed. The sudden view of things from their reverse, unusually unnoticed, side, comes upon us as a revelation, and such revelations are precisely those of Art. In this most general sense, Distance is a factor in all Art.[4]

However, Bullough also recognizes another psychical extreme—one of overdistancing. If, when we engage a work of art, we find ourselves unable to connect with it, greeting it with indifference or with abstract analysis rather than with personal identification and emotional resonance, we will be overdistanced from the work and lack aesthetic appreciation. Failure to engage a situation in terms of aesthetic experience can occur because of its own faults that fail to prompt our personal connection to it, or by our own inability to invest in our interaction with it. For many people, minimalist and modern forms of art can be stereotypical sites of overdistancing, especially when we lack the context and concepts that surround the work that would help make sense of its significance. In other cases, we can be overdistanced to an experience because of abstraction or aloofness. For example, we might glance at a beautiful river and, instead of being underdistanced and consumed by practical concerns like Twain was, be completely indifferent to it, either treating it like any other river or perhaps ignoring its particular aesthetic potential in the moment. Overdistancing undermines aesthetic experience because it shields us from the emotional and personal engagement required to feel connected to our world. As Bullough puts it, "Distance does not imply an impersonal, purely intellectually interested relation of such a kind. On the contrary, it describes a *personal relation, often highly emotionally coloured, but of a peculiar character.* Its peculiarity lies in that the personal character of the relation has been, so to speak, filtered. It has been cleared of the practical, concrete nature of its appeal, without, however, thereby losing its original constitution."[5]

While it remains open to debate whether these concepts identify something unique or essential about the nature of aesthetic experience, Bullough's distinctions help us see that there is a wide spectrum of approaching the world in terms of artistic appreciation, and the closer we get in terms of practical necessities and desires or the farther we are removed in terms of reflection, indifference, or abstraction, the harder it is to experience a connection to objects and entities in their own right. This was obviously not a passing thought for Twain. The struggle between cognitive reflection and aesthetic appreciation appeared in numerous places in his writing. In an 1867 letter to *Alta California*, Twain expresses something similar to what he wrote in *Life on the Mississippi*:

> I am thankful that the good God creates us all ignorant. I am glad that when we change His plans in this regard, we have to do it at our own risk. It is a gratification to me to know that I am ignorant of art, and ignorant also of surgery. Because people who understand art find nothing in pictures but blemishes, and surgeons and anatomists see no beautiful women in all their lives, but only a ghastly stack of bones with Latin names to them, and a network of nerves and muscles and tissues inflamed by disease. The very point in a picture that fascinates me with its beauty, is to the cultured artist a monstrous crime against the laws of coloring; and the very flush that charms me in a lovely face, is, to the critical surgeon, nothing but a sign hung out to advertise a decaying lung. Accursed be all such knowledge. I want none of it.[6]

This selection raises a more pointed issue in the discussion of aesthetic experience. Upon accepting Twain's remarks at face value, one might think *knowledge itself* is the key factor in ruining the appropriate psychical distance required for aesthetic appreciation. Twain's appeals to "ignorance," his warnings about "understanding" art or becoming a professional doctor, all are meant to caution us about the dangers of losing our innocent awe and wonder about the world. Indeed, if we become consumed by the intellectualization of our environment at the cost of gratitude, appreciation, surprise, pleasure, and joy, we indeed have lost more than we have gained. But must our growth in understanding costs and benefits, means and ends, and practical applications cause us to compress our psychical distance into a shallow preoccupation? In maintaining an innocent perspective toward our experiences, is ignorance truly bliss?

It need not be. In fact, there is great potential in applying our intellect to the aesthetic as long as we are aware of the dangers Twain alerts us to. Deepening our understanding of art, or of human physiology, or even the expansion of practical and scientific knowledge about the world, can actually increase our ability to appreciate things aesthetically. It is not knowledge *itself* that ruins psychical distance, but rather our inability to make the appropriate moves of perspective in the midst of our knowledge. Gaining a deeper understanding of things can actually provide *more* opportunities for aesthetic experience, if we are able to develop psychical distance about those various and deepened areas of knowledge themselves. Bullough recognized the challenge in this maintenance of distance in the midst of deepened understanding. He writes,

> The jealous spectator of "Othello" will indeed appreciate and enter into the play the more keenly, the greater the resemblance with his own experience— *provided* that he succeeds in keeping the Distance between the action of the play and his personal feelings: a very difficult performance in the circumstances. It is on account of the same difficulty that the expert and the professional critic makes a bad audience, since their expertness and critical professionalism are *practical* activities, involving their concrete personality and constantly endangering their Distance.[7]

Clearly, critics of art face fresh challenges in maintaining aesthetic experiences of art, just as medical doctors will face unique challenges in appreciating the beauty of people apart from seeing them as cases for treatment. But not only can recontextualization or environmental factors help rekindle psychical distance (imagine a doctor on a dinner date with their spouse as opposed to speaking with them in an exam room), but the very knowledge a learned person possesses can be a source of aesthetic inspiration. We can be in awe of the way the human body works, or by understanding the structural elements of a play we might find new levels of appreciation for its artistic nature. Immediate emotional phenomena are not the only source and standard of the aesthetic.

Instead of condemning knowledge or wisdom as the culprit in losing awe and wonder, we should continue to develop psychical distance concerning not only the original experiences we have, but also the deepened levels of understanding that we reach. Developing that ability is no easy task, and neither is creating art in such a way that it enables people to do so in their own lives. As we have seen, the approach with which we engage our experiences is the key to maintaining the aesthetic in our lives. But in examining the work of Twain and other great artists, we find not only the personal struggle to maintain that psychical distance but also the profound ability to *create* works that inspire such distancing in the experience of others. In the world of literature and, more broadly, in communication itself, it is the artful use of style and language that can help an audience rediscover this aesthetic perspective in their dealings with art and with the world as a whole.

Creating Psychical Distance

Fiction (be it literary or dramatic), when skillfully crafted, can help create the appropriate psychical distance required for aesthetic appreciation. Part of the appeal of Twain's work, including his most well-known and beloved fiction, is its ability to draw us in and to feel empathy with its characters. As we saw earlier, Bullough clarifies that it is not the removal of personal interest or personal connection that indicates distance. Instead it is the "filtering" of our relationship to the work, distilling the simultaneously universal and personal themes of the work and how they relate to us, along with the work's emotional impact upon us, while seeing past the concrete and practical necessities and details that would turn the work into a means to some other end. The distance involves appreciation and engagement, while avoiding obsession or indulgence. Fictional stories have the implicit advantage of creating such distance from practical concern, while remaining able to pull us close as they convey truth about the human experience.

The progressively developing themes of Twain's greatest works exemplify this well. We are introduced to a lighter-hearted world in *The Adventures of Tom Sawyer*, where we engage Twain's characters and their playful stories. Here we become disarmed through resonance with childhood feelings and the drama of exciting adventures that cross over into the adult world, including its lessons of friendship and community. *The Adventures of Huckleberry Finn* intensifies the social dimensions of Twain's work, and as we follow the story our concepts of loyalty, justice, and freedom become challenged and enlarged. In a work like *The Prince and the Pauper*, we are confronted with the theme of empathy itself as Edward Tudor and Tom Canty cross class lines and engage each other's world. Such moments create opportunities to experience psychical distance, in that they keep us close enough to the action of a story to feel relevance, developing our relationship with character and plot, but also keep us far enough away to provide perspective and aesthetic appreciation as we consider the themes being developed. Through it all, our perspective is shifted because Twain is able to artfully craft the context and characters that serve as sites of aesthetic engagement and personal development. These are the results of our own psychical distance coupled with the keen moral sense that emanates throughout his writings.

Indeed, character and plot are some of the main elements that provide this opportunity for our aesthetic enjoyment and moral development. But the literary *style* of Mark Twain also contributes to his ability to simultaneously draw us in and engage our intellect and emotions while avoiding hitting us on the head with moral and literary themes. His humorous situations and dialogue disarm us, poking and prodding us while drawing us into thoughtful contemplation. His detailed descriptions are coupled with whimsical and poetic reflections. Fiction, humor, irony, poetry, art—these are all examples of what Danish philosopher Søren Kierkegaard referred to as "indirect communication." While direct communication aims to convey meaning through the content of the words themselves, indirect communication seeks to prompt personal understanding through engagement with elusive and inspiring moments of experience. In creative domains such as the arts, the message of an author is not treated as an objective and settled piece of information. Rather, the truth and power of such forms of communication are to be found in the form and means by which the content is communicated. This artistic form recognizes that aesthetic experience—and its unique ability to reveal existential, personal truth—must be carefully prompted and preserved in the work. Artistic communication is not done with blunt instruments; it requires special handling. Since the truth of an author's feelings, thoughts, and hopes, coupled with the content of their broader life, cannot all be merely reduced to objective information on the page, Kierkegaard argues that the existential communicator must use indirect forms to engage the reader and facilitate the development of meaning. This need not be a complex or convoluted exercise; even the simplest children's story can have a profound impact on our lives as we engage the plot and characters and "feel" the meaning of a tale. In connection with psychical distance, the concept of indirect communication helps illuminate the appropriate balance of engagement and reflection so as to provide the context within which we can process the truth of the author's message.

Kierkegaard writes, "An example of such indirect communication is so to compose jest and earnest that the composition is a dialectical knot—and with this to be nobody. If anyone is to profit by this sort of communication, he must himself undo the knot for himself."[8] This "knot" is exactly the kind of message Twain so artfully constructs in his fiction. He provides us a chance to personally engage Tom and Huck, Edward and Tom Canty, and even the author himself in all their various circumstances so that we might not fall prey to the complacency of familiarity and practical concern, and be awakened to the aesthetic experience that accompanies any true work of art. Twain's style of communication throughout his stories, articles, and memoirs engages us and draws into self-reflection, philosophical inquiry, and social critique. This process is more than story-telling; it is constructing the tale in such a way that we are caught up in its rhythm and rhyme, its humor and insightfulness, until at once we realize something deeper about ourselves and about our world. Kierkegaard once wrote in his *Journals*, "The truth is a trap: you cannot get it without it getting you; you cannot get the truth by capturing it, only by its capturing you."[9] One might think he was predicting the style of Mark Twain.

Finally, because of the subjectivity involved in the truth of indirect communication, there is indeed something poignant in the construction and creation of artistic content. The author of such messages, while no doubt inspired by personal experience and aesthetic experience, must shift into a different mode to construct and convey their content. Twain must have wrestled with the construction of his own work as a "professional" writer and speaker. The very words meant to inspire and enthrall others could easily have become tools of the trade for Twain, and the underdistancing threat to aesthetic experience that a profession can bring is an all-too-common phenomenon. Bullough writes,

> The same qualification applies to the artist. He will prove artistically most effective in the formulation of an intensely *personal* experience, but he can formulate it artistically only on condition of a detachment from the experience *qua personal*. Hence the statement of so many artists that artistic formulation was to them a kind of catharsis, a means of ridding themselves of feelings and ideas the acuteness of which they felt almost as a kind of obsession.[10]

The secret is of course to find a way to maintain a personal connection to one's own work without practical obsession, constantly developing new levels of appreciation for the craft in order to maintain the fertile ground of aesthetic experience from which great, well-crafted works arise.

No doubt, despite the desire to bring about personal meaning through a work, the author's experience cannot be fully understood by others who themselves must struggle for interpretive significance. But good work at least provides the possibility for significance. Kierkegaard himself recognized the heartache and struggle in artistic creation and the critical interpretation of an audience:

> What is a poet? An unhappy man who conceals profound anguish in his heart, but whose lips are so fashioned that when sighs and groans pass over them they sound like beautiful music. His fate resembles that of the unhappy men who were slowly roasted by a gentle fire in the tyrant Phalaris' bull—their shrieks could not reach his ear to terrify him, to him they sounded like sweet music. And people flock about the poet and say to him: do sing again; Which

means, would that new sufferings tormented your soul, and: would that your lips stayed fashioned as before, for your cries would only terrify us, but your music is delightful.[11]

It is indeed a labor of love, and a personal sacrifice, to risk the misunderstanding that inevitably occurs in the creation and subsequent interpretation of a work. But the risks of misunderstanding are coordinate with sites of aesthetic impact and experience. The same work that stirs discord can inspire revelation. Twain was no doubt a master of such artful communication.

Distance Makes the Heart Grow Fonder

In A Connecticut Yankee in King Arthur's Court, Twain wrote, "You can't depend on your eyes when your imagination is out of focus."[12] That work, as much as any, blends Twain's wit and story-telling creativity with scathing social critique and moral insight concerning issues ranging from slavery, to class oppression, to the potential dangers of religious institutions. All the while, our imaginations are cultivated so that our eyes might see. Twain's art is his ability to woo us into an affectionate relation to his stories, and then to initiate just the right psychical distance from the plot and characters so that we realize the powerful truth of the themes he unfolds therein. We don't just see boys adventuring on the Mississippi; we are struck by the power of friendship and justice. We don't merely travel through time to a fanciful world; we realize the transcendent truths of a good society and the value of human relationships. It's a distance that makes our heart grow fonder and our minds grow wiser.

It takes a rare combination of personal reflection, contextual understanding, and artistic skill to excel in creating opportunities for aesthetic experience through psychical distance. One must be rooted enough in the realities of an audience to bring them close enough to their subject. Things must register, they must hit close to home, they must reflect the world that people recognize and relate to. In the midst of this, one must also be imaginative and artful enough to push people to awareness and contemplation, to the right distance where they can see something bigger than themselves or the circumstantial façade. Aesthetic experience hangs in the tension between that awareness and a deep emotional connection. Twain's provocative wit and intelligence coupled with his deep connection to real, authentic life fueled the artistry in his writing. It is why he is able to help us "gain most" in the area that all of us have the greatest inertial tendency to lose most: our perspective.

~

Notes

Chapter 1. The Conscience of Huckleberry Finn

1. This chapter began life as the Potter Memorial Lecture, given at Washington State University in Pullman, Washington, in 1972.

2. M. J. Sidnell, "Huck Finn and Jim," *The Cambridge Quarterly*, 2 (1967): 205–6.

3. Quoted in William L. Shirer, *The Rise and Fall of the Third Reich* (New York, 1960), 937–38.

4. Ibid., 966.

5. Roger Manwell and Heinrich Fraenkel, *Heinrich Himmler* (London, 1965), 132.

6. Ibid., 197.

7. Ibid., 184.

8. Ibid.

9. Ibid., 187.

10. Vergilius Ferm (ed.), *Puritan Sage: Collected Writings of Jonathan Edwards* (New York, 1953), 370.

11. Ibid., 366.

12. Ibid., 294.

13. Ibid., 372.

14. Jonathan Edwards, "The End of the Wicked Contemplated by the Righteous: or, The Torments of the Wicked in Hell, no Occasion of Grief to the Saints in Heaven," from *The Works of President Edwards* (London, r8r7), vol. IV, 507–8.

15. Ibid., 511–12.

16. Ibid., 509.

17. I am grateful to the executors of the estate of Harold Owen, and to Chatto and Windus Ltd., for permission to quote from Wilfred Owen's "Dulce et Decorum Est" and "Insensibility."

Chapter 2. Huckleberry Finn and Moral Motivation

1. A previous version of this essay appeared as "Huckleberry Finn and Moral Motivation," in *Philosophy and Literature*, volume 34 (2010).

2. Jonathan Bennett, "The Conscience of Huckleberry Finn," *Philosophy*, 49 (1974): 123–34.

3. Nomy Arpaly and Timothy Schroeder, "Praise, Blame and the Whole Self," *Philosophical Studies*, 93 (1999): 161–88.

4. Jenny Teichman, "Mr. Bennett on Huckleberry Finn," *Philosophy*, 50 (1975): 358–59. In this brief response to Bennett, she argues on this ground that emotions can oppose moral principles in a "rational" way.

5. For expansion on this point and further references, see A. Goldman, "Desire, Depression, and Rationality," *Philosophical Psychology*, 20 (2007): 711–30.

6. One interpreter who agrees is Thomas Crocker, "An American Novelist in the Philosopher King's Court," *Philosophy and Literature*, 26 (2002): 57–74.

7. For expansion on this requirement, see, for example, A. Goldman, *Practical Rules: When We Need Them and When We Don't* (Cambridge: Cambridge University Press, 2002), chapter 4; *Moral Knowledge* (London: Routledge, 1990), chapter 5.

8. For a recent version of this debate, see Shaun Nichols, *Sentimental Rules* (Oxford: Oxford University Press, 2004), chapter 3.

Chapter 3. Sympathy, Principles, and Conscience: Getting to the Heart of Huck Finn's Moral Praiseworthiness

1. Mark Twain, *Adventures of Huckleberry Finn* (New York: Signet Classic, 1987), 10.

2. Ibid., 92.

3. Ibid., 93.

4. Ibid., 93.

5. Ibid., 95–96.

6. Jonathan Bennett, "The Conscience of Huckleberry Finn," *Philosophy*, 49 (1974): 123–34.

7. Ibid., 127.

8. Ibid., 132.

9. Ibid., 132.

10. Nomy Arpaly and Timothy Schroeder, "Praise, Blame and the Whole Self," *Philosophical Studies*, 93 (1999): 161–88.

11. Ibid., 163.

12. Ibid., 172.

13. Ibid., 177–78.

14. Adam Smith, *The Theory of Moral Sentiments* (Indianapolis: Liberty Fund, 1982), 10.

15. Ibid., 69.

16. Ibid., 130.

17. Ibid., 159.

18. Anders Schinkel, "Huck Finn, Moral Language and Moral Education," *Journal of Philosophy of Education*, 45 (2011): 511.

19. Alan Goldman, "Huckleberry Finn and Moral Imagination," *Philosophy and Literature*, 34 (2010): 3.

20. Bennett, "Conscience," 124.

21. Goldman, "Huckleberry Finn," 3. See also Schinkel, "Huck Finn," 513–14.

22. Twain, *Huckleberry Finn*, 95.

Chapter 4. Huckleberry Finn's Struggle between Sympathy and Moral Principle Reconsidered

1. Jonathan Bennett "The Conscience of Huckleberry Finn," *Philosophy*, 49 (1974): 123–34. Also found as chapter 1 in this volume.

2. Mark Twain, *The Adventures of Huckleberry Finn* (London: Folio Society, 1993). (Original work published 1884.)

3. Ibid., 87.

4. Ibid., 88.

5. Ibid.

6. Ibid.

7. Ibid., 90.

8. Bennett, "The Conscience of Huckleberry Finn," 124.

9. Ibid.

10. Although Bennett noted the number as being four and a half million based on estimates at the time he published his paper (see Bennett, "The Conscience of Huckleberry Finn," 123), more recent estimates put the number as not fewer than five million, and potentially up to six million or more. For more information, see Franciszek Piper, "The Number of Victims," in *Anatomy of the Auschwitz Death Camp*, ed. Michael Berenbaum & Yisrael Gutman (Bloomington: Indiana University Press, 1998), 70–72.

11. Bennett, "The Conscience of Huckleberry Finn," 123.

12. Ibid., 129.

13. Ibid.

14. Ibid.

15. See Philip Montague, "Re-examining Huck Finn's Conscience," *Philosophy*, 55 (1980): 542–46.

16. Bennett, "The Conscience of Huckleberry Finn," 133.

17. Russ Shafer-Landau, *Whatever Happened to Good and Evil?* (New York: Oxford University Press, 2004), x.

18. Jonathan Dancy, *Ethics Without Principles* (New York: Oxford University Press, 2004), 2.

19. Bennett, "The Conscience of Huckleberry Finn," 131.

20. Ibid.

21. Twain, *Huckleberry Finn*, 91.

22. Colin Ward, "Introduction," in *The Adventures of Huckleberry Finn*, by Mark Twain (London: Folio Society, 1993), ix.

23. Ibid., x.

24. Bennett, "The Conscience of Huckleberry Finn," 131.

25. Ward, "Introduction," xv.

Chapter 5. Twain's Last Laugh

1. Arne Naess, "Self-Realization: An Ecological Approach to Being in the World," in *Ecology of Wisdom: Writings by Arne Naess*, ed. Alan Drengson and Bill Devall (Berkeley: Counterpoint Press, 2008), 81.

2. Ibid., 84–85.

3. For one thing, in the absence of language, how could one ever tell the difference between true kinship, and mere projection of one's feelings onto the other being? In this connection, see Thomas Nagel's famous essay, "What Is It Like to Be a Bat?" *The Philosophical Review* 83 (1974): 435–50.

4. Mark Twain, *The Adventures of Huckleberry Finn* (London: Transatlantic Press, 2012), 246, chapter 31. Note that I have included both chapter and page number in references to this work, following the practice of the editors of *Satire or Evasion? Black Perspectives on* Huckleberry Finn.

5. Fredrick Woodard and Donnarae MacCann, "Minstrel Shackles and Nineteenth-Century 'Liberality' in *Huckleberry Finn*," in *Satire or Evasion? Black Perspectives on* Huckleberry Finn, ed. James S. Leonard et al (Durham: Duke University Press, 1992). See also Woodard and MacCann's earlier essay on this topic, "*Huckleberry Finn* and the Traditions of Blackface Minstrelsy," in *The Black American in Books for Children: Readings in Racism*, 2nd ed., ed. Donnarae MacCann and Gloria Woodard (Metuchen, NJ: Scarecrow Press, 1985), 75–103; Ralph Ellison, "Change the Joke and Slip the Yoke," in *Shadow and Act* (New York: Random House, 1964); and the other essays in section three of *Satire or Evasion*.

6. Peaches Henry, "The Struggle for Tolerance: Race and Censorship in *Huckleberry Finn*," in *Satire or Evasion? Black Perspectives on* Huckleberry Finn, ed. James S. Leonard et al (Durham: Duke University Press, 1992), 32.

7. Kristina Gehrman, "The Character of Huckleberry Finn," forthcoming in *Philosophy and Literature*.

8. Iris Murdoch, "The Idea of Perfection," in *The Sovereignty of Good* (New York: Routledge, 2010), 33.

9. Aristotle, *The Basic Works of Aristotle*, ed. Richard McKeon (New York: Random House, 1941), 952, 1103a34-b2. Emphasis added.

10. Ibid., 952, 1103b9. Emphasis added.

11. Ibid., 953, 1103b24-5.

12. Murdoch, "The Idea of Perfection," 17.

13. Ibid., 22.

14. For the relevant passages, see Murdoch, "The Idea of Perfection," 103–04, chapter 15. For full discussion of these passages and their significance in this context, see the author's "The Character of Huckleberry Finn," cited above.

15. See, for example, Huck's musings at Murdoch, "The Idea of Perfection," 20–21, chapter 3.

16. Twain, *The Adventures of Huckleberry Finn*, 216, chapter 28.

17. Ibid., 147, chapter 19.

18. Henry, "The Struggle for Tolerance: Race and Censorship in *Huckleberry Finn*," 32.

19. Twain, *The Adventures of Huckleberry Finn*, 180, chapter 23.

20. Ibid., 314, chapter 40.

21. Ibid., 334, chapter The Last (43).

22. This fundamental form of moral wisdom is demonstrated not only throughout Jim's relationship with Huck but also in a story he tells about unfairly punishing his own daughter (Twain, *The Adventures of Huckleberry Finn*, 180–81, chapter 23), and finally in his superlatively selfless actions toward Tom in chapters 40 to 42, whose heartless and thoughtless behavior toward Jim surely gives Jim every reason to abandon him.

23. See Bernard W. Bell, "Twain's 'Nigger' Jim: The Tragic Face Behind the Minstrel Mask," in *Satire or Evasion? Black Perspectives on* Huckleberry Finn, ed. James S. Leonard et al (Durham: Duke University Press, 1992). The synopsis included with the Transatlantic Press edition of the novel that I have cited here, for example, refers to Jim and Huck as "the two absconders."

24. Plato, *The Trial and Death of Socrates*, trans. G. M. A. Grube, rev. John M. Cooper (Indianapolis: Hacket, 2000), 30e2–5.

25. This, too, is a very Socratic point: Socrates believed that "a good man cannot be harmed in life or in death," because the only real harm that can come to a person is to be wicked, and whether a person is good or bad is up to no one but that person. Plato, *The Trial and Death of Socrates*, 41d.

26. The author would like to thank Paul Nichols, Amber Franklin, Geralyn Timler, Richard and Lois Gehrman, and Alan Goldman for sustained discussion and suggestions that greatly benefited this paper.

Chapter 6. The Gospel According to Mark (Twain)

1. Benjamin Griffin and Harriet Elinor Smith, eds. *Autobiography of Mark Twain*, *volume 3* (Oakland: University of California Press, 2016), 130.

2. Mark Twain, *Letters from the Earth*, ed. Bernard DeVoto (Greenwich: Fawcett Publications, 1962). See also *Mark Twain on the Damned Human Race*, ed. Janet Smith (New York: Hill and Wang, 1962).

3. Twain, *Letters from the Earth*, 12.

4. Ibid., 13.

5. Ibid., 15.

6. Ibid., 105.

7. Ibid., 107.

8. Ibid., 17.

9. Ibid., 19.

10. Ibid., 76.

11. Ibid., 78.

12. Ibid., 71.

13. Ibid., 25.

14. Ibid., 42.

15. Ibid., 51.

16. Ibid., 33.

17. Ibid., 33.

18. Ibid., 33.

19. Ibid., 35.

20. Ibid., 19.

21. Ibid., 24.

22. Ibid., Editor's Preface, viii. See also: Gelb, Arthur (August 24, 1962). "Anti-Religious Work by Twain, Long Withheld, to Be Published." *The New York Times*, 23.

23. Griffin and Smith, *Autobiography*, vol. 3, 126.

24. Twain, *Letters from the Earth*, 19.

25. Ibid., 46.

26. Friedrich Nietzsche, *On the Genealogy of Morality*, trans. Maudemarie Clarke and Alan Swensen (Indianapolis: Hackett, 1998), 28.

27. Nietzsche, *On the Genealogy of Morality*, 64.

28. Griffin and Smith, *Autobiography*, vol. 3, 197.

29. Griffin and Smith, *Autobiography*, vol. 3, 130.

Chapter 7. Mark Twain and the Problem of Evil: *The Mysterious Stranger, Letters from the Earth,* and *The Diaries of Adam and Eve*

1. Mark Twain, *The Mysterious Stranger Manuscripts*, ed. William W. Gibson (Berkeley: University of California Press, 1969), 404–05.

2. Albert Camus, *The Plague*, trans. Stuart Gilbert (New York: Vintage Books, 1991), 127.

3. Mark Twain, *Letters from the Earth*, ed. Bernard DeVoto (New York: Harper & Row, 1962), 44.

4. Camus, *The Plague*, 127.

5. Albert Camus, *The Rebel: An Essay on Man in Revolt*, trans. Anthony Bower (New York: Vintage Books, 1992), 100–3.

6. Most versions of the "free will" defense ultimately end up offering an aesthetic justification for creatures being blessed with free wills thus making a richer world for the glory of God. Even John Hick's soul making theodicy ends up resting on aesthetic considerations. God has created a more glorious universe because of the development of beings toward perfection. What all of these theodicies still defend is a perfect being theology in which God's perfection is demonstrated but in no way enhanced by the creation of the world. Philip Clayton, *The Problem of God in Modern Thought* (Grand Rapids: Eerdmans, 2000).

7. *The Mysterious Stranger, A Romance* published in 1916 by Harper & Brothers Publishing Company, and still appearing in many anthologies of Twain's shorter works has been revealed by Twain scholars to be an editorial fraud perpetrated by Alfred Bigalow Paine and Frederick A. Duneka. Paine was Twain's official biographer and his literary executor. It is a compilation of several manuscripts that Twain never completed or published in his lifetime. The bulk of the work comes from Twain's *The Chronicle of Young Satan*. Paine attaches to this the conclusion of *No. 44, The Mysterious Stranger*, and adds some bridging and modifications of his own including the person of "The Astrologer" who in *The Chronicle of Young Satan* is a priest. William W. Gibson, "Introduction," in *The Mysterious Stranger Manuscripts*, 1.

8. David Hume, *Dialogues Concerning Natural Religion*, ed. Richard H. Popkin (Indianapolis: Hackett, 1980), 63.

9. David Ray Griffin, *God, Power, and Evil: A Process Theodicy* (Philadelphia: The Westminster Press, 1976), 19.

10. Edgar Sheffield Brightman, *A Philosophy of Religion* (New York: Prentice Hall, 1940), 245.

11. Plotinus, *The Enneads: Third Ennead: Second Tractate: Section 11*, http://www.sacred-texts.com/cla/plotenn/enn197.htm (accessed August 7, 2016).

12. Augustine of Hippo, *Confessions*, trans. Henry Chadwick (Oxford: Oxford University Press, 1998), 7:13.

13. The complete quotation reads:

> 51. I shall say no more, except that to us is promised a vision of beauty—the beauty of whose imitation all other things are beautiful, and by comparison which all other things are unsightly, Whosoever will have glimpsed this beauty—and he will see it, who lives well, prays well, studies well—how will it ever trouble him why one man, desiring to have children, has them not, while another man casts out his own offspring as being unduly numerous; why one man hates children before they are born, and another man loves them after birth, or how it is not absurd that nothing will come to pass which is not with God—and therefore it is inevitable that all things come into being in accordance with order—and nevertheless God is not petitioned in vain?
>
> Finally, how will any burdens, dangers, scorns, or smiles of fortune disturb a just man? In this world of sense, it is indeed necessary to examine carefully what time and place are, so that what delights in a portion of place or time, may be understood to be far less beauti-

ful than the whole of which it is a portion. And furthermore, it is clear to a learned man that what displeases in a potion, displeases for no other reason than because the whole with which that portion harmonizes wonderfully, is not see; but that in the intelligible world, every part is as beautiful and perfect as the whole.

Augustine, *De Ordine*, trans. Robert P. Russell, in *Philosophies of Art and Beauty: Selected Reading in Aesthetics from Plato to Heidegger*, eds. Albert Hofstadter and Richard Kuhns (Chicago: University of Chicago Press, 1964), 185, chapter 19.

14. Dante Alighieri, *The Divine Comedy, III Parodiso*, tr. Charles Singleton (Princeton: Princeton University Press, 1975), Canto XXXIII: 123, p. 379.

15. John Bunyan, *The Pilgrim's Progress* (New York: Oxford University Press, 1962), 13–14.

16. Letter to W. D. Howells, in Boston: ELMIRA, July 21, 1885. Mark Twain, *The Complete Works of Mark Twain: The Novels, Short Stories, Essays and Satires, Travel Writing, Non-fiction, the Complete Letters, the Complete Speeches, and the Autobiography of Mark Twain*, Kindle Locations 126807–08. e-artnow. Kindle Edition.

17. The angels explain to Stormfield after he gives up the choir that no one can take it too long.

I'll set you right on that point very quick. People take the figurative language of the Bible and the allegorists for literal, and the first thing they ask for when they get here is a halo and a harp, and so on. Nothing that's harmless and reasonable is refused a body here, if he asks it in the right spirit. So they are outfitted with these things without a word. They go and sing and play just about one day, and that's the last you'll ever see them in the choir. They don't need anybody to tell them that that sort of thing wouldn't make a heaven—at least not a heaven that a sane man could stand a week and remain sane. That cloud-bank is placed where the noise can't disturb the old inhabitants, and so there ain't any harm in letting everybody get up there and cure himself as soon as he comes.

Mark Twain, "Captain Stormfield's Visit to Heaven," in *The Best Short Stories of Mark Twain* (Modern Library Classics), Kindle Locations 4741–46. Random House Publishing Group. Kindle Edition.

18. Mark Twain, *Letters from the Earth*, 9.

19. Quoted in Stanley Brodwin, "Mark Twain's Theology: The Gods of a Brevet Presbyterian," in *The Cambridge Companion to Mark Twain*, ed. Forrest G. Robinson (Cambridge: Cambridge University Press, 1996), 242.

20. Mark Twain, *The Complete Works of Mark Twain*, Kindle Locations 24395–407.

21. Brodwin, "Mark Twain's Theology"; Lawrence I. Berkeove and Joseph Csicicsila, *Heretical Fictions: Religion in the Literature of Mark Twain* (Iowa City: University of Iowa Press, 2010); Joe B. Fulton, *The Reverent Mark Twain: Theological Burlesque, Form, and Content* (Columbus, OH: The Ohio State University Press, 2006).

22. Augustine, *The City of God*, XI 18.

23. John Calvin, *Institutes of the Christian Religion*, ed. John McNeill, trans. Ford Lewis Battles (Philadelphia: Westminster John Knox Press, 1960), vol. III, xxiii1 xiv.15

24. Ibid., vol. III, xxiii1 xiv.15.

25. Ibid., vol. XX, xxiii, 6.

26. Ibid., vol. XX, xxiii 7; xxiii, 2.

27. Twain, "Interpolated Extracts from Eve's Diary," in *Letters from the Earth*, 81–82.

28. Mark Twain, *The Bible According to Mark Twain: Irreverent Writings on Eden, Heaven, and the Flood by America's Master Satirist*, eds. Howard G. Baetzhold and Joseph B. McCullough (New York: Simon and Schuster, 1995), 213–17.

29. Twain, *Letters from the Earth*, 5.

30. Ibid., 5–6.

31. Twain, *The Mysterious Stranger Manuscripts*, 404–05.

32. Mark Twain, "Captain Stormfield's Visit to Heaven," in *The Best Short Stories of Mark Twain* (Modern Library Classics), Kindle Locations 5384–90. Random House Publishing Group. Kindle Edition (2007).

33. William Lane Craig, "'No Other Name': A Middle Knowledge Perspective on the Exclusivity of Salvation through Christ," *Faith and Philosophy*, 6 (1989): 172–88.

34. Mark Twain, *The Adventures of Tom Sawyer* (Garden City, NY: Doubleday: 1936), 34.

35. Twain, *The Mysterious Stranger Manuscripts*, 49.

36. Ibid., 49–50.

37. They are also "happiness machines" but the suffering seems to greatly predominate. Twain, *The Mysterious Stranger Manuscripts*, 112.

38. Twain, *Letters from the Earth*, 29–30.

39. Mark Twain, "The Autobiography of Eve," in *The Bible According to Mark Twain*, 54.

40. The incarnation of God in Christ rather than the evolution of God toward and kinder, gentler creature than the one presented in the Hebrew Bible is actually the opposite. The God of the new testament is worse. Berkeove and Csicicsila cite a passage in Twain's Notebooks that describes the incarnation and atonement in terms of Anselms satisfaction theory as a great act of revenge and resentment on the part of the deity.

> God as Christ If Christ was God he is in the attitude of one whose . . . anger against Adam has grown so uncontrollable . . . that nothing but a sacrifice of life can appease it; & so, without noticing how illogical the act is going to be, God condemns Himself self to death commits suicide on the cross, & in this ingenious way wipes off that old score. (Notebook 290)

Cited in Berkeove and Csicicsila, 10.

In *Letters from the Earth*, it is Christ who invents hell that he may pursue the sufferer beyond the grave.

> Now here is a curious thing. It is believed by everybody that while he was in heaven he was stern, hard, resentful, jealous, and cruel; but that when he came down to earth and

assumed the name of Jesus Christ, he became the opposite of what he was before: that is to say, he became sweet, and gentle, merciful, and all harshness disappeared from his nature and a deep and yearning love for his poor human children took its place. Whereas it was as Jesus Christ that he devised hell and proclaimed it!

Which is to say, that as the meek and gentle Savior he was a thousand billion times crueler than ever he was in the Old Testament-oh, incomparably more atrocious than ever he was when he was at the very worst in those old days.

Twain, *Letters from the Earth*, 45.

41. Twain, "Eve's Diary," in *The Bible According to Mark Twain*, 31–33.

Chapter 8. The Noble Art of Lying

1. Mark Twain, from Opie Read, *Mark Twain and I*, quoted in *The Wit and Wisdom of Mark Twain* (Mineola, NY: Dover Publications, 2013), 62.

2. A University of California, Berkeley, extension course on "The Philosophy of Mark Twain" includes "the ethics of lying" as one topic covered in the course: http://extension.berkeley.edu/search/publicCourseSearchDetails.do?method=load &courseId=10464593 [accessed 09/17/2016]. But there is little or nothing published specifically on Twain's contribution to our understanding of lying and the ethics of lying. Twain is cited a number of times by Martin Jay in *The Virtues of Mendacity: On Lying in Politics* (Charlottesville, VA: University of Virginia Press, 2010), but only in passing.

3. Oscar Wilde, "The Decay of Lying: An Observation," in *The Collected Oscar Wilde*, with Introduction and Notes by Angus Fletcher (New York, NY: Barnes and Noble Classics, 2007), 363. An early version of the essay first appeared in *The Nineteenth Century: A Monthly Review*, No. 143, January 1889. The final version appeared in Wilde's collection of essays, *Intentions* (London: James A. Osgood, McIlvaine & Co., 1891), 1–56.

4. Twain, "On the Decay of the Art of Lying," in *The Writings of Mark Twain*, vol. 20, 355–62.

5. Ibid., 355.

6. R. Kent Rasmussen, *Critical Companion to Mark Twain: A Literary Reference to His Life and Work* (New York, NY: Facts on File, 2007), 797; cf. Peter B. Messent, *The Short Works of Mark Twain: A Critical Study* (Philadelphia: University of Pennsylvania Press, 2001), 80.

7. Twain, "On the Decay of the Art of Lying," in *The Stolen White Elephant, Etc.* (Boston, MA: James R. Osgood and Company, 1882), 217–25. Subsequent page numbers refer to this edition.

8. Twain, "My First Lie, and How I Got Out of It," in *The Writings of Mark Twain*, vol. 10 (New York: Harper & Brothers, 1915), 159–70.

9. Twain, "My First Lie, and How I Got Out of It," in *The Man That Corrupted Hadleyburg and Other Stories and Essays* (New York: Harper & Brothers, 1900), 167–80. Subsequent page numbers refer to this edition.

10. Twain, "On the Decay of the Art of Lying," 225.

11. Ibid., 218.

12. Ibid., 218.

13. See *Liar, Liar*, directed by Tom Shadyac (Universal Pictures, 1997).

14. See *The Invention of Lying*, directed by Ricky Gervais and Matthew Robinson (Warner Brothers, 2009).

15. Richmal Crompton, "William's Truthful Christmas," in *Still—William* (London: George Newnes, Ltd., 1925), 164–79.

16. Voltaire, *Candide, ou l'Optimisme* (Paris: Sirène, 1759).

17. Twain, "On the Decay of the Art of Lying," 218.

18. Ibid.

19. Ibid., 224.

20. Ibid., 219.

21. Ibid.

22. Ibid.

23. Ibid., 221.

24. Ibid.

25. Ibid., 219.

26. Ibid., 221.

27. See Amelia Opie, *Illustration of Lying in All Its Branches* (London: Longman, Hurst, Rees, Orme, Brown and Green, 1825).

28. Twain, "My First Lie, and How I Got Out of It," 169.

29. Twain, "On the Decay of the Art of Lying," 221.

30. Ibid., 222.

31. Ibid.

32. Ibid.

33. Ibid.

34. Ibid., 223.

35. Ibid.

36. Ibid., 224.

37. According to Paul J. Griffiths, Saint Augustine held that lies do not have to be deceptive. See *Lying: An Augustinian Theology of Duplicity* (Grand Rapids, MI: Brazos Press, 2004).

38. See Thomas L. Carson, "The Definition of Lying," *Noûs*, 40 (2006): 284–306; Roy Sorensen, "Bald-Faced Lies! Lying Without The Intent To Deceive," *Pacific Philosophical Quarterly*, 88 (2007): 251–64; Don Fallis, "What is Lying?" *Journal of Philosophy*, 106 (2009): 29–56; A. Andreas, Stokke, "Lying and Asserting," *Journal of Philosophy*, 110 (2013): 33–60.

39. Thomas Nagel, "Concealment and Exposure," reprinted in *Concealment and Exposure and Other Essays* (Oxford: Oxford University Press, 2003), 4.

40. Ibid., 6.

41. See my "The Definition of Lying and Deception," *Stanford Encyclopedia of Philosophy* (2015).

42. Twain, "My First Lie, and How I Got Out of It," 161.

43. Ibid.

44. Ibid.

45. Ibid.

46. Ibid.

47. Ibid.

48. Ibid., 161–62.

49. Ibid., 162.

50. Ibid.

51. Ibid.

52. Ibid.

53. Ibid.

54. Ibid., 169.

55. See Lawrence J. Oliver, summary of "My First Lie, and How I Got Out of It," in *The Routledge Encyclopedia of Mark Twain*, eds. J. R. LeMaster and James D. Wilson (London: Routledge, 2011), 530.

56. In his autobiography, Twain says that, "In my schoolboy days I had no aversion to slavery. I was not aware that there was anything wrong with it. No one arraigned it in my hearing; the local papers said nothing against it; the local pulpit taught us that God approved it, that it was a holy thing, and that the doubter need only look in the Bible if he wished to settle his mind—and then the texts were read aloud to us to make the matter sure; if the slaves themselves had an aversion to slavery they were wise and said nothing. In Hannibal we seldom saw a slave misused; on the farm, never." Nevertheless, he tells a story about complaining to his mother about the singing of a slave boy who was hired to work on the farm, and being told in response that the boy "will never see his mother again," and that "when he sings, it shows that he is not remembering" and that "If you were older, you would understand me; then that friendless child's noise would make you glad" (*The Autobiography of Mark Twain*, vol. I, ed. Harriet Elinor Smith [Berkeley, CA: University of California Press, 2010], 212).

57. Evan Carton, "Speech Acts and Social Action: Mark Twain and the Politics of Literary Performance," in *The Cambridge Companion to Mark Twain*, ed. Forrest G. Robinson (Cambridge: Cambridge University Press, 1995), 163.

58. See Forrest G. Robinson, *In Bath Faith: The Dynamics of Deception in Mark Twain's America* (Cambridge, MA: Harvard University Press, 1986); and *The Author-Cat: Clemens's Life in Fiction* (New York, NY: Fordham University Press, 2007).

59. Lynda Obst, *Hello, He Lied—and Other Truths from the Hollywood Trenches* (Boston, MA: Little, Brown, 1996).

60. Twain, "On the Decay of the Art of Lying," 220.

61. Ibid.

62. Ibid.

63. Ibid.

64. Ibid.

65. Ibid.

66. Ibid., 220–21.
67. Ibid., 219.
68. Ibid.
69. Ibid., 219–20.
70. Twain, "My First Lie, and How I Got Out of It," 160.
71. Twain, "On the Decay of the Art of Lying," 219.
72. Ibid.
73. Twain, "My First Lie, and How I Got Out of It," 159.
74. Ibid.
75. Ibid.
76. Ibid., 160.
77. Ibid.
78. Ibid.
79. Ibid., 170.
80. Ibid., 165.
81. Ibid.
82. Ibid.
83. Ibid.
84. Ibid., 166.
85. Ibid., 164.
86. Frederick Schauer and Richard Zeckhauser, "Paltering," in *Deception: From Ancient Empires to Internet Dating*, ed. Brooke Harrington (Stanford, CA: Stanford University Press, 2009), 38–54.
87. Twain, "My First Lie, and How I Got Out of It," 164.
88. Ibid.
89. Ibid.
90. Ibid., 164–65.
91. Ibid., 165.
92. Ibid.
93. Twain, "On the Decay of the Art of Lying," 220.
94. Ibid.
95. Ibid.
96. Ibid.
97. Ibid., 224.
98. Ibid.
99. Quoted in "Twain Quotes—Lies," http://www.twainquotes.com/Lies.html (accessed October 8, 2016).
100. Twain, "On the Decay of the Art of Lying," 221.
101. Ibid., 219.
102. Ibid.
103. Ibid.
104. Ibid., 220.
105. Ibid., 221.

106. *Noonan v. Staples Inc.*, U.S. Court of Appeals, First Circuit, February 13, 2009. http://caselaw.findlaw.com/us-1st-circuit/1308763.html (accessed September 5, 2016).

107. Julie Hilden, "Can A True Statement Form the Basis for a Defamation Lawsuit? In a Controversial Ruling, the U.S. Court of Appeals for the First Circuit Says Yes," *FindLaw*, March 30, 2009, http://writ.news.findlaw.com/hilden/20090330.html (accessed September 5, 2016).

108. Hilden, "Can A True Statement Form the Basis for a Defamation Lawsuit? In a Controversial Ruling, the U.S. Court of Appeals for the First Circuit Says Yes."

109. Ibid.

110. Ibid.

111. Ibid.

112. Twain, "My First Lie, and How I Got Out of It," 160.

113. Ibid.

114. Ibid.

115. Ibid.

116. Ibid., 160–61.

117. Ibid., 169.

118. Ibid.

119. Ibid.

120. Ibid.

121. "Pudd'nhead Wilson's New Calendar," *Following the Equator*, chap. XIX, vol. II, quoted in *Mark Twain at Your Fingertips: A Book of Quotations*, ed. Caroline Thomas Harnsberger (Mineola, NY: Dover Publications, Inc., 2009), 237.

122. Twain, "My First Lie, and How I Got Out of It," 162–63.

123. "Bright People in Autograph Albums," *Fresno Republican Weekly*, 8 March 1884, 1. Quoted in "Twain Quotes—Lies."

124. Twain, "My First Lie, and How I Got Out of It," 163.

125. Ibid.

126. Twain, "On the Decay of the Art of Lying," 218.

127. Ibid., 217.

128. Ibid.

129. Ibid., 218.

130. "Advice to Youth," in *The Portable Mark Twain*, ed. Tom Quirk (New York, NY: Penguin Books, 2004), 548.

131. "The Ashcroft-Lyon Manuscript," in *The Autobiography of Mark Twain*, vol. III, eds. Benjamin Griffin and Harriet Elinor Smith, et al (Berkeley: University of California Press, 2015), 403.

132. Twain, "On the Decay of the Art of Lying," 217.

133. Ibid.

134. Ibid.

135. Ibid., 218.

136. Ibid.

137. Ibid.

138. Ibid.

139. Ibid., 224.

140. Ibid., 218.

141. Twain, "My First Lie, and How I Got Out of It," 160.

142. Twain, "On the Decay of the Art of Lying," 224.

143. Ibid., 223.

144. Ibid., 224.

145. Ibid.

146. Twain "Advice to Youth," 548.

147. Twain, "On the Decay of the Art of Lying," 224.

148. Ibid., 217–18.

149. Ibid., 225.

150. Ibid., 218.

151. Ibid., 225.

152. Letter to Revered Joseph H. Twichell, 1902, in *The Autobiography of Mark Twain*, vol. II, eds. Benjamin Griffin and Harriet Elinor Smith, et al (Berkeley: University of California Press, 2013), 104.

153. Philip Stratton-Lake, "Introduction," in *The Right and the Good*, W. D. Ross, ed. Philip Stratton-Lake (Oxford: Oxford University Press, 2002), xxxvi.

154. W. D. Ross, *The Right and the Good*, ed. Philip Stratton-Lake (Oxford: Oxford University Press, 2002), 21.

155. Twain, "On the Decay of the Art of Lying," 221.

156. Ibid.

157. W. D. Ross, *The Right and the Good*, 21.

158. J. J. C. Smart, "An Outline of a System of Utilitarian Ethics," in *Utilitarianism: For and Against* (Cambridge: Cambridge University Press, 1973), 32 (emphasis added).

159. Twain, "My First Lie, and How I Got Out of It," 164.

160. Twain, "On the Decay of the Art of Lying," 221.

161. Twain, "My First Lie, and How I Got Out of It," 166.

162. Ibid., 166–67.

163. Twain, "On the Decay of the Art of Lying," 223.

164. Ibid.

165. Twain, "My First Lie, and How I Got Out of It," 167.

166. Ibid.

167. Ibid.

168. Ibid.

169. It should be noted that the editors of Mark Twain's autobiography cannot find this quotation in Carlyle's writings: "'Nature admits of no lie,' Carlyle wrote in 'The Stump-Orator,' but no closer version of the quotation has been found" (Hirst et al., *The Autobiography of Mark Twain*, vol. II, 591).

170. *The Autobiography of Mark Twain*, vol. II, 304.

171. Twain, "My First Lie, and How I Got Out of It," 167.

172. Ibid.

173. Ibid., 167–68.

174. Ibid., 168.

175. Ibid., 167.

176. Ibid.

177. Ibid.

178. Letter to the *San Francisco Alta California*, dated May 17, 1867, published June 16, 1867, quoted in *The Wit and Wisdom of Mark Twain*, 62.

179. *The Autobiography of Mark Twain*, vol. II, 302.

180. Quoted in Peter S. Carmichael, "'Truth is mighty & will eventually prevail': Political Correctness, Neo-Confederates, and Robert E. Lee," *Southern Cultures* 17 (2011): 25. Carmichael may be said to agree with Twain that Lee was lying when he said this: "Despite Lee's assertion after Gettysburg that 'truth is mighty, & will eventually prevail,' the general knew better" (Ibid.).

181. It should be noted that the editors of Mark Twain's autobiography cannot find this quotation in Carlyle's writings: "'Nature admits of no lie,' Carlyle wrote in 'The Stump-Orator,' but no closer version of the quotation has been found" (Hirst et al., *The Autobiography of Mark Twain*, vol. II, 591).

182. Of course, the story about the young George Washington, first reported by Mason Locke Weems in his biography in 1800, *The Life of George Washington: With Curious Anecdotes, Equally honorable to Himself and Exemplary to his Young Countrymen*, is probably itself a lie (Ralph Keyes, *The Quote Verifier: Who Said What, Where, and When* [New York: St. Martin's Griffin, 2006], 121).

183. Twain, "My First Lie, and How I Got Out of It," 167.

184. Ibid., 168–69.

185. Ibid., 168.

186. Ibid.

187. Ibid.

188. Ibid., 169.

189. Ibid.

190. Ibid.

191. Twain, "Advice to Youth," 548.

192. My thanks to Mary Kate McGowan for suggesting that I write on this topic.

Chapter 9. Twain's Critique of Human Exceptionalism: "The Descent of Man" and the Antivivisection Movement

1. Mark Twain, *Mark Twain's Book of Animals*, ed. Shelley Fisher Fishkin (Berkeley: University of California Press, 2010), 125.

2. Ibid., 99 (emphasis is Twain's).

3. Ibid., 100.

4. Ibid., 102.

5. Ibid., 103.

6. Michel de Montaigne, *The Complete Essays of Montaigne*, trans. Donald M. Frame (Stanford: Stanford University Press, 1958), 331. Erica Fudge critiques Montaigne's human-centered perspective in this famous inquiry into the status of humans relative to animals. Erica Fudge, *Pets* (Stocksfield: Acumen, 2008): 78.

7. Twain, *Mark Twain's Book of Animals*, 125.

8. Jed Mayer notes this paradox that emerged in the late nineteenth century: "The evolutionary continuity between the species that helped inaugurate the emergence of this professional physiological regime also could be seen as implicitly challenging the ethical foundations of vivisection" (401). Jed Mayer, "The Expression of the Emotions in Man and Laboratory Animals," *Victorian Studies*, 50.3 (2005): 400–1

9. As the most famous spokesperson for evolutionary theory, Darwin's support was solicited by both sides of the vivisection controversy. On Darwin's complex relationship to the vivisection debates, see Paul White, "Darwin's Emotions: The Scientific Self and the Sentiment of Objectivity," *Isis*, 100.4 (2009): 823–24.

10. Jed Mayer notes that, "By reconfiguring the place of the emotions in evolutionary development, antivivisectionists effectively blurred the division between humans and nonhumans in order to question assumptions of human uniqueness." Mayer, "The Expression of the Emotions in Man and Laboratory Animals": 400.

11. Twain, *Mark Twain's Book of Animals*, 139.

12. Ibid., 139.

13. Jeremy Bentham, *An Introduction to the Principles of Morals and Legislation* (1789) (Oxford: Clarendon Press, 1907), Ch. XVII, note 122.

14. Mark Twain, "The Pains of Lowly Life" (London: Antivivisection Society, 1900). Mark Twain Papers, The Bancroft Library, University of California, Berkeley.

15. Joe B. Fulton notes that scholars have been reluctant to pay attention to Twain's "A Dog's Tale," because "many object to the story's rank sentimentality." Joe B. Fulton, "Jesus Christ and Vivisection: Mark Twain's Radical Empathy in 'A Dog's Tale,'" *CCTE Studies*, 71 (2006): 9.

16. Erica Fudge, *Animal* (London: Reaktion Books, 2002), 76–77.

17. Twain, *Mark Twain's Book of Animals*, 172, 173.

18. Ibid., 169.

19. W. D. Howells to Samuel Clemens, December 20, 1903. Mark Twain Papers, Bancroft Library, University of California, Berkeley.

20. Twain, *Mark Twain's Book of Animals*, 172.

21. Ibid., 173.

22. Ibid., 174.

23. Donna Haraway, *The Companion Species Manifesto* (Chicago: Prickly Paradigm Press, 2003): 49, 54.

24. Paul H. White, "The Experimental Animal in Victorian Britain," in *Thinking with Animals: New Perspectives on Anthropomorphism*, ed. Lorraine Daston and Gregg Mitman (New York: Columbia University Press, 2005): 75 (59–81).

25. Hayley Rose Glaholt, "Vivisection as War: The 'Moral Diseases' of Animal Experimentation and Slavery in British Victorian Quaker Pacifist Ethics," *Society & Animals* (2012): 166.

26. Twain, *Mark Twain's Book of Animals*, 174.

27. Such anxieties were grounded in reality. For the history of biomedical research with human subjects see Susan E. Lederer, *Subjected to Science: Human Experimentation in America Before the Second World War* (Baltimore: The Johns Hopkins University Press, 1997).

28. "Challenging the scientific models of social progress used by supporters of vivisection, antivivisectionists presented an alternative model of social progress in which the evolution of emotional sensitivity to suffering is central." Mayer, "The Expression of the Emotions in Man and Laboratory Animals," 411.

29. Elisabeth Arnould-Bloomfield, "Posthuman Compassions," *PMLA*, 130.5 (2015): 1474.

Chapter 10. Mark Twain's Serious Humor and That Peculiar Institution: Christianity

1. Manuel Davenport, "An Existentialist Philosophy of Humor," *Southwestern Journal of Philosophy*, 7 (1976): 171.

2. Justin Kaplan, *Mr. Clemens and Mark Twain* (New York: Simon and Schuster, 1966), 106, borrowing from the Cleveland Herald's review of *Innocents Abroad*.

3. Mark Twain, *Autobiography of Mark Twain: volume 2*, eds. Benjamin Griffin and Harriet Elinor Smith (Berkeley: University of California Press [The Mark Twain Project], 2010), 362.

4. Mark Twain, *The Complete Interviews*, ed. Gary Scharnhorst (Tuscaloosa: University of Alabama Press, 2006), 652.

5. Why react to human stupidity and misery with laughter rather than crying? Why not follow Heraclitus, the "weeping philosopher"? It would not be surprising or a weakness of character to respond to many of the serious issues Twain addresses with tears rather than laughter: "Man is the only animal that laughs and weeps; for he is the only animal that is struck with the difference between what things are, and what they ought to be" (William Hazlitt, "On Wit and Humor," in *The Philosophy of Laughter and Humor*, ed. John Morreall [New York: SUNY, 1987], 65). Let us rephrase this: Only *humans* laugh because they are *capable* of discovering this dissonance. Twain appears to be one who laughs rather than weeps over the moral incongruities in life, and I think he and his readers are better for it. To borrow from Sorensen, "humor [can be] a logical way of dealing with this absurdity in everyday life" (Majken Jul. Sorensen, "Humor as a Serious Strategy of Nonviolent Resistance to Oppression," *Peace and Change*, [2008]: 175).

6. Judith Jarvis Thompson, "A Defense of Abortion," *Philosophy & Public Affairs*, 1 (1971): 48–49.

7. This is true even of the self-proclaimed pessimist, Schopenhauer, who, according to Jennifer Michael Hecht, provides us with what might be the "funniest statement in the history of doubt": "For if we could guarantee them their dogma of immortality in some other way, the lively ardor for their gods would at once cool; and . . . if continued existence after death could be proved to be incompatible with the existence of gods . . . they would soon sacrifice these gods to their own immortality, and be hot for atheism" (quoted in Jennifer Hecht, *Doubt: A History* [New York: Harper Collins, 2003], 393).

8. Twain, *Interviews*, 633, 648.

9. Quoted in Matthew M. Hurley, Daniel Clement Dennett, and Reginald B. Adams, *Inside Jokes: Using Humor to Reverse-Engineer the Mind* (Cambridge, MA: MIT Press, 2011), 250.

10. Davenport, *An Existential Philosophy*, 170.

11. For just one example, see Mark Twain, *Helpful Hints for Good Living: A Handbook for the Damned Human Race*, eds. Lin Salamo, Victor Fischer, and Michael B. Frank (Berkeley: University of California Press, 2004), 1.

12. Arthur Schopenhauer, *The World as Will and Idea: volume II*, trans. R. B. Haldane and J. Kemp (Boston: Ticknor and Company, 1887), 280, my italics.

13. Hurley et al., *Inside Jokes*, 109.

14. Simone de Beauvoir, *The Ethics of Ambiguity*, trans. Bernard Frechtman (New York: Citadel Press, 1976), 85. Her analysis borrows heavily from Sartre: "The spirit of seriousness has two characteristics: it considers values as transcendent givens independent of human subjectivity, and it transfers the quality of 'desirable' from the ontological structure of things to their simple material constitution" (Jean-Paul Sartre, *Being and Nothingness: A Phenomenological Essay on Ontology*, trans. Hazel E. Barnes [New York: Washington Square Press, 1977], 796). These characteristics assume that human beings are simply static objects in the world wholly dependent upon certain and unchanging material conditions, and that any values or meaning are naturally laid down in such a way that individual persons are presumed to be bereft of responsibility for them. Furthermore, this notion of seriousness includes a desire for fixed essences of self and other; this is very easily maintained with the presumption that an all-powerful God has designed us and our morals.

15. Lewis Gordon, *Existentia Africana: Understanding Africana Existential Thought* (New York: Routledge, 2000), 72.

16. Mark Twain, "Letters from the Earth," in *Mark Twain on Religion*, ed. Henry Nash Smith (Easy Reading Series, 1962), 40, 44. (Forgotten Books), 0060803312. Ibooks. A similar sentiment is found in *The Mysterious Stranger* 17, and his *Autobiography*, vol. 2, 134.

17. Gordon, *Existentia Africana*, 88.

18. Twain, *Letters from the Earth*, 30–37.

19. John Morreall, *Comedy, Tragedy, and Religion* (Albany: State University of New York Press, 1999), 31.

20. John Morreall, *Comic Relief: A Comprehensive Philosophy of Humor* (Malden MA: Wiley and Sons Ltd, 2009), 102.

21. Mark Twain, *Autobiography of Mark Twain, vol. 1*, ed. Harriet Elinor Smith (Berkeley: University of California Press [The Mark Twain Project], 2010), 378.

22. Stanley Brodwin, in "Mark Twain's Theology: The Gods of a Brevet Presbyterian," in *The Cambridge Companion to Mark Twain*, ed. Forrest G. Robinson (New York: Cambridge University Press, 2003), details the oscillations of Twain's skeptical mind in both directions: with all of his scathing parodies of Christianity and his submission to hard determinism, Twain still recognizes that he "could not give up . . . his judgments of regret" and religiously infused guilt (232). Twain does not ignore this apparent inconsistency; instead he uses his humorous playful attitude to contemplate the ironies without becoming consumed by them.

23. Twain, *Autobiography, vol. 2*, 153, my italics.

24. Twain, *Interviews*, 652.

25. Bruce Michelson, *Mark Twain on the Loose: A Comic Writer and the American Self* (Amherst: University of Massachusetts Press, 1995), 9, my italics.

26. Twain, *Letters from the Earth*, 327.

27. Twain, *Helpful Hints*, 1, bolds in original.

28. Twain, *Letters from the Earth*, 60.

29. Quoted in Brodwin, *Mark Twain's Theology*, 228.

30. Twain, *Interviews*, 657.

31. Twain, *Autobiography, vol. 1*, 404.

32. Ibid., 405.

33. Twain, *Interviews*, 657.

34. Twain, "Little Bessie," http://www.payer.de/religionskritik/MarkTwain2.htm, accessed July 22, 2016, chapter 6.

35. Ibid.

36. Ibid., chapter 1.

37. Ibid

38. Quoted in Brodwin, *Mark Twain's Theology*, 227.

39. Twain, *Little Bessie*, chapter 6.

40. Quoted in Brodwin, *Mark Twain's Theology*, 229.

41. Even *Saint* Augustine was aware of this conundrum when, in his *Confessions*, he asked God to "Make me chaste. But not yet." His *nature* was telling him that he still had some *loving* to do.

42. Twain, *Letters from the Earth*, 19.

43. Ibid.

44. Ibid., 52.

45. Ibid., my italics.

46. Ibid., 324.

47. Hurley et al., *Inside Jokes*, 27–34, elaborate on the "Funny-ha-ha" and "Funny-huh" distinction.

48. Michelson, *Mark Twain on the Loose*, 212.

49. On God: "Dr. Clemens referred lightly to his belief, he stating that it was the general impression that he did not believe in a God. All on this score he would say

was that he believed in a great intellectual force which ruled this great universe. He emphatically stated that he did not concur in the belief of some that this big world came here by chance" (Twain, *Interviews*, 686).

50. Twain, *Autobiography*, vol. 2, 128.

51. Davenport, *An Existential Philosophy*, 171.

Chapter 11. Socratic Irony in Twain's Skeptical Religious Jeremiads

1. Professor Jacquette passed away during the production of this volume. We, and the philosophical community, mourn his loss as we celebrate his life and offer our condolences to his loved ones. What is produced here is his initial draft, edited only for minor typos or grammatical errors. It has otherwise been left unedited.

2. Richard K. Barksdale, "History, Slavery, and Thematic Irony in 'Huckleberry Finn,'" *Mark Twain Journal*, 22 (1984): 19.

3. Ibid., 19.

4. Mark Twain, *Christian Science*, ed. Vic Doyno (Buffalo: Prometheus Books, 1993), vi.

5. Gregory Vlastos, "Socratic Irony," in *Socrates: Ironist and Moral Philosopher* (Ithaca: Cornell University Press, 1991), 21.

6. Mark Twain, *The Innocents Abroad* (New York: Harper & Row, Publishers, Inc., 1980), 96.

7. Mark Twain, *Personal Recollections of Joan of Arc*, introduction by John Seelye (Hartford: The Stowe-Day Foundation, 1980), frontmatter.

8. Ibid., 461.

9. Ibid., xii.

10. Twain, *The Innocents Abroad*, 119.

11. Ibid., 119–20.

12. Ibid., 129.

13. Ibid., 196.

14. Ibid., 119.

15. Vlastos, "Socratic Irony," 44.

16. A jeremiad is a lengthy complaint. Twain makes lengthy, sometimes book-length complaints about what he considers to be unsubstantiable especially fraudulent religious beliefs and hypocrisy in religious practice. I am grateful to my research assistant Andreas Freivogel for hunting down elusive works of secondary literature relevant to understanding Twain's irony.

Chapter 12. The American Diogenes: Mark Twain's Sacred Profanity

1. William E. Phipps, *Mark Twain's Religion* (Macon: Mercer University Press, 2003), 136; Albert Bigelow Paine, ed. *Mark Twain's Letters* (New York: Harper, 1917), 348.

2. Gary Scharnhorst, ed. *Mark Twain on Potholes and Politics: Letters to the Editor* (Columbia: University of Missouri Press, 2014), 99f.; Phipps, *Religion*, 64f.

3. Albert Bigelow Paine, *Mark Twain: A Biography* (New York: Harper, 1912), 383.

4. Ibid., 336.

5. Mark Twain, *The Innocents Abroad* (New York: Penguin, 2004), ch. LXI.

6. Ibid., chapter XXXII.

7. Frederick Anderson, Michael Frank, Kenneth Sanderson, eds. *Mark Twain's Notebooks and Journals* (Berkeley: University of California Press), 3:144.

8. Diogenes Laertius, *The Lives of the Eminent Philosophers*, trans. C. D. Younge (London: Henry Bohn, 1853), 6.54. N.B. I have made some revisions to Younge's translation.

9. Ibid., 6.43.

10. Ibid., 6.33.

11. Ibid., 6.45.

12. Ibid., 6.22, 6.23, 6.46 and 6.69.

13. Ibid., 6.61.

14. Ibid., 6.33.

15. Ibid., 6.32, 6.40 and 6.60.

16. Ibid., 6.32.

17. Ibid., 6.27.

18. Ibid., 6.24. Compare Twain: "I would distrust a religious faith that came upon me suddenly—that came otherwise than deliberately, and *proven*, step by step as it came" Phipps, *Religion*, 124; Michael B. Frank and Harriet Elinor Smith, eds. *Mark Twain's Letters* (Berkeley: University of California Press, 2002), 3:13.

19. Diogenes Laertius, *Lives*, 6.37.

20. Ibid., 6.73. For Diogenes, this stance included the scandalous belief that cannibalism is not inherently wrong. This claim much embarrassed later admirers of Cynicism. Diogenes certainly did not favor murder or eating corpses as a matter of regular practice; later interpreters believed that what Diogenes meant is that, under dire circumstances, cannibalism might be acceptable. His claim was particular shocking to the ancient Greeks because religious customs made it taboo to harm a corpse under any circumstances.

21. William M. Gibson, ed., *The Mysterious Stranger Manuscripts* (Berkeley: University of California Press, 1969), 16; Albert Bigelow Paine, ed., *Mark Twain's Notebook* (New York: Harper 1935), 256.

22. Cf. Diogenes Laertius, *Lives*, 6.69.

23. Phipps, *Religion*, 230. The delicate nude illustrations for Twain's *Eve's Diary* provoked one library to ban the book. Twain spoke before Congress about it and mocked the prudery of the librarian.

24. Howard Baetzhold and Joseph McCullough, eds., *The Bible According to Mark Twain* (New York: Touchstone, 1995), 247.

25. Mark Twain, *Pudd'nhead* Wilson (New York: Penguin, 1969), chap. XVI; compare also "A Dog's Tale" in Tom Quirk, ed., *Tales, Speeches, Essays, and Sketches* (New York: Penguin, 1994), 288–98.

26. Baetzhold and McCullough, *Bible*, 213. Twain did use the words "Satanic" and "Satan" as terms of disapproval, e.g., Phipps, *Religion*, 189–90, but, as Gibson, *Mysterious Stranger*, 15 notes, Twain was intrigued by the idea of Satan even in boyhood and horrified his Sunday school teacher by proposing to write a biography of him.

27. On Diogenes's ability to parody or quote Homer at just the right moment, see Diogenes Laertius, Lives, 6.53 and 6.57.

28. Twain, *Innocents*, chap. XLVIII.

29. Diogenes *Laertius*, Lives, 6.38.

30. Ibid., 6.69.

31. Ibid., 6.34.

32. Paul Fatout, ed. *Mark Twain Speaking* (Iowa City: University of Iowa Press, 1976), 193.

33. Phipps, *Religion*, 136; Anderson, Frank, and Sanderson, *Notebooks and Journals*, 3:524.

34. Paine, *Notebook*, 345. However, Twain seems undecided about whether or not God laughs. Phipps, *Religion*, 237 and 275.

35. Phipps, *Religion*, 54; Letter to Orion, Clemens, October 19 and 20, 1865.

36. Paine, *Notebook*, 198.

37. Gibbon, *Mysterious Stranger*, 166.

38. Paine, *Letters*, 323.

39. Diogenes Laertius, *Lives*, 6.64.

40. Ibid., 6.24.

41. Ibid., 5.59.

42. Compare Diogenes, "On one occasion he saw a child drinking out of its hands, and so he threw away the cup which belonged to his leather pouch, saying, 'That child has beaten me in simplicity.'" Diogenes Laertius, *Lives*, 6.37.

43. Quirk, *Tales*, 323.

44. Cf. Phipps, *Religion*, 247, "flimsy nonsense"; see John S. Tuckey, Frederick Anderson, Kenneth M. Sanderson, and Bernard L. Stein, eds., *Mark Twain's Fables of Man* (Berkeley: University of California Press, 1972), 53–57.

45. Cf. Phipps, *Religion*, 280.

46. Quirk, *Tales*, 331.

47. Paine, *Notebook*, 190.

48. See Paine, *Biography*, chap. CCXCV.

49. Paine, *Letters*, 771.

50. Quirk, *Tales*, 48–52.

51. Ibid., 20.

52. Ibid., 23.

53. Gibbon, *The Mysterious Stranger Manuscripts*, 113–14.

54. Ibid., 51. Twain also objects to superstition because it holds back practical scientific progress. Phipps, *Religion*, 251. But such a thought would have been alien to Diogenes; in Diogenes's day, the sciences were seen as purely theoretical and so Diogenes objects to their study because he regarded them as useless. Diogenes Laertius, *Lives*, 6.39 and 6.73.

55. Diogenes Laertius, *Lives*, 6.27–28; compare 6.48 and 6.65.

56. Ibid., 6.43.

57. Ibid., 6.45.

58. "One of [Diogenes's] sayings was, 'That one ought to hold out one's hand to a friend without closing the fingers.'" Diogenes Laertius, *Lives*, 6.29; or in Twain's clever remark, "If a man compel thee to go with him a mile, go with him Twain." Phipps, *Religion*, 245; Frank and Smith, *Letters*, 2: 261.

59. Paine, *Letters*, 678.

60. Twain found God, as expressed in the Bible, to be not only hypocritical but far too small for the vastness of the cosmos as revealed by modern astronomy. Phipps, *Religion*, 273–74.

61. Reproduced in Hamlin Hill, ed., *Mark Twain: God's Fool* (Chicago: University of Chicago Press, 2010), 22.

62. For Twain's extended treatment of this sort of hypocrisy, see his essay "To the Person Sitting in Darkness" and his pamphlet, "King Leopold's Soliloquy: A Defense of His Congo Rule." Both of these essays are available online.

63. Twain, *Innocents*, chap. XXVI.

64. Baetzhold and McCullough, *Bible*, 317.

65. Paine, *Notebook*, 344.

66. "Little Bessie" in Quirk, *Tales*, 330.

67. Baetzhold and McCullough, *Bible*, 39.

68. Ibid., 315.

69. Chapter 5 of "Schoolhouse Hill," *The Mysterious Stranger Manuscripts*, 212 ff. Although Twain enjoyed riffing on the story of creation, he did not believe it. Twain actively followed and embraced the latest developments in biology (Darwin's defense of evolution) and geology (Lyell's view that the Earth is tens of millions of years old). Twain even traveled to meet Darwin in England. Phipps, *Religion*, 223, 284.

70. *The Bible According to Mark Twain*, 318.

71. Ibid., 320.

72. Diogenes Laertius, *Lives*, 6.71.

73. *Mark Twain's Notebook*, 348–49. Of course, the man without conscience *or* respect for the Golden Rule is, Twain recognized, quite dangerous; see his short story, "The Facts Concerning the Recent Carnival of Crime in Connecticut" about the man who murders his own conscience. But conscience alone can be quite dangerous as the consciences of allegedly decent folk can be turned against each other; see Twain's "The Man That Corrupted Hadleyburg." Plus, as Twain well knew, it was (in his boyhood) supposed to be a matter of conscience that a slave be returned to his owner. "In my schoolboy days I had no aversion to slavery. I was not aware that

there was anything wrong about it. . . . [T]he local pulpit taught us that God approved it, that it was a holy thing, and that the doubter need only look in the Bible if he wished to settle his mind—and then the texts were read aloud to us to make the matter sure" (Phipps, 28; *The Autobiography of Mark Twain*, 6). Hence, Twain has Huckleberry Finn wrestle with his own conscience which demands returning Jim; after deciding against returning his friend, Finn profanely declares, "All right, then, I'll go to hell." Mark Twain, *Adventures of Huckleberry Finn* (New York: Penguin, 2014), chap. XXXI.

74. See R. Bracht Branham and Marie-Odile Goulet-Cazé, eds., *The Cynics* (Berkeley: University of California Press, 2000), 35; also see Douglas Cairns, *Aidos: The Psychology and Ethics of Honour and Shame in Ancient Greek Literature* (Oxford: Clarendon Press, 1993). Diogenes himself did use the expression "are you not ashamed?" Diogenes Laertius, *Lives*, 6.65, but he also critiqued erroneous shame. Ibid., 6.35.

75. Paine, *Notebook*, 288.

76. Ibid., 242.

77. Ibid., 325. See also Twain's admiration for Japanese customs about nudity. Ibid., 288. Phipps, *Religion*, 230, also cites a quip about a Hawaiian wearing only spectacles but is otherwise naked.

78. Gibbon, *Mysterious Stranger*, 72–77.

79. Ibid., 72.

80. Ibid.

81. Ibid., 73.

82. Ibid., 74.

83. Ibid., 76.

84. Diogenes Laertius, *Lives*, 6.68.

85. Diogenes Laertius, *Lives*, 6.39.

86. Phipps, *Religion*, 303; Dixon Wecter, ed., *The Love Letters of Mark Twain* (New York: Harper, 1949), 344. See Phipps, *Religion*, 301–4, for a gathering of Twain's ambivalent statements. But, whatever came next, whether nothingness or an afterlife, Twain was convinced that it entailed nothing bad and that religious conceptions had it wrong (quite possibly for pernicious reasons).

87. Phipps, *Religion*, 301; Paul Baender, ed., *What Is Man? And Other Philosophical Writings* (Berkeley: University of California Press, 1973), 56–57.

88. Phipps, *Religion*, 304; Nieder, *Autobiography*, 249. These reflections are what led Twain to joke: "Why is it that we rejoice at a birth and grieve at a funeral? It is because we are not the person involved?" Twain, *Pudd'nhead Wilson*, chap. IX.

89. Quirk, *Tales*, 349. Compare: "Death, the only immortal who treats us all alike, whose pity and whose peace and whose refuge are for all—the soiled and the pure, the rich and the poor, the loved and the unloved." Paine, *Notebook*, 398.

90. Baetzhold and McCullough, *Bible*, 69–70.

91. Phipps, *Religion*, 301; Baender, *What is Man?* 56–57.

92. Phipps, *Religion*, 302; Wecter, *Love Letters*, 253–54.

93. Phipps, *Religion*, 370; Paine, Biography, 1584.

94. Phipps, *Religion*, 280 and 342; *The Bible According to Mark Twain*, 321.

95. Baetzhold and McCullough, *Bible*, 209.

96. Phipps, *Religion*, 309; Mark Twain, "Christmas Greetings," *Boston Daily Globe*, 25 December 1890: 3. Nevertheless, Twain seemed to be proud at having the first private telephone in Hartford, CT; he referred to it as "a time-saving, profanity-breeding, useful invention." Caroline Thomas Harnsberger, ed., *Mark Twain at Your Fingertips* (New York: Beechhurst Press, 1948), 469–70.

97. Mark Twain, *Roughing It* (New York: Penguin, 1981), 460–61.

98. However, Twain does fantasize, "It would be a wonderful experience to stand there in those enchanted surroundings and hear Shakespeare and Milton and Bunyan read from their noble works." Phipps, *Religion*, 303; from Twain's unpublished book review of The Cities of the Sun by George Warder, quoted in Ray Browne, ed., Mark Twain's Quarrel with Heaven (New Haven, CT: Rowman & Littlefield, 1970), 37.

99. Baetzhold and McCullough, *Bible*, 224–27.

100. Ibid., 155.

101. Ibid., 156.

102. Ibid., 157.

103. Ibid., 166.

104. Ibid., 170.

105. Ibid., 208, 209.

106. Ibid., 209.

107. Diogenes Laertius, *Lives*, 6.41.

108. *Anthropos* specifically means "human being" as opposed to *anêr* for male or *gunê* for female.

109. Paine, *Mark Twain's Letters*, 718.

110. Diogenes Laertius, *Lives*, 6.63; cf. 6.72.

111. Twain's "The Damned Human Race" is printed in Bernard DeVoto, ed., *Letters from the Earth* (Greenwich, CT: Fawcett, 1962), 209–32.

112. Diogenes Laertius, *Lives*, 6.42.

113. Baetzhold and McCullough, *Bible*, 95.

Chapter 13. An Epicurean Consideration of Superstitions in Mark Twain and in the Good Life

1. Mark Twain, *The Adventures of Tom Sawyer and Adventures of Huckleberry Finn* (London: Penguin, 2013), 1.

2. Joanne Cantor, *"Mommy, I'm Scared": How TV and Movies Frighten Children and What We Can Do to Protect Them* (San Diego, CA: Harcourt, 1998); "Fright Reactions to Mass Media," in *Media Effects: Advances in Theory and Research*, ed. Jennings Bryant and Dolf Zillmann (Mahwah, NJ: Erlbaum, 1994), 287–306; Joanne

Cantor and Glenn G. Sparks, "Children's Fear Responses to Mass Media: Testing Some Piagetian Predictions," *Journal of Communication*, 34 (1994): 90–103.

3. Wislawa Szymborska, *Nonrequired Reading: Prose Pieces* (Boston: Houghton Mifflin Harcourt, 2015), 4.

4. Mark Twain, *Autobiography of Mark Twain*, volume 2 (Berkeley: University of California Press, 2013), 69.

5. Julia Annas, "Virtue Ethics and Social Psychology," *A Priori* 2 (2003): 24–25.

6. In *Intelligent Virtue*, Annas explains that virtue "is part of the agent's happiness or flourishing," and she argues that, despite the idea's ancient origins, it is still "plausible to see virtue as actually constituting (wholly or in part) that happiness." Julia Annas, *Intelligent Virtue* (New York: Oxford University Press, 2011), 1. See also Lawrence Becker, *A New Stoicism* (Princeton, NJ: Princeton University Press, 1998), 20.

7. Mark Twain, *Tom Sawyer and Huckleberry Finn* (Hertfordshire, England: Wordsworth Editions, 1992), 235.

8. Twain, *Tom Sawyer and Huckleberry Finn*, 236.

9. Jonathan Bennett, "The Conscience of Huckleberry Finn," *Philosophy* 49 (1974): 123–34, 4, http://www.earlymoderntexts.com/assets/jfb/huckfinn.pdf (accessed October 19, 2016).

10. M. J. Sidnell, "Huck Finn and Jim," *The Cambridge Quarterly* 2 (1967): 205–6.

11. Bennett, "The Conscience of Huckleberry Finn," 4.

12. Ibid.

13. Ibid., 8.

14. Julia Annas, *The Morality of Happiness* (New York: Oxford University Press, 1998).

15. Mark Twain, *Sammlung* (Cambridge, MA. Da Capo Press, 2000), 447. Here is another passage of relevance, though a bit oblique, "During many ages there were witches. The Bible said so. The Bible commanded that they should not be allowed to live. Therefore the Church, after eight hundred years, gathered up its halters, thumb-screws, and firebrands, and set about its holy work in earnest. She worked hard at it night and day during nine centuries and imprisoned, tortured, hanged, and burned whole hordes and armies of witches, and washed the Christian world clean with their foul blood. Then it was discovered that there was no such thing as witches, and never had been. One does not know whether to laugh or to cry. Who discovered that there was no such thing as a witch—the priest, the parson? No, these never discover anything. . . . There are no witches. The witch text remains; only the practice has changed. Hell fire is gone, but the text remains. Infant damnation is gone, but the text remains. More than two hundred death penalties are gone from the law books, but the texts that authorized them remain" (571).

16. Martha Nussbaum offers a rather thorough explanation of how the Epicureans hold the views they do. The epistemic and moral psychological preliminaries include that perceptions are not always veridical; that desire and perception influence each other; that the mind rapidly extrapolates from perceptions; and that our psychologi-

cal state and habit influence desire. Martha Nussbaum, *The Therapy of Desire: Theory and Practice in Hellenistic Ethics* (Princeton: Princeton University Press, 2013), 165.

17. Epicurus, "Letter to Menoeceus," http://classics.mit.edu/Epicurus/menoec .html (accessed October 11, 2016).

18. Lucretius, *De Rerum Natura (On the Nature of Things)*, III. 37–4, http://classics .mit.edu/Carus/nature_things.html (accessed September 8, 2016).

19. Ibid., 1053–70.

20. Nussbaum, *The Therapy of Desire*, 197.

21. Twain, *The Adventures of Tom Sawyer and Adventures of Huckleberry Finn*, 36.

22. Mark Twain, *The Adventures of Tom Sawyer* (North Chelmsford, MA: Courier Corporation, 2012), 186.

Chapter 14. Moral Value and Moral Psychology in Twain's "Carnival of Crime"

1. Mark Twain, "The Facts Concerning the Recent Carnival of Crime in Connecticut," in *Selected Shorter Writings of Mark Twain*, ed. Walter Blair (Boston: Houghton Mifflin Company, 1962), 141.

2. Ibid., 143.

3. Mark Twain to William Howells, Hartford, January 11, 1876, in *Mark Twain— Howells Letters: The Correspondence of Samuel L. Clemens and William D. Howells 1872-1910*, eds. Henry Nash Smith and William M. Gibson (Cambridge: Harvard University Press, 1960), 119.

4. Mark Twain to William Howells, Hartford, January 18, 1876, in *Mark Twain— Howells Letters: The Correspondence of Samuel L. Clemens and William D. Howells 1872–1910*, eds. Henry Nash Smith and William M. Gibson (Cambridge: Harvard University Press, 1960), 122–23.

5. Albert Bigelow Paine, *Mark Twain: A Biography: The Personal and Literary Life of Samuel Langhorne Clemens* (New York: Harper & Brothers, 1912), 569.

6. William Howells in the *Century Magazine*. As quoted in Paine, *A Biography*, 733.

7. Friedrich Nietzsche, *On The Genealogy of Morality*, trans. Maudmarie Clark and Alan J. Swensen (Indianapolis: Hackett, 1998), 21.

8. David Hume, *Treatise of Human Nature* (Amherst: Prometheus Books, 1992), 457–63.

9. Ibid., 463.

10. Ibid., 469

11. Paine, *A Biography*, 569.

Chapter 15. Making the Heart Grow Fonder: Twain, Psychical Distance, and Aesthetic Experience

1. Mark Twain, *Life on the Mississippi*, electronic edition, chapter 9: 118–19, http://docsouth.unc.edu/southlit/twainlife/twain.html#twain112. This work is the

property of the University of North Carolina at Chapel Hill. It may be used freely by individuals for research, teaching, and personal use as long as this statement of availability is included in the text.

2. Twain, *Life on the Mississippi*, 121.

3. Edward Bullough, "'Psychical Distance' as a Factor in Art and as an Aesthetic Principle," *British Journal of Psychology*, 5 (1912): 87–118

4. Ibid., 89.

5. Ibid., 91.

6. Mark Twain, *Mark Twain's Travels with Mr. Brown*, eds. Franklin Walker and G. Ezra Dane, "Academy of Design," letter to San Francisco *Alta California*, July 28, 1867.

7. Bullough, "'Psychical Distance,'" 93.

8. Søren Kierkegaard, *Paper and Journals*, trans. Alstair Hannay (London: Penguin Classics, 1996), 355.

9. Søren Kierkegaard, *Papers and Journals: A Selection*, trans. Alastair Hannay (London: Penguin Classics, 1996), 54 XI I A 355.

10. Bullough, "'Psychical Distance,'" 93.

11. Søren Kierkegaard, *Either/Or, volume I*, trans. David and Lillian Swenson (Princeton: Princeton University Press, 1944), from "Diapsalmata," 17.

12. Mark Twain, *A Connecticut Yankee in King Arthur's Court*, Project Gutenberg edition, chapter 43, http://www.gutenberg.org/files/86/86-h/86-h.htm.

Index

About the Editor and Contributors

Jennifer Baker works on updating traditional virtue ethics for use today. An associate professor of philosophy at the College of Charleston, her published articles include "Who is Afraid of a Final End?" "Virtue Ethics and Practical Guidance," and "Virtue and Behavior." She recently edited *Economics and the Virtues* (2016) and is at work on a forthcoming monograph entitled "*Stoic Economics.*

Frank Boardman is currently a visiting assistant professor at Dickinson College, having received a PhD in philosophy from the City University of New York Graduate Center in 2016. Visit frankboardman.com if curiosity persists.

Jeffrey Dueck is associate professor of philosophy at Nyack College, where he teaches and writes on issues in philosophy of religion, rthics, and the arts. His current interests focus on the intersections of pragmatism and existentialism in issues of religious belief and aesthetic experience. He also works in ministry and music at a multicampus church in New York's Hudson Valley, where he and his family reside.

Robert Fudge is professor of philosophy at Weber State University in Ogden, Utah. His research and teaching center around issues in aesthetics and ethics, and he has a special interest in the interrelations between the two fields.

Kristina Gehrman is an assistant professor at the University of Tennessee, Knoxville, where she conducts research and teaches courses on Ethics, especially contemporary Aristotelian ethics and environmental ethics. A companion paper to her essay in this volume, "The Character of Huckleberry Finn," is forthcoming in the journal *Philosophy and Literature* in 2017.

An apparent victim of attention deficit, **Alan Goldman** has written in almost every area of philosophy. He is working on his ninth authored (and promised last) book. His most recent two were *Reasons from Within* and *Philosophy and the Novel*. He has more than 150 articles and retired from teaching after forty-seven years in the classroom last year.

Dale Jacquette (1953–2016) was senior professorial chair in theoretical philosophy at the University of Bern (Switzerland). Prior to moving to Bern in 2008, he was professor of philosophy at Penn State University. Professor Jacquette was quite prolific with a wide breadth of research interests including logic, metaphysics, philosophy of mind, Wittgenstein, ethics, aesthetics, epistemology, and the history of philosophy. It was an honor to have him attached to this project.

Brian E. Johnson is an assistant professor of philosophy at Fordham University. He specializes in ancient Greek and Roman philosophy, focusing on the ethics of Epictetus. Much to Epictetus's dismay, Johnson embraces the pathos of literature and devotes his free time to reading the classics. Johnson is only a recent "convert" to Twain but has already made a "pilgrimage" to Virginia City, Nevada, in order to see the "relics" of Twain's first years writing for the *Territorial Enterprise*.

Chris Kramer is an associate professor and academic chair of the Philosophy Department at Rock Valley College. He made the move to Rockford, Illinois, after a professional career in rock music in San Diego inconceivably proved to be elusive. His interests intersect across the philosophy of mind, humor, religion, informal logic, existentialism and phenomenology, and ethical issues surrounding oppression. He completed his PhD at Marquette University in May 2015, with his dissertation on "subversive humor." He lives in Rockford, Illinois, with his wife Lynne, and his two diminutive philosophers, Milo and Lola, who continually test his epistemological prowess with their infinitely regressive queries.

Michael Lyons is currently completing a PhD in philosophy at Trinity College Dublin. He studied philosophy at the University of Bristol, where he earned his BA, and at King's College London, where he earned his MA. He always thought it was good to do the right thing but is still trying to figure out exactly what that means. As such, his research focuses primarily on ethics, more specifically on the theoretical side.

James Edwin Mahon is professor and chair of the Department of Philosophy at City University of New York–Lehman College. His primary research interests are in moral philosophy, the history of moral philosophy, and the intersection of law and applied ethics. Recent publications include "The Definition of Lying and Deception" in the *Stanford Encyclopedia of Philosophy* and "Innocent Burdens" in *Washington and Lee Law Review*.

James McLachlan is professor of philosophy and religion at Western Carolina University. He is an author of books and articles on the problem of evil, including *The Desire to be God: Freedom and the Other in Sartre and Berdyaev*, "Beyond the Self, Beyond Ontology: Levinas' Reading of Shestov's Reading of Kierkegaard," "Mormonism and the Problem of Evil" in the *Oxford Handbook on Mormonism*, "Mystic Terror and Metaphysical Rebels: Active Evil and Active Love in Schelling and Dostoevsky," and "Satan: Romantic Hero or Just Another Asshole: The Desire to be God, The Devil, and the Demonic." He was founding co-chair of the Mormon Studies Group at the American Academy of Religion.

Emily E. VanDette is associate professor of English at the State University of New York at Fredonia. She is the author of *Sibling Romance in American Fiction, 1835–1900*, as well as numerous articles about nineteenth-century U.S. literature. Her current project focuses on the literary history of the advocacy movement during its formative years in the United States, 1866 to 1917.

Craig Vasey is professor of philosophy and chair of the Department of Classics, Philosophy, and Religion at University of Mary Washington in Fredericksburg, Virginia, where he has taught since 1986. He has a PhD in philosophy from Brown University and a doctorate from Université de Paris. He is translator and editor of *The Last Chance*, volume IV of Jean-Paul Sartre's *Roads of Freedom* (2009), and serves as treasurer of the North American Sartre Society.